BAD KARMA

Thinking Twice about the Social Consequences of Reincarnation Theory

William Garrett

University Press of America,® Inc.
Lanham · Boulder · New York · Toronto · Oxford

Copyright © 2005 by
University Press of America,® Inc.
4501 Forbes Boulevard
Suite 200
Lanham, Maryland 20706
UPA Acquisitions Department (301) 459-3366

PO Box 317
Oxford
OX2 9RU, UK

All rights reserved
Printed in the United States of America
British Library Cataloging in Publication Information Available

Library of Congress Control Number: 2005929545
ISBN 0-7618-3316-1 (paperback : alk. ppr.)

∞™ The paper used in this publication meets the minimum
requirements of American National Standard for Information
Sciences—Permanence of Paper for Printed Library Materials,
ANSI Z39.48—1984

To my wife, Judy Marie Wilson—for her love, her brassy cheer, and her invincible confidence.

Contents

ACKNOWLEDGMENTS vii

INTRODUCTION 1

1 The Drama of Reincarnation 17

2 Karma: The Dance of Consequence 35

3 A Passage Through India 53

4 Cannibals & Cavemen:
   Reincarnation in Ancient Greece 85

5 An Indian Breeze in Modern Europe 115

6 Evolution and Its Discontents 127

7 Theosophy & the Revolt Against Darwin 141

8 Tough Justice for Tough Minds:
   Social Darwinism in Its Season 167

9 O' Brave New World—Complete with Castes? 185

10 Postscript: The Emergence of Buddhism in America 207

BIBLIOGRAPHY	221
INDEX	229
ABOUT THE AUTHOR	237

Acknowledgments

I have had help with this work. I wish to acknowledge the diligent editing of Ms. Dawn Adams, the skillful manuscript preparation of Ms. Susan Peabody, and the superb indexing of Ms. Donalda Murphy. Acknowledgment is also due to my wife, Judy Wilson, for her generous reading and rereading of the manuscript at various phases of its development.

I am lucky enough to have challenging and relentlessly inquisitive students—and I here acknowledge their input to my thinking over the years.

I want to express my gratitude to John F. Kennedy University for allowing me time and resources to research and write this book. In addition, I want to give particular acknowledgment to my colleagues in the Liberal Arts Department at John F. Kennedy University: to Barry Martin (who sets an example for me more than he realizes), to Cyd Jenefsky (who makes me think twice more than she realizes) and to Susanne West (who fully realizes the extent to which she keeps me on my toes).

William Garrett
Alameda, California. 2005

Introduction

THE CONSEQUENCES OF BELIEF

... 27% [of the American people] believe in reincarnation, that they were once another person. This includes 40% of people aged 25 to 29 but only 14% of people aged 65 and over.

—Harris Poll, February 26, 2003[1]

Is it that a whole class of Americans—mainly poor, black Americans—have become more or less totally isolated from the rest of society, and are acquiring the status of a despised foreign presence? Is it that the wealthiest 20 or 30 percent of Americans are 'seceding,' as Robert Reich put it, into separate, often self-sufficient suburbs, where they rarely even meet members of non-wealthy classes, except in the latter's role as receptionists or repairmen? And is it the gnawing sense that, in *their* isolation, these richer Americans not only are passing their advantages on to their children, but are coming to think that those advantages are deserved, that they and their children are, at bottom, not just better off but *better?*

—Mickey Kaus, *The End of Equality*[2]

1

This book is intended to elicit concern over the potential confluence of the two trends described above. According to the 2003 Harris poll cited—and a recent Gallup poll concurs[3]—over a quarter of the American population claims to believe in reincarnation. This is not a trivial matter, I urge, because belief in reincarnation carries consequences not only for religion, but also for culture. And I will argue in what follows that the cultural consequences of a widespread belief in reincarnation are likely to be devastating. To set the stage for why I think this is so, let's move back in time a bit.

The earth was photographed from the moon in 1969. These photographic images evoked a sense of wonder and awe in nearly everyone who saw them. For many, these lovely photos also evoked hope. It allowed a view of the home of the entire human species in a single image. It allowed hope that, finally, the unity seen from the moon could find expression as a societal unity here on earth. One world—at long last.

Twenty years later, in 1989, the aspiration for one world had apparently been brought to fruition. The Berlin Wall had fallen. Instantaneous global communication had become commonplace. The world was unified. Not, however, in the way that many had hoped. The process has come to be called globalization, and it has indeed unified the world. However, this unity was realized not on humanistic values, but on corporate values. And these values, globalized, have brought about something historically unprecedented.

Globalization is changing the nature of employment in America; it is generating an ever-widening disparity in income and standard of living. While it is generating spectacular wealth for the few, globalization is bringing a bleak reality of underpaid, dead-end jobs, as well as the threat of unemployment, to many, many more. And, as Micky Kaus and other social critics have analyzed it, this social stratification seems disturbingly intransigent. These dynamics are prompting some to conclude that the social stratification produced by globalization reflects differences in people that run deeper than socioeconomic differences, differences that are rooted in genetics rather than culture.

The dynamics of globalization threaten to trigger circumstances of desperation, circumstances that historically would have torn at the consciences of Americans and brought them to demand remedy. But viewed through the prism of reincarnation theory, such dire circumstances take on a far more serene aspect; we are confronted not by a specter of outrage and injustice, but by a drama, and a sacred drama at that, in which people are "working out their karma." Steeped in reincarnation theory, the religious impulse that has been such a profound force in American history can easily find expression as a sunny Chardonnay spirituality—one in which more emotional conflict is felt over the fate of the chicken and veal that are served as *hors d'oeuvres* than is felt over abject human wretchedness in the impoverished neighborhoods through which we no longer need to drive. That is the concern of this book.

2

I argue in what follows that belief in reincarnation generates a mind-set that is conducive to the emergence of social castes. My concern is that, should belief in reincarnation come to predominate in American culture, then social caste—not social *class,* now, but social *caste*—will become a real possibility in America. What would that mean? Let's begin with a definition of caste as I'll be considering it here. G. D. Bereman, in his article on caste in the *International Encyclopedia of Social Sciences,* puts it this way:

> A caste system, then, can be said to occur when society is composed of birth-ascribed, hierarchically ordered, and culturally distinct groups. The hierarchy entails differential evaluation, differential rewards, and differential association.[4]

Bereman's crisp description of caste sounds like the very antithesis of the spirit of American culture. Caste, with its birth-ascribed advantages and disadvantages, is simply not "the American way." That the circumstances of one's birth would define the limits of one's potentials would—at present—strike most Americans as repugnant. It is inconsistent with our cultural ideals. Now it is hardly a news-flash that such ideals have been imperfectly realized. The story of American culture includes bigotry, intolerance, and oppression. Yet, in our favorite self-portrait, we Americans see America as a place in which caste—as Bereman describes it, as we will find it manifested in Indian culture—has no place. But America is changing, and fast. And the popularity of reincarnation doctrine is capable of playing an unseen but important role in the social dramas that are unfolding here at the beginning of the 21st century.

But surely, it might be objected, this goes too far. Reincarnation is only an *idea*—it is only a theory. I caution that to put it thus is to misunderstand what ideas are, and therefore to underestimate their power. True enough, some ideas are "only ideas": the idea of a computer mouse, the idea of canned beans, the idea of a fur glove. Reincarnation is not such an idea. Reincarnation is what might be called a master-idea: it is an idea, like that of God or damnation or Fate, that puts our entire experience into a certain perspective. Such master-ideas potently impact the mind in which they inhere. They structure our sense of reality and of human well-being; they serve to identify problems and suggest strategies for the solution of those problems; they condition our hopes and anticipations.

Master-ideas are at the heart of great religions and philosophies of life. Such ideas are not like coins that may or may not be in one's pocket. Coins are *things*, and ideas—especially the ideas we'll be considering in this study—are best thought of as *activities*. And activities produce effects. To hold a master-idea is to engage in a certain way of thinking; such ideas are, as it were, generative of certain modes of behavior. And as such, these ideas have a characteristic and therefore predictable dynamic.

Consider as an example another master-idea, the idea of *Apocalypse*. This is the idea that there is a great confrontation afoot—a confrontation between good and evil, between light and darkness, between God and Satan, between the human followers of God and the human followers of Satan. The enemy is implacable: any hope for negotiation is a naive delusion; redemption is to be found in victory alone, and total victory at that. The onset of war is imminent, the precise starting time is not known but—it will be soon. The world is presently in thrall to Satan and the forces of darkness. But soon God will break forcibly into history to end Satan's reign and set all right with the world. The present corrupt age is at an end—almost. As we who live at the dawn of the 21st century are all-too-familiar, the idea of Apocalypse remains at the heart of certain strains of monotheist religions throughout the world—emphatically including America.

But let's return to the notion of the dynamics inherent in master-ideas. To believe in the Apocalypse will condition one's thinking in regard to the crises that confront us today. To name only two: approaches to conflict resolution will disdain compromise and have ready resort to battles that are taken to be inevitable; concerns about environmental sustainability will be given blithe dismissal in the face of certainties that God is coming soon and all will be well. These collateral attitudes are *predictable consequences* of embracing the master-idea of Apocalypse in that they are extrapolations of the values and explanations inherent in the idea of Apocalypse.

And likewise, I argue in what follows, the master-idea of reincarnation has inherent within it values and explanations that will powerfully condition our approach to the various crises that confront us. The idea of reincarnation has a predictable dynamic that will prompt America, as a culture, to embrace the reality (if not the name) of castes as inevitable—however regrettable that inevitability may be.

3

I want to take time, now, to discuss how the consequences of master-ideas find expression in history. How can an idea like reincarnation, a *religious* doctrine, so significantly impact culture? More specifically, how can belief in reincarnation impact the economic and political realities manifesting themselves in the vertical stratification of American society? Historian David Gress, in his comprehensive study, *From Plato to NATO: The Idea of the West and Its Opponents,* makes a point that is central to this study. The present state of the West's self-understanding, what he calls the "standard story," is deeply compromised by an underestimation of the role of *religion* in culture. He says,

> ... the standard story was deaf to religion and theology as cultural forces in their own right ... Thus, the standard story could use parts of what came to be called the Judeo-Christian tradition: dignity of the individual, value of each life, and the hopes and struggles for human rights and moral equality that flowed from that tradition. But it could not easily use others: the belief that the next life was as important as, if not more important than, this and that worldly success was therefore not to be sought; the value of contemplation over action; doctrinal orthodoxy; intolerance; religious wars; anti-Semitism. Because it was deaf to religion, the standard story presented both classical religion and Christianity as peripheral, derivative, and largely irrelevant, except as providers of ideas whose true role was to function as stepping stones in the great secular drama of Western ascendancy from Plato to NATO.[5]

Religious views are not a cultural accessory. At issue is never "just religion." The values and beliefs that constitute religion serve to *define* us—they shape both our understanding of present circumstances and our aspirations for the future. A shift in religious assumptions is therefore inevitably a shift in culture. For example, Europe's culture changed decisively when Christianity replaced the various indigenous pagan religions. Consider as an example the religious views of Vikings of pre-Christian Europe. One feature of this religion is that it took blood vengeance to be not just personal or social retaliation, but as a religious obligation. Any culture predicated on the duty for vengeance has a tendency, if not toward self-destruction, then toward a rude self-limitation. There will, perhaps, be splendid warlords, there will be mighty clans and tribes—but amidst those rough theatrics there will be no advanced civilization. People in those tribal cultures are typically too busy cherishing ancestral hatreds and slaughtering each other to be able to cooperate, at least for very long. Our admiration of the various Viking sagas, for example, and also the *Epic of Beowulf,* is made possible largely through our capacity to suppress any sense of historical realism. Such realism would confront us with accounts of pirate bands engaged in ghastly and revolting behavior—behavior more akin to what is depicted in the Australian film *Mad Max* than the relatively serene portrayals of Viking episodes in romantic 19th century paintings.

With the arrival of Christianity in northern Europe, the religious *ideal* became one that urged a turning away from violence. Yes, religious ideals make us cynical when we don't live up to them. And certainly the subsequent history of Christian Europe suggests that living by the ideal of Christianity was more the exception than the rule. But religious ideals, however poorly realized, serve nonetheless to transform a culture, to shape it on a subtle level. Nordic, pagan Europe, in embracing Christianity, embraced an ethos and a model of personal excellence in which seeking a peaceful resolution to problems was not taken as a sign of *weakness*. The transition from a warrior to a non-warrior religious and cultural ideal—from one that makes revenge a religious duty to one in which religious duty is just the opposite—was a transition that brought with it different cultural possibilities. This momentous transition is characterized by historian James Reston this way:

> At the turn of the last millennium, Europe Christianized, almost all at once ... No more dramatic change can be imagined, not because it was Christian per se, but because Christianity in 999 A.D. represented civilization and learning and nationhood against the darkness of heathenism, illiteracy, and tribal chaos.[6]

When the Nordic pagans adopted new religious assumptions, the tribal lands of the north simultaneously found themselves with new potentials. For one thing, those former pagans developed the potential to become key players in the emergence of what historians call "the first Europe." And by adopting new religious assumptions today, we are, whether we realize it or not, setting the stage for our future cultural possibilities. To repeat: religious views are not a trivial matter; they are never "just religion." That is why it is urgently important that we pay careful attention to the dynamics of transition that are underway.

4

Since the heady days of the 1960s, the attitude toward religion on the part of many Americans has been *exploratory*. There has been an openness to new ways of thinking. No small part of this openness was generated by an evolutionary process in the course of religion that is both inevitable and healthy—a sense of dissatisfaction and impatience with traditional practices and worldviews that, over time, had become outdated. And this impatience did not begin in the 1960's.

Since the emergence of the Enlightenment—the philosophical movement exemplified by 18th century thinkers like John Locke and Thomas Jefferson—and the later development in the 19th century of classic Liberalism—exemplified by John Stuart Mill—certain aspects of traditional Christianity have elicited an uneasiness, even a sense of repugnance. One such aspect is the view that God condemns human souls to everlasting torment in Hell. The idea—and we shall examine it in greater detail later—is that God, through his own inscrutable ways, singles out some people for salvation, others for damnation. In his 1873 *Autobiography,* John Stuart Mill tells of his father's (and his own) revulsion at the idea:

> Think (he used to say) of a being who would make a Hell—who would create the human race with the infallible foreknowledge, and therefore with the intention, that the great majority of them were to be consigned to horrible and everlasting torment. The time, I believe, is drawing near when this dreadful conception of an object of worship will be no longer identified with Christianity ... [7]

The time Mill looked forward to has come. Setting aside dogmatic Fundamentalism for the moment, the Christian vision is, for many if not for all Christians, changing with the times. Pre-modern baggage like the doctrine of eternal damnation is being quietly but decisively left behind. But again, the times are changing *fast,* and the rapidly widening gap between ancient tradition and modern sensibilities has generated an urgent sense of dissatisfaction. This dissatisfaction has prompted many people, especially in Europe and America, to turn to views from outside the religious traditions of the West.

One of the most potent sources of ideas from outside the historical traditions of the West has been the great religious and philosophical traditions of Asia. And one of the most important ideas to arrive from the Asian traditions is from India—*reincarnation theory*. I don't claim that reincarnation theory is the most *important* aspect of the Asian religious traditions. Nor do I take the current trend toward a convergence of traditional Asian and traditional Western views to be misdirected: in fact it is my enthusiastic view that the West will benefit significantly from an incorporation of many aspects of Asian traditions. But my focus in this book is on reincarnation. That is because I believe that reincarnation theory poses a unique threat to American culture—a threat which has been all-too-thoroughly realized in one of the greatest of Asian cultures, the culture of its origin, India.

The attraction to reincarnation theory has manifested itself in several ways in the West, and especially in America. Sometimes the religious outlooks featuring reincarnation simply *replace* traditional Western religious beliefs; people who were born into the Christian tradition, for example, cease to be Christians and embrace Hinduism, or any of a variety of forms of Buddhism. But this is not always the case. It is not uncommon for a belief in reincarnation to be incorporated into the Christian outlook. It is possible, in other words, to remain Christian and embrace the doctrine of reincarnation as an adjunct doctrine to Christianity. Some of that 27% of Americans who are reported to believe in reincarnation are Christians and Jews. An illustration of this is found in the *Catholic World News* reports. In its August 13, 1998, online edition, this Catholic periodical announced that "About 20 percent of Christians believe in reincarnation."[8] This was not, I should add, a joyous disclosure on their part.

5

Here at the turn of the century, then, the West has evidenced a readiness for religious change—whether by way of reformation of existing traditions or their replacement. Especially in America, this readiness for change has at times taken on a sense of urgency. As a result, the present period of transition is sometimes characterized by those who live through it as being somewhat *flighty*. Consider the assessment of social critic Walter Truett Anderson:

> Like hermit crabs who skitter about in the tide pools wearing the shells of dead snails, we don old belief systems that do not always fit too well, and go about our business. Most of us now are not so much believers as possessors of beliefs. Conversion comes easy and often. The seeker after religious faith tries on not just one religion, but any number of them.[9]

And to say it again, many important elements of this late 20th/early 21st century religious free market originated in Asia. Indeed, the predictions of renowned historian Arnold Toynbee, written in 1948, have proven prescient:

> Our own descendants are not going to be just Western, like ourselves. They are going to be heirs of Confucius and Lao-Tse as well as Socrates, Plato, and Plotinus; heirs of Gautama Buddha as well as Deutero-Isaiah and Jesus Christ ... heirs of Shankara and Ramanuja as well as Clement and Origen ...[10]

No matter if you haven't heard of Shankara or Ramanuja, the convergence of traditional Asian views with Western traditions that Toynbee forecast is well underway. And an important accelerant of that process is a growing dissatisfaction on the part of many Americans with certain traditional Western religious assumptions. Incoming Asian views entice many Americans with exciting and plausible alternatives to what seem to them to be outdated Western views on the nature of reality and on the self and its destiny.

It's worth repeating that this combination of dissatisfaction and excitement was not born in the 1960's. As we shall see later in this discussion, ideas from Asia have been electrifying intellectuals in the West since the 18th century. And while that impact was significant, its scope was restricted to intellectuals. What is different about the last decades of the 20th century is the extraordinary *popularity* and general acceptance of Asian religious assumptions about the self. Among the most important of those assumptions, and the focus of the present study, is the doctrine of reincarnation.

The discussion that follows is stridently critical of reincarnation theory and its potential effects on 21st century American culture. What I have to say may at times, I fear, tilt toward the jeremiad in its tone. But this should not be misconstrued. What follows is not a nativist rant about the perils of foreign cultural imports. It is not part of the conservative "take back our culture" agenda that has developed an increasingly shrill voice in the last two decades.

To reiterate: the convergences presently underway between traditional Asian and traditional Western outlooks are a cause for excitement and hope. My optimism here is rooted in my belief that, just as it is possible to embrace Christianity without accepting the toxic doctrine of everlasting damnation, so it is equally possible to embrace traditional Asian religious outlooks without accepting what I argue to be the toxic doctrine of reincarnation.

6

But before we proceed, a word about cultural change. My assumption is that ongoing change is *essential* to culture, not something that may or may not happen to it. The cultural preservationist disposition—whether it is invested in preserving traditional, so-called mainstream American culture, or in preserving the traditions of cultural sub-groups within American society—is based on a different view. It is based on the view, not always explicitly stated, that cultural traditions are a finished product, something established and sacrosanct, something to which loyalty and allegiance is due.

Against this view, I take the position that culture is an ongoing activity, ever in process, ever unfinished. Culture not only changes, it *grows*. For a culture, the alternative to change and growth is *atrophy*. Culture is best understood as being a *verb* rather than a *noun,* as a *process* rather than as a *thing*. To speak of a process as a thing constitutes a fallacy called *reification*—literally, from the Latin *re,* meaning thing, "thingifying." Now, recognizing that we would be involved in the fallacy of reification if we say that culture *is* a living thing, we can nonetheless observe that culture is very *like* a living thing in that it has a dynamic existence. It is more *like* an organism, in other words, than it is *like* a mechanism. Culture is not something like a car, for example. One can take a car and remove a hood-ornament or add a trailer-hitch, and still have the same car—the same car minus a hood-ornament or plus a hitch. Changes in culture are different. I take my cue here from Neil Postman's assessment of the consequences of *technological* innovation, in this case television, within a culture. He says:

> Technological change is neither additive nor subtractive. It is ecological ... One significant change generates total change. If you remove the caterpillars from a given habitat, you are not left with the same environment minus caterpillars: you have a new environment ... This is how the ecology of media works as well. A new technology does not add or subtract something. It changes everything ... After television, the United States was not America plus television; television gave a new coloration to every political campaign, to every home, to every school, to every church, to every industry.[11]

Postman cautions that there is no such thing as an isolated event in the significant moments of culture. Culture is an ecological system, and therefore any change introduced will resonate throughout—it will not remain localized, but will inevitably transform the entire system. And as American culture was decisively transformed through the introduction of the technology of television, so it will be decisively transformed through the introduction of the religious concept of reincarnation. The result will not be "America-plus"—America plus some different religious assumptions; the result will be a different America. And what will that different America be like? Just that is my concern in this study.

7

It is by now clear that I want to invest the reader with a sense of concern, even a sense of alarm, over what I take to be the harmful aspects of the doctrine of reincarnation. But there is a very basic question to be faced. What if it's true? All objections and predictions of dire outcomes notwithstanding, what if the doctrine of reincarnation is simply how things work in the world? My response to such questions might seem frivolous at first blush: in this book I am not concerned with truth. That is, I am not concerned to establish either the truth or the non-truth of the doctrine of reincarnation. My is assumption is that attaining to the *truth*—understood as objective, unchanging, absolute, or "pure" truth—is not an authentic human possibility. This assumption is not a new one. Since the publication of Immanuel Kant's *Critique of Pure Reason* in 1781, a consensus among laborers in the field of ideas have conceded that the hope to attain absolute truth is illusory.

Especially in regard to speculation about what happens after death—whether heaven or hell, simple oblivion, or reincarnation—Kant's denial of truth as a human possibility carries a certain credibility. If the truth about such an urgent issue were possible, we would by now have attained it. Or at least there would be a reasonable consensus. And such a consensus is conspicuously absent; expert testimony is countered by expert testimony. There is something of a Newtonian dynamic operative in the vigorous contest over public opinion: for every Ph.D. there is an equal and opposite Ph.D. The master-ideas dealt with in this book will never be settled in regard to truth. Never.

But the fact that we cannot attain the truth doesn't mean that we are reduced to silence. We can discuss the existence of God or the operation of karma over successive lives, we can examine the views on such topics put forward by eminent philosophers or authentic mystics. My assumption, however, is that the most realistic engagement of such issues trades not in certainties and claims to absolute truth, but in multiple perspectives, in hypotheses that are taken as *working* hypotheses, subject to correction, refinement, and rejection over time. In saying this I do not suggest that the issue of the truth should remain unaddressed in regard to reincarnation theory. Paul Edwards' book, *Reincarnation: A Critical Examination,* assesses the truth and scientific cogency of the theories of karma and reincarnation, and his discussion is useful. He states at the outset of his study what he takes to be his task:

> ... the question with which I am primarily concerned in this book ... [is] with what may be called the logical standing of reincarnation: Is it true or false or neither?[12]

By contrast, in this book I will explore and assess not the *truth* of the doctrines of karma and reincarnation, but the *consequences* of those doctrines—specifically their *social* consequences. And I must point out that this mode of engaging and assessing philosophical issues is not a new one, nor is it one alien to the domain of American discourse.

8

Nearly a century ago, the American philosopher and psychologist William James asserted that all theories and descriptions of reality are alike in that none of them are the absolute truth. But—and this is the important part—they are not all alike in their *consequences*. They are not all alike in the practical results they generate, results that are realized in the life of an individual or the life of a culture. James' criterion for evaluating theories is straightforward and pragmatic: what makes a theory a good one is determined by how well it *works,* by what effects it produces. This approach to philosophy is called *Pragmatism,* and was articulated by James and Charles S. Peirce. Of his rejection of truth in favor of utility, James said: "I am well aware how odd it must seem to some of you to hear me say that an idea is 'true' so long as to believe it is profitable to our lives."[13] For James, the vitality conferred by a belief in one's life is its whole justification. He insisted that this committed him to no *specific* world-view or religion or philosophy, but only to a method of assessing philosophical and religious views. The sole evaluative principle for a theory is—how does it *work?* What does it *do?* Again in James' words:

> *Theories thus become instruments, not answers to enigmas in which we can rest.* We don't lie back on them, we move forward, and, on occasion, make nature over again by their aid. Pragmatism unstiffens all our theories, limbers them up and sets each one at work.[14]

At issue is the central concern of this book. Ideas, especially those I've called master-ideas, are powerful. Whether we recognize it or not, they *do* something. The master-ideas embodied in religious doctrines are *instruments*—tools—and never "just ideas." Do you believe in God, in heaven and hell? That will *do* something in your life. What does it do? And do you really want that effect in your life? Do you believe in reincarnation? That too will *do* something. It will do something not just on the personal level, but, when enough other people also believe it, on a cultural level as well.

Yet, one might ask, is a pragmatic approach really appropriate for religious ideas? Such an approach may be fine, may *work* fine, in the domain of secular concerns. But religion goes deeper; religion touches on our core values; religion is the domain of the *sacred,* not the merely *useful.* Anyone with a glancing acquaintance with his work knows that William James does indeed make bold to submit the claims of religion and mysticism to the sweaty criterion of pragmatism. Speaking metaphorically of philosophical pragmatism as *feminine,* he tells us that:

> She will count [=approve] mystical experiences if they have practical consequences ... Her only test of probable truth is what works best in the way of leading us, what fits every part of life best and combines with the collectivity of experience's demands, nothing being omitted.[15]

And his pragmatic rigor in regard to mysticism is fully endorsed by the noted scholar and practitioner of mysticism, Evelyn Underhill. Embracing James' pragmatic criterion in assessing the authenticity of the mystical experience, Underhill says:

> The ecstatic condition is no guarantee of mystic vision. It is frequently pathological ... we have a test which we can apply to the ecstatic; and which separates the results of nervous disorder from those of spiritual transcendence. "What fruit dost thou bring back from this thy vision?" is the final question ... to the mystic's soul. And the answer is: "An orderly life in every state."[16]

Underhill endorses the pragmatic criterion—indeed throughout her writings she regularly cites James with approval. We see, then, that a pragmatic criterion was embraced by an extraordinary philosopher of religion and a renowned scholar of mysticism. And in what follows, I will take my cue from James and Underhill. My task, that is to say, is to assess not the truth of reincarnation doctrine, but its *consequences*. What are the consequences for the individual who believes in reincarnation? And as important—what are the consequences for society when a critical mass of its members come to believe in reincarnation?

9

Will reincarnation come to be embraced as a mainstream outlook in American culture? Conjecture is possible, of course, but that is not the purpose of this book. My purpose here is to explore the *consequences* of such a development, should it occur. And I want to close this Introduction on a special note of caution.

The ideas to be treated in this book are "hot" in that they touch on issues that evoke strong emotional responses. Emotional responses tend to be simplistic, and to be characterized by impatience and anger. Neither accusation nor vilification is my purpose in this discussion. Specifically, it is not my intention to impugn the character or integrity of those in the past, or those here in American culture at the dawn of the 21st century, who are committed to the doctrine of reincarnation.

At stake is far more than politeness or diplomacy. It is a matter of the utmost importance to emphasize, indeed to *insist*, that adherents of reincarnation theory are typically among the best of us. To believe in reincarnation, to be *dedicated* to that doctrine, is not thereby to be wicked. It is not a character flaw that attracts people to the theory. Nor do good folks inadvertently *develop* a mean streak through their embrace of the doctrine. Entirely to the contrary, those who embrace the doctrine of reincarnation tend to be people of a philosophical bent, thoughtful people, people who are often deeply committed to a more just society.

As we'll see in Chapter 1, belief in reincarnation, like the Christian belief in an afterlife, can be understood as an expression of the human need to find a balancing of the scales, to find some degree of consolation through embracing an explanation based on familiar social ideals of compensation and repayment in kind. The facts of life can be savage. And in the face of what can easily seem a brute and mute life-force, people have a need to tell themselves that somehow, someway, it all makes sense—that terrible and otherwise incomprehensible experiences do not reduce life to being, as a despairing Macbeth cried out, "a tale told by an idiot, full of sound and fury, signifying nothing."

To repeat: those who believe in reincarnation are typically among the best of us. But precisely this is the most dangerous aspect of reincarnation theory in the contemporary world, at least as I see it. One of the most irresponsible of assumptions is that theories of disastrous consequence are thought up and embraced by nasty people. Since few identify themselves as "nasty," the implication is that decent folks—folks like you and me, my friend—don't need to worry about what views *we* hold. Right?

I often meet people, exceptionally well-educated people possessed of high intelligence and equally high integrity, who believe fervently in reincarnation. And some of them claim to believe in the doctrine for the best of reasons: direct experience—they have, they believe, been brought to remember a past life, sometimes many past lives, sometimes in copious detail. Their sincerity is beyond reproach. But history shows us that sincerity does not confer immunity against horrific social outcomes.

Notes

1. Harris survey, cited at http://www.harrisinteractive.com/harris_poll/ index.asp?PID=359.
2. Kaus, M. *The End of Equality.* New York: Basic Books, 1996, p.17.
3. "In a 1990 study conducted by The Gallup Poll, 21% of adults said they believed in reincarnation. By 1994 that figure had grown to 27%." Gallup, G., Jr. and D. M. Lindsay *Surveying the Religious Landscape: Trends in U.S. Beliefs.* Harrisburg, PA: Morehouse Publishing, 1999, p.33-4.
4. Bereman, G. D. "The Concept of Caste" in the *International Encyclopedia of Social Sciences, v.II.* New York: Crowell, Collier, and Macmillan, 1968, p.334.
5. Gress, D. *From Plato to NATO: the Idea of the West and Its Opponents.* New York: The Free Press, 1998, p.24.
6. Reston, J. *The Last Apocalypse: Europe at the Year 1000 A.D.* New York: Anchor Books, 1998, p.7.
7. Mill, J. S. *Autobiography.* New York: Bobbs-Merrill Co., Inc., 1957, pp.27-8.
8. *Catholic World News Online.* http://www.cwnews.com/ news/viewrec.cfm?RefNum=8270, 8-13-98.
9. Anderson, W. T. *Reality Isn't What It Used to Be.* New York: Harper and Row, 1990, p.9.
10. Toynbee, A. J. *Civilization on Trial.* New York: Oxford Univ. Press, 1948, p.90.

11. Postman, N. *Amusing Ourselves to Death.* New York: Penguin Books, 1986, p.18.
12. Edwards, P. *Reincarnation: a Critical Examination.* Amherst, NY: Prometheus Books, 1996, p.26.
13. James, W. *Pragmatism.* Buffalo, New York: Prometheus Books, 1991, p.36.
14. James, 1991, p.26. Emphasis in the original.
15. James, 1991, p.38.
16. Underhill, E. "The Essentials of Mysticism" in *The Essentials of Mysticism and Other Essays.* New York: E. P. Dutton & Co., 1920, pp.22-23.

1

THE DRAMA OF REINCARNATION

> Do you have any idea how many lives we must have gone through before we even got the first idea that there is more to life than eating, or fighting, or power in the Flock? A thousand lives, Jon, ten thousand! And then another hundred lives until we began to learn that there is such a thing as perfection, and another hundred again to get the idea that our purpose for living is to find that perfection and show it forth. The same rule holds for us now, of course: we choose our next world through what we learn in this one. Learn nothing, and the next world is the same as this one, all the same limitations and lead weights to overcome.
>
> —Richard Bach, *Jonathan Livingston Seagull*[1]

1

The drama of reincarnation is twofold. First, there is the dramatic unfolding of serial lives purported to be the destiny of each individual. Second, there is the often dramatic debate over the desirability of having reincarnation doctrine incorporated into the collective psyche of the West. I call this debate a drama because it is so often attended by towering certainties on all sides. This book is, of course, a part of the latter drama. Like many of the sources I cite, I am not impartial. I find reincarnation to be a deeply problematic doctrine. The passage used as the epigraph of this chapter is from a so-called "New Age" fictional work that enjoyed huge popularity. But, it might be objected at the outset, how relevant is a popular book, one written largely as *entertainment*, to this discussion? *Enormously* relevant, from the standpoint of my concerns. My primary interest here is not with philosophers or theologians, although I will regularly invoke their ideas. In this study, I am not concerned with whether an attraction to reincarnation has taken root among intellectuals or occultists. My concern is with the popular mind—with the mind that ultimately determines the character of American culture. And that collective mind is tilting in favor of reincarnation theory.

2

We begin by considering some details. Reincarnation theory is not, as they say, rocket science. The gist of the theory can be stated fairly succinctly: death is not final, but is a transition to another life—not a life in Heaven as conceived by traditional Christianity, but another earthly life in human or animal or sometimes even vegetable form. Our true identity, what is subject to being reborn in another life, is a nonmaterial, spiritual essence. It is this essence that undergoes a succession of rebirths in bodies and personalities—bodies and personalities that are no more than temporary vehicles of the *true self* in its journey toward liberation. That's pretty simple; again, the core of the doctrine requires no special philosophical training. More to the point of the present discussion: how *dangerous* can such an idea be? It is clear from talking to the doctrine's adherents that believing in reincarnation makes people *feel* good. What can possibly be the harm in that?

The danger is not in the fact *that* people believe in reincarnation; the danger lies in the *way* in which they believe in reincarnation, as well as in other religious ideas. Reincarnation is one of the master-ideas spoken of in the previous chapter, ideas that powerfully condition the mind and structure our understanding of reality. Typically, religious master-ideas are presented through narratives, and these narratives can be understood in two ways—literally or metaphorically.

The literalist approach takes the words of a religious narrative to be literally and objectively true. These words are taken to mean exactly what they say, and what they say is taken to be the one and only truth. By contrast, the metaphoric approach takes the words and stories of the religious narrative as having a *psychological,* rather than a literal meaning. Also, and equally important, the metaphoric approach accepts that multiple interpretations of the narrative are both possible and *legitimate*—there is, in this view, no definitive interpretation.

The importance of the distinction between a literal and a metaphoric understanding of religious narratives becomes apparent when we consider how such narratives find expression in history. Take as an example the master-idea mentioned in the previous chapter, the idea of the Apocalypse. The Apocalypse narrative is a pivotal feature of the monotheistic religions; it centers on the drama of a cosmic battle for the earth, a battle waged between the forces of Good and Evil—a battle between God and his followers and Satan and his followers. Is a metaphoric understanding of such dire events possible? In fact it is. For the Jew or Christian or Muslim who is willing to think in non-literalist terms, Apocalypse may well serve as a metaphor for the spiritual struggle endemic to the individual human psyche, a struggle to transcend personal limitations. The dead weight of habitual response, the insistent tug of appetite, the emotional fire of rage and anger, the secret impulses to preen and strut in subtle ways—all these could be seen metaphorically as demonic. The quest to subdue them, the aspiration toward spiritual growth, can in this psychological context be framed as "fighting the good fight"—engaging in the Apocalypse.

The fact that a metaphoric approach to the idea of Apocalypse is possible should not mislead us. History shows us that when a foundation narrative like the Apocalypse is brought to the streets—when it is popularized—it finds expression not in metaphor but in metaphysical certainty. And as a certainty, out on the street, it possesses the minds of all-too-many who are eager to die and kill in the realization of an apocalyptic Armageddon. Metaphor is not the understanding of the street: adherents to the apocalyptic vision from Waco to Washington, from Jerusalem to Qum, see themselves as engaged in war against "the Evil One." It is a physical battle against a very real Satan—an entity of pure malice whose will is being asserted by corrupt humans who are his agents and executors. Despite its claims to spiritual sensitivity, the apocalyptic scenario has unvarnished cruelty built into it.

This dimension of the popular understanding is given lucid if distasteful expression in the series of religious novels by Tim LaHaye and Jerry B. Jenkins, a series under the general title *Left Behind*. In the final novel of the series, *Glorious Appearing,* LaHaye and Jenkins present grotesque and vivid images of the events surrounding the second coming of Christ. We read of the sudden and horrific massacre of those who do not share the vision of evangelical Christians. In reviewing the novel, New York Times commentator Nicholas D. Kristof says this:

> These are the best-selling novels for adults in the United States, and they have sold more than 60 million copies worldwide. The latest is "Glorious Appearing," which has Jesus returning to Earth to wipe all non-Christians from the planet. It's disconcerting to find ethnic cleansing celebrated as the height of piety... this portrayal of a bloody Second Coming reflects a shift in American portrayals of Jesus, from a gentle Mister Rogers figure to a martial messiah presiding over a sea of blood... "Tens of thousands of foot soldiers dropped their weapons, grabbed their heads or their chests, fell to their knees, and writhed as they were invisibly sliced asunder. Their innards and entrails gushed to the desert floor, and as those around them turned to run, they too were slain, their blood pooling and rising in the unforgiving brightness of the glory of Christ."[2]

An ugly vision, this unforgiving brightness of the glory of Christ. Here is a disposition to celebrate savagery as divine intention. And it must be insisted that such an encomium of cruelty is a travesty of the Christianity by which most American Christians live. Yet just such extremes are predictable in the translation of religious metaphors into street certainties.

Reincarnation theory, too, can be construed as an elegant metaphor—a metaphor of connectedness and consequence. As a master-idea it can foster a sense of empathy with any station of life—human or non-human—because the spiritual essence that is the true self can be incarnated at any of those stations. This generalized empathy can in turn generate, at least in theory, a recognition of the interconnections that underlie myriad life-forms and the feeling of reciprocity implicit in that recognition. The narrative of reincarnation might bring us to conclude that we are, after all, our brother's and sister's care-takers.

But again, this isn't how it plays out in the street. As with the master-idea of Apocalypse, the concept of reincarnation has found expression in the street not as metaphor, but as metaphysical certainty. Reincarnation has been taken to be an objective account that scripts social disparities in terms of *just deserts*. As such it becomes a blueprint for indifference in the face of injustice and grinding human misery. The scenario of reincarnation is less overtly violent than the myth of apocalypse. It finds expression not through thunderous upheavals attendant on Jesus' angry return; it works quietly and unobtrusively within a culture. Where there is cruelty and swagger inherent in the Apocalypse narrative, there is a gentleness and ostensible humaneness that attends reincarnation theory. And I contend in what follows that its gentle and humane demeanor is one of its most dangerous aspects.

3

Let's proceed by looking more closely at the *appeal* of reincarnation theory. The renowned Buddhist scholar Edward Conze, in a passage that is both wicked and wise, makes a variety of observations about some of the believers in reincarnation that he encountered in his travels:

> The doctrine of reincarnation attracts them for three reasons, (1) because it allows them to believe that they have spent much of their time in the past as Egyptian princesses and the like, (2) because it frees them from the sense of social guilt which is endemic in the bourgeoisie of the twentieth century, by persuading them that they deserve their money and privileges as a reward for merit gained in the past and (3) because it convinces them that their precious selves will not be lost when they die.[3]

Lest anyone think that he was speaking only of spiritual dilettantes or beginners in Buddhist practice, Conze adds a footnote to point (1) in this passage in which he includes his colleague, the noted Buddhist scholar and adept Christmas Humphreys:

> Nor does Christmas Humphreys himself disappoint us in this respect, when he tells us of "an incident in Egypt when Rene and I were together in the reign of Rameses II. I was immensely proud of my gold breastplate as an officer in the royal bodyguard, and she was a Virgin of Isis. We loved, somehow, and unlawfully to the point of death for both of us"; and so we go on.[4]

A cheeky presentation, yes, but deeply perceptive as well. Of the three reasons cited by Conze for belief in reincarnation, the first and the third tend to be focused upon by those who see reincarnation as a harmless doctrine. That is, the doctrine is seen as innocuous when conceived as either romantic wish fulfillment (reason 1), or as a harmless anodyne in the face of the terrors of death (reason 3). I will not disparage romance and its appeals. And it should be noted, in the interests of fairness, that not every recalled past life is that of a princess or an officer in a praetorian guard. Some accounts speak of past lives that are grubby, anonymous, and dishonorable. Taken as a series, however, accounts of past lives are, well, *interesting*. Taken as a series, past lives could not but be more interesting than the present life, the life in which those past lives are recalled.

But we mustn't make things easy for ourselves by supposing that believers in reincarnation are romantics or wispy sentimentalists. There are gritty realists as well. And two of the grittiest of these might be said to be a pair of redoubtable figures from 20th century American history—the industrialist Henry Ford and General George Patton. Speaking of the importance of reincarnation theory to his life, Henry Ford said:

> I adopted the theory of Reincarnation when I was twenty-six ... Religion offered nothing to the point ... Even work could not give me complete satisfaction. Work is futile if we cannot utilize the experience we collect in one life in the next. When I discovered Reincarnation ... time was no longer limited. I was no longer a slave to the clock ... The discovery of Reincarnation put my mind at ease ... I would like to communicate to others the calmness that the long view of life gives to us.[5]

Colonel Roger H. Nye, family friend and biographer of General George Patton, wrote copiously in his papers and letters on the General. His remarks and recollections of Patton are included in historian Stanley P. Hirshson's 2002 study, *General Patton: A Soldier's Life*. Hirshson cites a paper by Nye in which Patton's views on reincarnation are summarized:

> Patton wrote that he may have initiated his many lives as a caveman hunting for meat, and he may have been a soldier who stabbed Christ on the cross. He fought alongside the Greeks, Alexander at Tyre, and the Roman legionnaires. He was once a pirate, a cavalryman with Napoleon, and finally a tanker in the Great War.[6]

But whether it is embraced by vintage tough-guys or less heroic grocery clerks, how can an embrace of reincarnation doctrine be harmful? Belief in past lives, as well as hopes in regard to future lives, can confer a sense of consolation and meaning in the midst of moments of dire crisis, industrial or military. And it can confer a delicious secret on the person schlepping along in a dreary and underappreciated job. A flighty variant of Walter Mitty's inner theater, perhaps—but a congenial boost to self-esteem that does no real damage to anyone, not even the person who embraces the adventures. Eccentric?—maybe; harmless?—maybe not.

4

For now, we take a more somber turn and consider the third reason proposed above by Conze as to the appeal of reincarnation—"that their precious selves will not be lost when they die." Humans ancient and modern exhibit a deep-seated abhorrence of nonbeing. This, of course, is the great appeal of Christianity with its promise of personal immortality. Such a promise is no trivial matter.

Consider the view espoused by many who have renounced Christianity and embrace a more scientific view of human identity. Cosmologists tell us that every atom in our body was once in the interior of a star—that we are, all of us, stardust. Nice. We smile. But when we hear that from stardust we came, and to stardust we shall return, the smile fades. To be human is to hope for something a bit more than that. It's fine to hear that I'm stardust. The problem is that I don't really *identify* with stardust. I identify with a quite specific concatenation of stardust known as "Bill." But "Bill" describes a *personality,* and science argues compellingly that the fate of the personality is inextricably bound to the fate of the body. And the fate of the body is no mystery: at death, it must be buried, burned, or refrigerated lest it constitute a public health hazard.

But here the doctrine of reincarnation, like the Christian doctrine of personal immortality, comes to the rescue. For reincarnation theory holds that there is a spiritual essence that is deeper than either the body or any one personality. The body that dies is not really *me*—it is like an overcoat that my true self, my essential self, discards when it is worn out. And this essential self incarnates again and again; again and again personalities develop in conjunction with each incarnation.

This scenario has proven especially attractive to educated Westerners. Reincarnation allows those who see themselves as sophisticated and "grown up" about religion to persist in the hope for the persistence of identity. Reincarnation is not, after all, about the vulgar hope for *personal* immortality. But a closer look suggests otherwise. Immediately in the wings of the drama of reincarnation is the breathless suggestion that, with appropriate training, past lives can be *recalled.* All those personal lives can be woven together into a single awareness, a single consciousness—one that might constitute a kind of super-person. How often do we say of our youth, "Of course, I was a different person then." As that super-person who recalls the "persons" of childhood and youth serves to unite and claim identity with *all* those subordinates, so the evolved soul who remembers a spray of past persons could claim identity with the entire collection. If this isn't actual immortality (we don't know that this recollecting soul might not, after many a lifetime, terminate), then it allows for a significantly longer span than the three-score and ten allotted to us. And thus it provides hope that, to quote

Conze's words yet again, "their precious selves will not be lost when they die."

Considered from the perspective of the overall career of the reincarnating essential self, from the perspective of *eons*, individual lives come to seem like days—mere episodes in the career of the essence that evolves toward beatification. Death thus is no more than the end of a day, a hiatus of no great consequence. But the ticket to this easement is shadowed forth in the very terms in which it is expressed: as death is a mere sunset of no consequence, so any one life—and in particular *this* life—is a mere day, and of no great consequence. Again, as with the romantic gratifications attendant upon it, this aspect of reincarnation theory may seem harmless enough. But as we'll see, not all that *seems* harmless actually *is* harmless.

There is still another reason, one not mentioned by Conze, as to why people come to embrace the theory of reincarnation. This reason is not, as in some of his wry conjectures, silly or pretentious; it reflects one of the things that makes us human. It is rooted, I suggest, in our natural sense of *wonder*. We look up at the stars on a clear night; we have been schooled by Carl Sagan to think in terms of "billions and billions" of potential worlds. We want to see those worlds, we want to somehow experience them. Knowing they are there, we have a yearning, an emotional tug, a kind of ache (albeit a delicious ache) to *experience* them. Reincarnation promises, not exactly many worlds, but something quite as good: many *lives*, many personalities. Few are unimpressed by the potential richness of a single human life. Might it not be grand to amplify that richness a thousandfold? Ten thousandfold? Reincarnation allows for just that. While most folks experience only one life at a time, we are told of adepts who remember many past lives. We even hear of experts who are able to lead ordinary people through a process called *past life regression*. To be able to embrace a grand multiplicity of personalities without having to endure all the fuss and bother of a psychiatric diagnosis—the prospect is a heady one, and an attraction to it is entirely understandable.

I want to take time, now, to acknowledge that the presentation of reincarnation offered here is *selective*. The doctrine of reincarnation is, of course, susceptible of a wide variety of interpretations. The one that is popular in America, and so the focus of this study, is the one just described—an individual spiritual essence, something that might be thought of as a "deep soul," that migrates from one life to the next. It should be noted, however, that this is not the only understanding of reincarnation. In concluding his detailed and perceptive analysis of case-study evidence for reincarnation, the psychologist D. Scott Rogo, says this:

So, in conclusion, do I "believe" in reincarnation? Based on the evidence, I suppose I should say that I do: but not in the reincarnation of the soul, but in the fact that certain apparently vanished memories and traits of personality *can* actually be born again.[7]

Rogo presents an interesting version of reincarnation theory, consistent with certain schools of Buddhism, but one which he himself allows is out of step with the mainstream. And it is *not* the mainstream view, I suggest, because it offers precious little by way of psychological consolation. No princesses or officers with golden breastplates here—no soul to travel from one splendid or poignant adventure to the next. Again, my focus is on reincarnation understood as the successive rebirths of a continuous self, a "deep soul" whose previous lives can be recalled under the right circumstances, because it is the understanding of reincarnation held by adherents to the theory as diverse as Christmas Humphreys and Henry Ford, as well as Richard Bach and Shirley MacLaine. It is the understanding of reincarnation that currently enjoys such popularity in America; it is the understanding of the doctrine that I take to be so dangerous.

5

We return to Conze's analysis. I want to look closer at the second reason he cites as to why people believe in reincarnation—that the belief in reincarnation "frees them from the sense of social guilt which is endemic in the bourgeoisie of the twentieth century, by persuading them that they deserve their money and privileges." Despite his blithe presentation, this is a point that Conze himself took very seriously. The downside of believing in reincarnation is that the theory embodies a perspective on life that allows people to assuage feelings of responsibility, to assume that their privileged life is deserved, and to assume that the misfortune of others is equally deserved. Still worse, belief in reincarnation can bring people—people who are good and generous-hearted—to assume that attempts to mitigate social inequities may be well-intentioned, but are, in the last analysis, *misdirected*. Put otherwise, reincarnation theory can produce two kinds of mischief in American culture. First, it can *license* social indifference for those inclined to it. Second, and more serious, reincarnation theory can *generate* social indifference in those who might otherwise be disposed to work to change the social and economic disparities that can prove to be dehumanizing.

Consider, for example, the remarkable popularity of Shirley MacLaine's 1983 book, *Out on a Limb*. This is a book which many people—Americans intellectual and non-intellectual—loudly acclaimed as a pivotal experience in their lives. The message of the book is summarized in the words of one of Ms. MacLaine's resources, a man named John, who we are told is the owner of the Bodhi Tree bookstore. Here:

> It's so important ... see, to the people like Pythagoras or Plato or any of those guys, all the misfortunes in life like disease, deformities, injustices, and all that, were explained by the fact that each life embodiment was a reward or punishment of a preceding life embodiment, and as each soul progressed, that person was rewarded with more choices of how to reincarnate, all with the moral purpose, of course, to work out his or her own individual karma.[8]

This enormously successful book, like *Jonathan Livingston Seagull* before it, did more than introduce the ideas of karma and reincarnation to a vast number of Americans, it generated an unprecedented popular *enthusiasm* for those ideas. And, I will be repeatedly urging, this was hardly a moment in American history to celebrate. Recall the point made in the Introduction, that a master-idea like reincarnation has predictable dynamics. To a degree, we can see those dynamics unfolding before our eyes. People of good intentions, many of them committed to implementing justice in society, are brought to believe that "disease, deformities, injustices" are somehow the *choices* of the people afflicted by them—that there is a "moral purpose" operative, allowing each "to work out his or her individual karma."

It is no doubt salutary in contemporary America to call attention to the fact that acts have *consequences*. It is good to emphasize that the choices we make *matter*. Yes, our choices matter. But one of those choices is not who our parents are; we do not choose the situation into which we are born. To assume that we do is to exempt ourselves from serious concern over those who have made "choices of how to reincarnate, all with the moral purpose, of course, to work out his or her own individual karma." The suggestion that we *choose* our birth, and thereby our social circumstances in life can be, as Gilbert and Sullivan showed us in their delightful *H. M. S. Pinafore*, an entertaining one:

> He is an Englishman!
>
> For he himself has said it and it's greatly to his credit,
> That he is an Englishman!

For he might have been a Roosian, a French or Turk or Proosian ...

Or perhaps Itali-an!

But in spite of all temptations to belong to other nations,
He remains an Englishman!

In comic opera, entertaining; as an analysis of social circumstances out there in the streets in which we live, not a bit entertaining. Why not? Because the theory of reincarnation presented by MacLaine offers more than an *explanation* of social disparities; it offers a *justification* of social disparities—a full-dress, *moral* justification. And my intention in this writing is to provoke an awareness of the extent to which such moral justifications of human misery are implicit in the doctrine of reincarnation. They are part of the innate dynamic of the master-idea of reincarnation. And this is why a growing belief in reincarnation is anything but harmless. But for now, let's look at another aspect of reincarnation theory.

6

I return to the image with which this chapter opened, that of the *drama* of reincarnation. The dramatic dimensions of the theory of reincarnation will be promptly evident to anyone who presumes to question it—or outright oppose it—in a public forum. Consider the account of the Indian scholar S. Bhattacharji. In the preface to his book, *Fatalism in India,* he says this:

> In 1981, I attended a conference on religion in Winnipeg, Canada. My paper was on "Fatalism in ancient India." In the course of my discourse, I had mentioned that the theories of Karman and rebirth were two of the most vicious ever invented by man. I was attacked vehemently by all and sundry; I realized that the fatalism with which these theories were intrinsically linked was a vested interest, or, the apathy and passivity it produced were.[9]

I cannot agree with Bhattacharji that there is a "vested interested" in apathy and passivity produced by fatalism behind the response to his paper. The vested interest, and I think there is one, is an interest in *certainty*. It is an interest in protecting cherished beliefs from the often rude process of interrogation, a rudeness that is essential to the scientific method. And the remarkable thing is that such a disposition can be found among trained scientists.

7

Stanislav Grof was raised in Czechoslovakia and was trained as a physician and psychiatrist in Prague. He came to the United States in 1960, and has since become a celebrated figure in the fields of consciousness studies and transpersonal psychology. I focus on Dr. Grof for two reasons. First, he is a trained scientist, a world-class intellectual, and therefore cannot be lightly dismissed as a superstitious ignoramus. Second, Grof's attitudes toward reincarnation are representative, if not of professional psychologists and scientists, then of a majority of the people in America who accept the doctrine of reincarnation. In his 1998 book, *The Cosmic Game: Explorations of the Frontiers of Human Consciousness,* he says:

> The concept of reincarnation and karma is not a "belief" in the usual sense of the word, meaning an ungrounded and arbitrary theoretical and emotional position that is not supported by facts ... It is an eminently empirical issue, based on very specific experiences and observations.[10]

Grof's assertion is that reincarnation is an empirical fact, self-evident through immediate, personal experience, and not merely through theoretical abstractions or arcane metaphysics. Direct experience, not the strictures of the scientific method, is the touchstone by which the doctrine of reincarnation is to be assessed. He continues further on in his discussion:

> The existence of past life experiences with all their remarkable characteristics is an *unquestionable fact* that can be verified by any *serious* researcher who is *sufficiently open-minded* and interested to check the evidence. It is also clear that there is no plausible explanation for these phenomena within the conceptual framework of mainstream psychiatry and psychology ... The popular understanding of reincarnation as a repeated cycle of life, death, and rebirth of the same individual is a reasonable conclusion from the available evidence. It is certainly far superior to the attitude of traditional psychologists and psychiatrists, who ignore all the available evidence and rigidly adhere to the established ways of thinking.[11]

The italics in this passage are mine, but it is Grof's phrasing that is important. Past lives and reincarnation, we are told, are a matter of *unquestionable fact.* And the suggestion is clear, no matter if unstated, that those who demur are likely to be unserious and closed minded, people who don't give a damn about checking the evidence. We should, I suggest, feel a dawning sense of alarm when any purported fact is deemed to be beyond question. The problem is not *what* Grof believes—or, to allow him to correct me, what he *knows*—but the *way* that he knows it. He disparages what he calls the "established ways of thinking" of traditional psychiatrists. But these "established ways" are grounded in the scientific method—a method of testing hypotheses and thereby confirming or disconfirming them. By contrast, Grof maintains his views in such a way that they are immune from disconfirmation. Indeed, any attempt at questioning reincarnation would be not only misdirected, but somehow improper. The very act of inquiry would, for those who think like him, call into suspicion the credibility of the questioner, even the *integrity* of the questioner.

But surely there is a problem here. Have we not veered toward the mindset typically associated with fundamentalism? To place a theory in a position immune to falsification on the basis of the strength of one's beliefs about that theory is to stand in dubious company—one has joined with people who *know beyond question* about alien abductions, poltergeists, demonic possessions, and the sinister presence of black helicopters.

Those who assertively embrace reincarnation theory in this fashion invite the speculation that, despite their protestations of higher consciousness, they are somewhat thin on critical self-reflection. To elaborate this point, let me bring into our discussion another psychiatrist, Sigmund Freud. Freud makes a distinction between illusion and delusion. A delusion, in Freud's view, is simply a mistake. An illusion, however, is more interesting. He says:

> An illusion is not the same thing as an error; nor is it necessarily an error. Aristotle's belief that vermin are developed out of dung was an error ... It would be incorrect to call these errors illusions. On the other hand, it was an illusion of Columbus's that he had discovered a new sea-route to the Indies. The part played by his wish in this error is very clear ... What is characteristic of illusions is that they are derived from human wishes. Illusions need not necessarily be false ... For instance, a middle-class girl may have the illusion that a prince will come and marry her. This is possible; and a few such cases have occurred. That the Messiah will come and found a golden age is much less likely ... Thus we call a belief an illusion when a wish-fulfilment is a prominent factor in its motivation, and in doing so we disregard its relations to reality, just as the illusion itself sets no store by verification.[12]

Because the beliefs that Freud categorizes as illusions are so deeply grounded in wishes, submitting them to the processes of verification and potential disconfirmation can trigger a strong reaction. And this strong reaction can take the form of an insistence, for example, that these beliefs are really not beliefs at all, that they are *unquestionable facts*. The irony here is that such a tactic is entirely counterproductive.

The theory of evolution, for example, is a successful theory not because it hasn't been questioned, but precisely because it *has* been questioned—and questioned with tenacity, ingenuity, and vigor. The theory holds a high degree of credibility in the modern world because it has proved stoutly resistant to even the most dogged attempts to disconfirm it. If reincarnation theory should be as resistant to disconfirmation, its usefulness as a theory would rival that of evolution. And we do ourselves a disservice if we allow a theory of such stunning potential significance to humanity to be exempted from the very processes that would give it credibility. Admittedly these testing processes are often rough and tumble. But if we attempt to immunize the doctrine of reincarnation from that turbulent process, if we wrap it in pieties and take it to be beyond legitimate question, then we treat it like the emperor's new clothes—visible only to the wise, invisible to the coarse and foolish. As we'll see, the impulse to shield reincarnation theory from the rigors of vulgar interrogation arises regularly among its advocates.

Americans who accept the doctrine of reincarnation tend to hold attitudes toward their belief similar to the one expressed by Grof. "I don't *believe* in reincarnation; I *know* it to be true." This mindset, in addition to being disturbing, is, to say it again, unnecessary and counterproductive. One can be deeply committed to reincarnation in conjunction with transpersonal psychology, or in connection to any of a number of Asian religions. One can maintain that commitment, but without holding fast to reincarnation theory dogmatically, without insisting that it is beyond question. I'll go into greater detail on this issue later; for now, consider the attitude of Stephen Batchelor, a scholar and practitioner of Buddhism. Speaking of reincarnation, he says: "It may seem that there are two options: either to believe in rebirth or not. But there is a third alternative: to acknowledge, in all honesty, *I do not know.*"[13] Such a view is refreshing because, among other things, it allows us to discuss this issue, and to *differ* on the issue, without mutual disparagement.

8

One of the marks of the new attitudes of religious rethinking and exploration that are sweeping the West is a tangible excitement over the rapprochement between the great antagonists of the Modern era—religion and science. With enthusiasm, those looking for religious renaissance are reading books with titles like *God and the New Physics;* they are eagerly embracing crossover science-religion issues, issues like deep ecology and the Gaia hypothesis. Why not, then, bring the disposition characteristic of science to the enterprise of rethinking religion for the 21st century? Of course it won't be all sweetness and light; no process in which people have strong psychological investments is ever without a degree of acrimony. But at its best, the scientific method—all the crisp and icy business of questioning, testing, and even falsifying theories—can be a context for camaraderie, large-heartedness, and all that we admire in the human endeavor. The famous British scientist and philosopher Richard Dawkins offers a splendid illustration:

> One of the formative experiences of my Oxford undergraduate years occurred when a visiting lecturer from America presented evidence that conclusively disproved the pet theory of a deeply respected elder statesman of our zoology department, the theory that we had all been brought up on. At the end of the lecture, the old man rose, strode to the front of the hall, shook the American warmly by the hand and declared, in ringing emotional tones, "My dear fellow, I wish to thank you. I have been wrong these fifteen years." We clapped our hands red.[14]

Truth or falsity, right or wrong—these aren't what is ultimately at issue in this delightful story. At issue is whether one feels compelled to treat the present state of one's understanding as the last word, as final and incontrovertible, as beyond question. And the concern is entirely practical: from the latter state of mind one cannot *grow.* One can travel no further because the working assumption is that one has already *arrived.* The delicious joy of learning is precluded—an experience that is somehow delicious even when what you learn is that your position is no longer tenable. And, to leave the realm of hard science behind, this approach is not alien to workers in the field of transpersonal psychology. Two of the most prominent figures in that field, Roger N. Walsh and Frances Vaughan, sound this caution to those who would be taken seriously as transpersonal psychologists:

> ... if the transpersonal is truly to be an effective synthesis of Eastern wisdom and Western science, then its practitioners need to do all they can to ensure that their work is indeed subjected to careful scientific scrutiny ... While there is a growing body of research on meditation ... few other transpersonal areas have been examined closely.[15]

And if a more authoritative voice is wanted, we can find it in the man who is almost certainly the most prominent and influential spokesperson for Buddhism in the world today—the fourteenth Dalai Lama. In an interview with scientist Carl Sagan, he was questioned about the status of reincarnation theory within Buddhism. Sagan recounts the exchange:

> In theological discussion with religious leaders, I often ask what their response would be if a central tenet of their faith were disproved by science. When I put this question to the current, Fourteenth, Dalai Lama, he unhesitatingly replied as no conservative or fundamentalist religious leaders do: In such a case, he said, Tibetan Buddhism would have to change.
>
> Even, I asked, if it's a *really* central tenet, like (I searched for an example) reincarnation?
>
> Even then, he answered.
>
> However—he added with a twinkle—it's going to be hard to disprove reincarnation.[16]

It is clear that, for the Dalai Lama, reincarnation is not beyond question. For all the undoubted sincerity of Stanislav Grof's position regarding the doctrine, his attitude toward reincarnation is not the only one; nor, *pacé* Dr. Grof, is it the only respectable one. Certainly the Dalai Lama is not about to jettison belief in reincarnation—not, at least, until there is scientific proof that he should do so. But should evidence be forthcoming, one senses that he would not reject that evidence for the sake of maintaining his belief in reincarnation.

Notes

1. Bach, R. *Jonathan Livingston Seagull.* New York, MacMillan Co., 1970, p.54.
2. Kristof, N. D. "Jesus and Jihad." New York Times, July 17, 2004, online edition.

3. Conze, E. *The Memoirs of a Modern Gnostic, Parts I & II.* Sherborne, England: Samizdat Publishing Co., 1979, Part I, p.33.
4. Conze, 1979, p.33.
5. Ford, H. Cited in *Reincarnation: an East-West Anthology,* ed. J. Head and S. L. Cranston. Wheaton, Ill.: Quest Book, 1975, pp.270-1.
6. Hirshson, S. P. *General Patton: A Soldier's Life.* New York: HarperCollins, 2002, p.703.
7. Rogo, D. S. *The Search for Yesterday: a Critical Examination of the Evidence for Reincarnation.* Englewood Cliffs, NJ: Prentice-Hall, 1985, p.218.
8. MacLaine, S. *Out on a Limb.* New York: Bantam Books, 1983, p.107.
9. Bhattacharji, S. *Fatalism in India.* Calcutta: Sarmistha Roy, 1995, p.i.
10. Grof, S. *The Cosmic Game: Explorations of the Frontiers of Human Consciousness.* Albany: SUNY Press, 1998, p.161-2.
11. Grof, 1998, p.178-9, my emphasis.
12. Freud, S. *The Future of an Illusion.* (Translated by J. Strachey) New York: W. W. Norton & Co., 1961, pp.30-1.
13. Batchelor, S. *Buddhism without Beliefs.* New York: Riverhead Books, 1997, pp.37-8.
14. Dawkins, R. *Unweaving the Rainbow: Science, Delusion, and the Appetite for Wonder.* New York: Mariner Books, 2000, p.31.
15. Walsh, R. N. And F. Vaughan, "A Comparison of Psychotherapies" in *Beyond Ego: Transpersonal Dimensions in Psychology,* ed. Walsh, R. N. and F. Vaughan. Los Angeles: Jeremy Tarcher, Inc, 1980, p.173.
16. Sagan, C. *The Demon-haunted World: Science as a Candle in the Dark.* New York: Ballantine Books, 1996, p. 278.

2

KARMA: THE DANCE OF CONSEQUENCE

From the physical agony inflicted results physical agony endured, for karma is the restoration of the equilibrium disturbed ... Hereditary and congenital diseases, again, are the reaction from past misdeeds. The drunkard of a previous life will be born into a family in which drunkenness has left diseases of the nerves—epilepsy and the like. The profligate will be born into a family tainted with diseases which spring from sexual vice. A "bad heredity" is the reaction from wrong activities in the past. Often the man who is reaping these sad harvests shows in his moral nature that he has purged himself from the evil, though the physical harvesting remains.

—Annie Besant, *A Study in Karma*[1]

1

In the previous chapter, the doctrine of reincarnation and its various appeals were discussed. There is, however, more to the story. Reincarnation is never a stand-alone doctrine. The cycle of rebirths that is the core of reincarnation theory is never taken to be haphazard. Whenever belief in reincarnation arises, it does so in tandem with a belief that the process of rebirth is guided by an order that insures *justice*—an order that adjusts circumstances of rebirth to merit previously earned. Put otherwise, reincarnation theory demands an *orderly* progression of rebirths. Again we see a dynamic inherent in the master-idea of reincarnation, a dynamic that generates a principle according to which reincarnation takes place, a dynamic that generates a sense of rightness about the social positions to which this or that person was born. There is thus established a correspondence between virtue and circumstance. This correspondence assures that some sort of *justice* is woven into the order of reality, an assurance that satisfies a deep human psychological need. We are assured that virtue and tenacity will be rewarded (in future incarnations), and that villainy will be repaid (in future incarnations).

What reincarnation theory presumes to explain was poetically characterized by Shakespeare as "the slings and arrows of outrageous fortune." Fortune is outrageous in this view not so much because of the pain attending it, but because of its *capriciousness*. The crash of an airliner, a child's being born into circumstances of ignorance and rude violence, catastrophic diseases in infants—is life no more than a protracted crapshoot? The human mind recoils in horror at the prospect. And the doctrine of reincarnation assuages that horror by proposing that there is an *order*, a law, according to which events occur.

The order that governs the specifics of rebirth is taken to be one that reflects natural and divine law. In ancient and modern India, and in the modern West, that order is called *karma*. Belief in reincarnation, if it is to satisfy our need for a sense of justice in the world, inevitably generates a belief in an order, an order deeper than the social order, that guides the processes of rebirth. That is why reincarnation is never a stand-alone doctrine. In what follows, we will see that elaborations of reincarnation theory, ancient and modern, East and West, invariably bring into play the related theory that there is an order and a rightness operative in the succession of rebirths to which the individual soul is subject.

And this brings us back to why I take reincarnation theory to be so dangerous. Looked at through the lens of reincarnation theory, life becomes a domain in which suffering is lamentably pervasive, but no longer capricious. Suffering is seen to serve a *purpose*. The poor, the underprivileged, even victims of war and genocide, are seen to be—*working out their karma*. The often devastating realities of disease or malnutrition, of a lack of education, of bigotry expressed in terms of gender, race, or religion—all these come to be seen not as an *affront* to justice, but as *expression* of justice. But justice on a deeper level. To repeat the point made earlier: reincarnation offers more than an *explanation* of social disparities; it offers a *moral justification* of social disparities.

We turn now to a more fulsome consideration of the order that guides the processes of rebirth. To be born may be a matter of hazard, but to be reborn—and reborn again and again and again—prompts us to think in terms of a guiding principle. That principle, we have seen, has come to be known in the modern world by its Indian name—*karma*.

Although they are regularly coupled together, reincarnation and karma are logically independent doctrines. In theory, if seldom in practice, one can subscribe to one and not the other. It is possible to believe that there is reincarnation, but that the sequence of rebirth is utterly capricious. No karma, just reincarnation. It is also possible to believe that something like karma occurs in life (in the minimalist sense that acts have consequences), but that no karmic effect is freighted from one life to another. No reincarnation, just karma. This theoretical independence of reincarnation and karma, however, is not found in practice. In practice, in the street, the two are found in tandem. Part of the reason for that has already been referred to—reincarnation theory *needs* a doctrine like that of karma to establish that there is, somehow, a rightness, a justness, to the drama of rebirth. In this chapter, we will give that claim closer analysis. For now, however, let's consider the basics.

2

The word *karma* (or sometimes *karman*) is a word from Sanskrit, the language of ancient India. The word literally means "work" or "activity." The theory of karma is, at its most basic, a theory about how activity occurs; it is a theory that turns on *causality*. We can say that the theory of karma is a simple insight into how experience works: *acts have consequences*. And in general, experience bears out this commonplace. We hear it stated frequently, though in different words: "As you sow, so shall you reap" "What goes around comes around." Simple enough, but let's dig a little deeper.

First, although karma involves causality, karma and causality are not equivalent concepts. Causality is a *descriptive* law; it tells us how things are, how things happen. Karma is descriptive, yes, but it is also inevitably *prescriptive*. That is, karma speaks not only of how things *are,* but also of how they *ought* to be. Where causality simply describes the reality we experience, the doctrine of karma prompts us *how* to live, it speaks the language of *should.* This is because karma, unlike causality, is a doctrine that carries with it an investment in an personal agenda—more than mere description, karma points the way toward a goal, the goal of liberation or enlightenment or some other variant of self-realization.

More: while causality is blind to *intentions,* karma is not. Karma is emphatically focused on the state of mind (or, the state of heart) of the agent acting in the world. The consequences wrought through karma, the doctrine goes, are powerfully conditioned by the *intentions* behind the doing. Karma holds that like produces like in a *moral* sense: good acts produce good effects, bad acts, bad effects. Causality holds no such parallelism. Causality is concerned with events in the world; karma is concerned with events in the world, yes, but also with the state of the agent acting in the world.

3

The order governing the particulars of rebirth has typically been seen as a *moral* order. There are good reasons for this, and I will elaborate on them in more detail soon. For now, note that despite its moral bias in positing "good" and "bad" acts that elicit parallel consequences, karma does not establish a system of rewards and punishments. Karma is taken to be an impersonal principle. The concepts of punishment and reward are couched in the language of theism: they imply the existence of a judge, a *Mediator,* who assesses individual actions, and through a deliberative process metes out rewards and punishments. Karmic results, by contrast, are not the product of a deliberative process—they are a direct, unmediated, and natural consequence of those actions. For example, a hangover is not *punishment* for unwise drinking, it is a *natural consequence* of unwise drinking. Gods or any other cosmic police are not necessary; indeed, they are rendered mere *accessories* in the context of karma doctrine. Stated simply: karma traffics in neither rewards or punishments—karma traffics exclusively in natural consequences. Historian Wendy Doniger O'Flaherty presents it this way:

> ... the retributive function of rebirth is of secondary significance; indeed, as a Tamil Brahmin woman said to me, karma means that we are punished not *for* our actions, but *by* our actions.[2]

4

Another point about karma that will be relevant to subsequent concerns in this book turns on a contrast between karma and the scientific theory of genetics. The inherited characteristics of genetic inheritance are transferred between two distinct individuals. Not so with karma: the transference of characteristics occurs not between two individuals, but, in the last analysis, *one* individual—one individual born first as *this* person, and then later as *that* person. We can say, then, that a crucial difference between karma and genetics is this: for geneticists the root of our inheritance depends not on *us*, but on our *ancestors*. And this is not the case in the doctrine of karma, where transmitted traits and tendencies are rooted directly in the individual being born, not his/her ancestors.

A religious variant of this point can be found in the Biblical view that human hardships are the result of unwise ancestors. We read in *Exodus,* for example,

> ... I the LORD your God am a jealous God, visiting the iniquity of the fathers upon the children to the third and the fourth generation of those who hate me ... Exodus 20:5[3]

And in the Gospel of Matthew, we find the same outlook asserted. Pilate is depicted as reticent to execute Jesus, and turning to the crowd of assembled Jews says to them:

> "I am innocent of this man's blood; see to it yourselves." And all the people answered, "His blood be on us and on our children!" Matthew 27:24-5

Again, according to the theory of karma, individuals never endure the consequences of their ancestors' actions, but only of their own. It should not escape us that, at least in this regard, there is a strain of fairness in the doctrine of karma. But it should be noted that the highly individualistic bias of the doctrine of karma emphasized here is not the only understanding of the doctrine. There is an understanding of karma, both in India and in America, that moves beyond a focus on the individual to a concept of *collective* karma. Consider this statement by philosopher Christopher M. Bache:

> Sometimes there is simply too much pain in a person's life to see it as deriving from their former lives alone, even a long series of such lives. A new dimension to the problem of suffering opens when we begin to recognize that our lives reflect and embody collective as well as personal karma ...[4]

That's an American perspective on the issue. The Indian sage and teacher Sivananda gives voice to the same idea:

> The collective Karma of a race or a nation is as much a fact in Nature as an individual one. The same principles underlying the Karmic laws apply, without much wide difference, to national and collective Karma. Nations rise and fall, empires flourish and are dismembered on the same ground. The wise heads in a nation should not neglect the dominating sway of this law. In the midst of a national calamity it is well to remember that nothing can come to us which we have not deserved. We may not be able to see the immediate cause of the catastrophe, but it does not follow that it took place without sufficient cause.[5]

This understanding of collective karma has arisen at different points in history—sometimes, as we'll see, with consequences that were especially insidious. At present, however, it is not the dominant understanding of karma in America. The current popular understanding in America is one that focuses on the individual and the successive incarnations of the individual. And so my focus is on individual karma.[6]

In the passage cited above, Christopher Bache says "there is simply too much pain in a person's life to see it as deriving from their former lives alone." That may make sense in terms of the Western experience of the world ("Life ain't fair"), but it affronts a basic human need—specifically, the need for a sense of justice. Justice is served only when each *individual* gets what she or he deserves. Sivananda, perhaps more seasoned in the art of thinking about karma, asserts that "In the midst of a national calamity it is well to remember that nothing can come to us which we [that is, each of us as individuals] have not deserved." Unlike Bache, Sivananda keeps a sense of justice intact. And this, as we'll see, is important.

5

In light of the doctrine of karma, we've seen that the proverbial buck stops with *you*. What has been done in the past, the sequence of actions of which your present state is a consequence, centers squarely on each individual. And at least as important, what will happen both now and in the future is rooted in the individual—what choices, what intentions, what aspirations you bring to the present moment will condition your future state. This brings us to an important aspect of karma: as it burdens the individual with responsibility for present circumstances, so it also confers on the individual a vital control over *future* circumstances.

The doctrine of karma asserts that past actions determine present circumstance. But—and this is the important part—past actions do not determine how one will *act* in the present. Freedom of choice is left intact.

The operation of karma has been likened to a poker game: past acts determine which cards you'll be dealt, but not how you'll *play* those cards. This is no insignificant point. Because if in addition to present circumstances being conditioned by the past, present *choices* are also so conditioned, one of the most important benefits conferred by believing in karma is lost—the sense of *justice* in the world, a sense of *control* over circumstances. No choice, no justice; no choice, no control.

The renowned Indian scholar Sarvepalli Radhakrishnan is among the most lucid explicators of Hindu doctrine. And he has a special interest in the details of the doctrine of karma—and in the ways that the doctrine can be misunderstood. Pursuing this interest, he insists of karma theory that:

> While it regards the past as determined, it allows that the future is only conditioned. The spiritual element in man allows him freedom within the limits of his nature ... What the individual will be cannot be predicted beforehand, though there is no caprice. We can predict an individual's acts so far as they are governed by habit, that is, to the extent his actions are mechanical and not affected by choice.[7]

This states it nicely: our present acts are *conditioned*, but not determined by our past acts. This is so, incidentally, whether or not one subscribes to the doctrine of reincarnation. It is naive to assume, Radhakrishnan points out, that what we call free will is mere caprice; our will, our actions, are conditioned by *habit*. And again, whether those habits developed in the present life or in previous lives is not the crucial point here; we are concerned only with the fact that, according to Radhakrishnan's view, the theory of karma leaves us with a degree of choice. Without choice in the present, we are left with a fatalism in which pain and horror are simply written in to a film-loop, we are left helpless. But karma is not determinism; it is not fatalism, either in its Greek or its traditional Indian formulations.[8] The issue of control, and *individual* control, is central to karma.

6

Religion in the context of karma theory offers a model of *self-realization*, not salvation. It is a "do it yourself" scenario, and for the best of reasons—no one else can do it *for* you. Many modern Westerners find this aspect of karma theory to be particularly appealing. To see why, let's briefly consider the alternative to karma offered by the mainstream religion in the West, the Christian doctrine of *salvation*. There are of course many versions of this doctrine. But a version that has been particularly influential historically is that of St. Augustine. Here is a representative statement of his view:

> For men are separated from God only by sins, from which we are in this life cleansed not by our own virtue, but by the divine compassion; through His indulgence, not through our own power. For, whatever virtue we call our own is itself bestowed upon us by His goodness. *The City of God, x.22.*[9]

Note that Augustine puts all the control in the hands of God. He emphasizes here, and throughout his writings, that the individual human is powerless to impact his own predicament. What is needed is "divine compassion," or "His indulgence"—that is, God's grace. Where the doctrine of karma puts control and responsibility squarely on the individual, the doctrine of salvation—at least in its influential Augustinian form, followed by Reformation figures like Luther and Calvin—leaves the individual with little to do but recognize an abject need for God's grace. Again, the control conferred on the individual by the doctrine of karma is doubtlessly one of its appeals to those Westerners dissatisfied with their religious traditions. Also at issue here, and notoriously so, is the question of *justice*. Gallons of ink have been expended on either defending or condemning what, from the human perspective, seems to be the sheer caprice of God's grace. To some, He grants it; to others, He withholds it. And the stakes are momentous: the alternative to God's grace is *damnation*. This, recall from the Introduction, is what elicited the revulsion of John Stuart Mill and his father. At issue here, however, is something different. Capricious damnation is an outrage to our sense of justice, yes, but there is a concern that some have seen as running even deeper than that. What are the roots of the human sense of justice? Why is justice so important to us? And how is it, in regard to our sense of justice, that the doctrine of karma has an advantage over traditional Christian views of salvation?

7

Robert Wright, a prominent explicator of evolutionary psychology, discusses the universality of a sense of justice and its evolution. He speaks of anthropologists who point out that:

Beneath the global crazy quilt of rituals and customs, they see recurring patterns in the structure of family, friendship, politics, courtship, [and] morality. They believe the evolutionary design of human beings explains these patterns: ... why people everywhere feel guilt, and feel it in broadly predictable circumstances; why people everywhere have a deep sense of justice, so that the axioms "One good turn deserves another" and "An eye for an eye, a tooth for a tooth" shape human life everywhere on this planet.[10]

Wright's point is that a sense of justice is woven deeply into the human psyche; it is a primordial demand, one installed through the process of our biological evolution. This theory is compelling to many, but it remains a hypothesis; whether the hypothesis will withstand the tests of scientific rigor is yet to be seen. But the theory purports to explain an observation that few will dispute—the ubiquity of a sense of justice, indeed a *demand* for justice, among human beings. And this ubiquitous demand for justice finds expression through the doctrine of karma.

The demand for justice is a vital aspect of the human story, yes. But for some thinkers, this tells only a part of the story. Underlying the demand for justice is an even more primordial human need—the need for *control*. And we want control because we, that is, the human species over millennia, have lived in a world that is unpredictable and menacing. In the face of threat from the world outside us, our impulse is to somehow, by whatever means, *control* it. Our desire for justice, the suggestion goes, is in the last analysis a desire for control; we want justice *because* we want control.

Again we can profitably consult the ever-insightful Dr. Freud. In *The Future of an Illusion*, he suggests that the psychological root of all religious belief is *control*—or more precisely, the *illusion* of control. He says:

But how does he [=humanity] defend himself against the superior powers of nature, of Fate, which threaten him as they threaten all the rest? ... The task is a manifold one. Man's self-regard, seriously menaced, calls for consolation; life and the universe must be robbed of their terrors; moreover his curiosity, moved, it is true, by the strongest practical interest, demands an answer. A great deal is already gained by the first step: the humanization of nature. Impersonal forces and destinies cannot be approached; they remain eternally remote. But if the elements have passions that rage as they do in our own souls, if death itself is not something spontaneous but the violent act of an evil Will ... We are still defenseless, perhaps, but we are no longer helplessly paralyzed ... We can try to adjure them [the powers of Nature], to appease them, to bribe them, and by so influencing them, we may rob them of a part of their power.[11]

And, in Freud's assessment, this ploy to wrest control for ourselves *works*. But the way in which it works is not to deliver control of the uncertainties of life through prayer and ritual—religion does not, in Freud's view, deliver on its promises. But it *does* work in another way, a way that is vital to human beings: religion gives humans the *illusion* of control. And without that illusion, we would be, in his words, "helplessly paralyzed."

We find the same idea confirmed in more recent research. In his book *The Lucifer Principle,* Howard Bloom summarizes research on the effects, not of actual control, but of the *feeling* of control. He describes controlled studies in which two groups of people are given tasks like working puzzles and proofreading in a room filled with distracting noises. One group had a button on the table on which they worked, a button they were told would control the irritating sound. The another group was given no such button. An important aspect of the experiment was that the buttons given the one group were not connected to anything—pressing them did nothing. Bloom presents the results of the experiments, results that dramatically illustrate the importance of the *belief* that one has control:

> The group with the control buttons on their desks sailed through the puzzles and made only a modest number of errors in their proofreading. The group with no control did miserably ... The deprivation of control had clouded their minds. Strangest of all, the group with the button never actually pushed that button once. It wasn't the noise or lack of it that affected their performance; it was the mere *idea* that if they'd wanted to, they could shut it off. It was the thought of control.[12]

We return now to the psychological effects of the idea of karma. The great advantage of the doctrine of karma over traditional Christian salvation is clearly that, in terms of karma doctrine, the illusion of control (if illusion it be) is a more *potent* one. Christianity offers control in terms of appeal to God, a God whose dispensation of the grace necessary for salvation could seem, from the human perspective at least, to be something of a Divine Lottery. Karma theory obviates the need for such a God or His grace. As stated earlier, karma sets the individual in circumstances of significant control over her or his own future experience. In the marketplace of illusions, then, karma has an edge, a competitive edge that doubtlessly accounts in part for its steady increase in popularity in the West of the 21st century.

8

There's karma, and there's karma. My intention, again, is to call attention to the dangerous aspects of the tandem doctrines of reincarnation and karma. And because that is my focus, it is important to assert, at this point, that not every understanding of karma is pernicious. Let me explain.

"What goes around comes around." Simple, perhaps, but all too easy to put out of mind. Stated otherwise, we humans often lose sight of the fact that acts have consequence because we *want* to lose sight of it, because it serves our immediate impulses to not be aware of consequences. Consider, for example, Shakespeare's character Macbeth, as he contemplates the murder of his king—a deed that is clearly dishonorable in his eyes:

> "If the assassination could trammel up the consequence and catch, with his surcease, success; that but this blow might be the be-all and the end-all ..."
> *Macbeth* I.vii.1-5

Macbeth's dark hope is that his act of murder (done just this once; never, ever again) might somehow be immune from consequences. That this single deed, the assassination of King Duncan, might, just might, only this one time, trammel up—that is, swallow up, or negate—its consequences. Oh, that just this one act could be done without consequences! Macbeth's hope is clearly a desperate one, but in fact it is an instance, writ large, of an entirely commonplace tendency in human thinking. We need not be contemplating a spectacular crime like murder; acts of far less moment, the petty compromise and corner-cutting that characterize ordinary experience, are often accompanied by the hopeful assumption that somehow this "might be the be-all and the end-all." Too bad for Macbeth; too bad for the rest of us. It just doesn't work that way. Or at least it shouldn't. And mostly, it *doesn't*.

But sometimes, damn it, it *does*. Sometimes, the pattern of consequences evident in life, whether called karma or by any other name, just doesn't "kick in." That is because, I suggest, the process of consequence that we find in life is not a mechanistic, foolproof one—it is a *tendency,* one that serves as the basis for a very real wisdom that can be useful in negotiating the complexities of life. As such, this wisdom is useful—as far as it goes. But tendencies always have exceptions. It is at least conceivable that Macbeth might have pulled it off. Conceivable, but not likely. And this brings us to a consideration of how the pattern of consequence called karma has been understood.

9

Historically, the operation of karma has been designated as "the *law* of karma." In that phrasing lies the problem, a problem that centers not on the word karma, but on the word *law*. The *law* of karma. What *kind* of law is at issue here? There is a way of understanding the term *law* that makes the *law of karma* a good thing. And there is a way of understanding the term *law* that makes the *law of karma* not just a bad thing, but a *very* bad thing. But let's look at the brighter side first.

A benign understanding of the law of karma is possible if we come to see the law as a *statistical* law. So taken, the law of karma describes, more or less reliably, the probabilities that follow on any given course of behavior. Understood in this way, karma fosters dispositions that are salutary for the individual and society. Consider only two:

1. Karma as a statistical law fosters the idea that the individual is not an isolated, atomistic entity, but is embedded in a context of reciprocity with both society and nature. The idea of connectedness that is implicit in this view serves as a needed corrective for the misdirected valuation of independence that has so characterized modern culture, especially in the West, even more especially in America.

2. Karma urges us to see that, on average, living honorably and with responsibility may well be good, but it is more than good, it is *smart,* and *street smart* at that—smart in terms of the ways of the world. Living responsibly puts the odds in our favor. This is an insight that seats ethical discourse on a refreshingly realistic basis. Ethical prescriptions that speak the language of *smart* (rather than preach the language of *good)* have a far better chance of being heard in the ambience of corporate culture, in which the ultimate value is, without apology, the bottom line.

Cooperative behavior, self-control, personal integrity: these will typically produce good results. Typically, but again, not necessarily. Unlike a mechanistic law such as gravitation, which trades in results that are *certain,* a statistical law like karma produces only *probabilities.* The fact that karma, taken now as a statistical law, does not produce *certainties* does not mean that it has no *predictive* value. This is a point on which I disagree with philosopher Paul Edwards. In his extensive study referred to earlier,

Reincarnation: A Critical Examination, I feel that he makes too strong a claim:

> ... the Law of Karma has no predictive value whatever. A simple example will make this clear. Let us suppose that a plane takes off in which all the crew and passengers are, as far as we can tell, thoroughly decent people. The believer in Karma cannot predict any more or less confidently than the unbeliever that the plane will not crash.[13]

But in fact the law of karma, taken as a statistical law, *is* predictive. Its predictions, however, are framed as *probabilities,* not as certainties. And these predictions become more probable as the level of generality becomes higher. On the day to day level of particular events, probability decreases; on the level of events taken in a broader, more general view, probability increases. For example, it can be predicted that x-hundred people will be killed in traffic fatalities on a given holiday weekend. And, when made by qualified statisticians, that prediction has a reasonably high probability. But a prediction that this or that person will be killed on the weekend in question is very different. It is of course *possible* that Fred or Mabel will be killed, but the probability of that prediction is far lower, far less reliable, than the more general prediction about x-hundred people. Edwards looks for predictive value in terms of individuals and specific events—on the level of this decent person, or that one, or even a whole crowd of decent people on that particular plane. And he looks for predictive value for those individual people on that particular plane in terms of a single, unique event—a plane crash. At such a concrete level of specificity, the statistical law of karma confers less probability, and is less predictive. But that the statistical law of karma is *less* predictive at the level of individual events does not mean that it is *not* predictive.

A parallel to a statistical understanding of karma, and one that will figure significantly in this study, may be found in what Charles Darwin took to be the engine of evolution—natural selection. Natural selection is a *statistical* law. As such, its function in Darwin's theories is unlike Newtonian mechanistic laws with their certainties. Natural selection does not state that an individual possessed of adaptive characteristics *will* survive. Instead, the theory of natural selection states that such a well adapted individual will have a higher *probability* of surviving. That is, the *odds* of that individual are better. Better odds, yes; guarantees, no. Consider the fate of some splendidly adapted animals, the dinosaurs—indeed entire species of dinosaurs—that dominated the planet until some sixty-five million years ago. All their adaptive success was of no avail when a huge meteorite struck the earth in the general area known today as the Gulf of Mexico. Natural selection theory describes odds, probabilities. And sometimes, against all odds, the improbable happens. The dreadful happens. The unspeakable happens.

It is clear, then, that a statistical understanding of the law of karma is predictive and therefore practical. For all its practicality, though, a statistical approach to karma generates consternation. Why? Precisely because it allows for *exceptions*. And those exceptions grate on human sensibilities. This might be said to be the bad news about good karma: a theory of consequence based on probabilities has *loopholes*. Consider the following wisdom that is addressed to this very point:

> In my vain life I have seen everything; there is a righteous man who perishes in his righteousness, and there is a wicked man who prolongs his life in his evil-doing. *Ecclesiastes* 7:15

Not only does the righteous man sometimes perish of his righteousness, the wicked man sometimes thrives through his very wickedness. Sometimes, that is to say, the bastards get away clean, with their ill-gotten gains intact. And sometimes, as poignantly detailed in Harold S. Kushner's book *When Bad Things Happen to Good People*, sometimes bad things—*really* bad things—happen to good people, to those we love, to the children we cherish.

There is authentic wisdom, I believe, in learning to reconcile oneself to the capricious sorrow and tragedy woven into life. But when the baleful events of life are understood through a process of *probable* consequences, indignation and outrage are all but inevitable. When terrible tragedy touches home, many are left with a keen sense of dissatisfaction. It leaves the scales of life, as it were, *unbalanced*. The human need for a sense of *justice* is left unsatisfied.

Perhaps it was this frustration that brought people to construe karma not as a statistical law, but as a *mechanical* law. Perhaps it was a need for certainty, the kind of certainty found in mathematics. In any case, similar to the ways in which the Christian concepts of Heaven and Hell functioned, thinking of karma as a mechanical law established with *certainty* that goodness would be compensated, that wickedness would meet retribution—if not in this life, then in a life subsequent to this one. Comfort there may be in this view, but it is an expensive comfort.

10

Taken as a statistical law, the doctrine of karma might provide a basis for living a disciplined life with a general—a probabilistic—standard of justice. History has shown us that in the face of adversity, we humans hanker for more precision. And so karma has come to be understood in *mechanistic* terms. Indeed, in contemporary America what comes to mind almost automatically when the law of karma is spoken of is a *mechanical* law. And this *mechanistic* understanding of the law of consequences, the reader will understand, is what I mean by *bad karma.*

A useful illustration of mechanical law is the Newtonian law of gravitation. And a term commonly associated with such laws is *inexorable.* Mechanical laws do not admit of exceptions; mechanical laws are universal, invariable, and inviolable. If, for example, someone credibly asserts that an exception to the law of gravitation has been found, scientists will dash in from every quarter to confirm or disconfirm that stunning claim. And confirmation of the claim would be *very* big news—it would amount to a veritable tectonic shift in the domain of theoretical physics. Understand, please, that a mechanistic approach to consequences is not being disparaged here. It is exquisite when applied, for example, to physics or engineering. The problems arise when a mechanistic approach is misapplied—specifically, when it is applied to the law of karma. And one of those problems is that a mechanistic approach to karma makes a belief in reincarnation *inevitable.* And, as is being argued throughout this study, the doctrine of reincarnation—no matter how well-intentioned it may be—generates social realities that are at the very least *questionable.* Let's look more closely.

When the law of karma is taken to be a *mechanistic* law, we confront a mirror image of what we found in our earlier discussion of reincarnation. It was stated that a belief in reincarnation generates, in the interest of some sense of justice, a belief in karma. The details of this reasoning are given a clear, if somewhat chilling, exposition by Christopher W. Gowans. In his 2003 study titled *Philosophy of the Buddha,* he says this:

> To a large extent, *kamma* [karma] is implausible without rebirth. As the Buddha recognized, in this lifetime sometimes good persons suffer and immoral persons prosper. This would be a decisive refutation of *kamma* in the absence of rebirth ... For example, it is sometimes said that *kamma* is cruel because it requires us to believe that a young child suffering from

cancer deserves his or her fate. But we probably would not think this cruel if the child was the rebirth of Joseph Stalin.[14]

But Gowans' claim that the absence of rebirth would be a decisive refutation of karma is plausible, however, only if karma is taken to be a mechanistic law rather than a statistical law. It is a mechanistic understanding of karma that *forces* an embrace of reincarnation. And it does so not only in the interest of logical consistency, but also—maddeningly, I would urge—in the interest of *justice*. Cheek to jowl with Gowans' concern for theoretical coherence is a breezy contention that is the core concern of this study. If we could see the whole story of that child stricken with cancer, the contention goes, we'd see that our spontaneous feelings of outrage, our sense of unfairness, are quite misdirected. The kid was probably something monstrous in a previous life—you know, something like Stalin. Or maybe just a garden variety thug. As we contemplate the child's desperate situation, such an analysis might make us feel better. And how much easier, I'll be urging later in this discussion, how much easier will it be to look at kids living not in the throes of cancer, but of dehumanizing poverty, and to allow ourselves to *feel better* through a sophisticated awareness that their present state does not tell the whole story. Relax: they've somehow *earned* their present condition; what we see here is not an affront to justice, but an *expression* of justice. But how is such an understanding of justice possible?

Taken as a *mechanical* law, karma presses the investigation into human misery from the general to the acutely specific. No longer trading in tendencies and probabilities, a retail explanation is required, explanation on a per-incident basis. Conceived as mechanistic law, the doctrine of karma asserts flatly and unconditionally that everything that happens in the life of a person is caused by previous actions on the part of *that* person. Period. And when karma is so construed, we are impelled to pursue an inquiry as to why a very young child suffers horribly into the domain of *previous lives*—just as we saw Professor Gowens do. A consideration of the life of a young child can yield no plausible cause—no wicked deed requiring retribution—of, say, a catastrophic genetic defect, or an (apparently) random accident, or criminal predation. In his discussion of karma in Indian thought, the philosopher Ramakrishna Puligandla states the case for a mechanistic understanding of the operation of karma. He says this:

> ... the present existence of a man is dependent upon his past existence; that is, his present existence is the effect of his thoughts, words, and actions in his past existence. Similarly his future existence is dependent

upon his present existence. This is precisely the law of karma: *every event, be it thought, word, or action, produces its effects, which in turn become causes for other effects, and so on, thus generating the karmic chain.*[15]

It is this assumption, that karmic effect is wrought by a *mechanistic* law, that has historically bound the idea of karma to the idea of reincarnation. And just such a mechanistic understanding of karma has prevailed in those thought systems in which the doctrine of reincarnation has been embraced. Worse, the story does not stop there.

We turn now to the operational dynamics of the conjunction of karma—understood now as a mechanistic law—and reincarnation. These theories, taken together, are also connected to (and supportive of) another doctrine, this one more sinister—the doctrine of *social castes*. When we examine ancient India and Greece in the following two chapters, we'll see that the idea of social caste is endemic to reincarnation theory. The castes we'll encounter in those cultures are manifested in society, yes, but they are taken to reflect an order far deeper than the social order; social castes are presumed to be woven into the order of nature. According to this view, human beings are classifiable into social categories that are both vertical and hereditary, categories in which prospects are more or less *fixed* at birth, categories supported by unique behavior patterns, educational levels, and economic status. And—this is the important part—these social categories are not taken to be *unjust:* the operation of karma is taken to warrant membership in these categories. Whether high status or low, one's position in society is *earned*, it is *deserved*. And I repeat that my concerns about the emergence of caste-thinking (and of *de facto* castes) in American culture reflect a dynamic innate to the idea of reincarnation itself. A culture that embraces reincarnation theory is one that will develop, by whatever name, a caste system. Over time, reincarnation and caste will weave into a single fabric.

Notes

1. Besant, A. *A Study in Karma*, 1917. "Perfect Justice." http://www.theosophical.ca/StudyKarma.htm.
2. O'Flaherty, W. D. "Karma and Rebirth in the Vedas and Puranas," in O'Flaherty, W. D., ed., *Karma and Rebirth in Classical Indian Traditions*. Berkeley: University of California Press, 1980, p.37.
3. All quotations from the Bible are from the Revised Standard Version.
4. Bache, C. M. *Dark Night, Early Dawn: Steps to an Ecology of Mind*. Albany: SUNY Press, 2000, p.174.

5. Sivananda, S. *Practice of Karma Yoga*. Divine Life Trust Society, 1995, p.23. Online edition. http://www.SivanandaDlshq.org/.
6. We may note in passing that the concept of group karma, in accounting for the fact that peoples, nations, or tribes suffer a common fate, assumes the primacy of individual karma. For according to the logic of karma, the individuals that comprise a given group find their way to being born in that group through their past behaviors *as individuals*. Stated simply, to be included in this or that group, the individual—*each* individual—must uniquely generate the appropriate set of consequences. But the concept of group karma will make another appearance in this study—and in a particularly ugly form.
7. Radhakrishnan, S. *The Hindu View of Life*. New York: The Macmillan Co., 1965, p.54.
8. That karma is not fatalism is true *in theory*. But—as we'll see in considering the historical manifestations of these doctrines in India—*in practice* the story is typically quite different, as we'll see in the next chapter.
9. Augustine, St. *The City of God*. Translated by M. Dods. New York: The Modern Library, 1950, p.327.
10. Wright, R. *The Moral Animal: the New Science of Evolutionary Psychology*. New York: Vintage Books, 1994, p.7-8.
11. Freud, S. *The Future of an Illusion*. New York: W.W. Norton & Co., 1961, p.16-17.
12. Bloom, H. *The Lucifer Principle: a Scientific Expedition into the Forces of History*. New York: Atlantic Monthly Press, 1995, p.113-4.
13. Edwards, *Reincarnation: a Critical Examination*. Amherst, New York: Prometheus Books, 1996, p.35-6.
14. Gowans, C. W. *Philosophy of the Buddha*. New York: Routledge, 2003, p.111.
15. Puligandla, R. *Fundamentals of Indian Philosophy*. New York: Abington Press, 1975, p.63-4. Emphasis added.

3

A Passage Through India

There are still people who would not—still today [1999]—allow a Dalit person into their kitchen or into their house ... I have had relatives who told me "Well, you know, they smell different" and things like this. It's barbaric, there's no other word for it ... My grandmother told me stories about how they would have to walk backwards and sweep away their footprints because somebody stepping into their footprints would be polluted. A Dalit might even now—I know somebody, who works in my mother's school—and he talks like this [holding her hand in front of her mouth]. He doesn't want his breath to pollute the rest of the air. He's an old man. He does it, you know, sort of instinctively I think. Traditionally, the Dalits were supposed to live *downstream,* so that they don't pollute the water.

—Arundati Roy, author of *The God of Small Things,*
speaking in the PBS documentary *Out of India*[1]

1

Why India? The topic of this book—reincarnation—is by no means an exclusively Indian story. Belief in reincarnation has arisen in many parts of the world. Indeed, it is taken by many historians to be a predictable phase in the religious development of primal cultures. Consider, for example, what the eminent British scholar, F. M. Cornford, says of these phases:

The most primitive of these is Reincarnation (*palingensis*). The essence of this belief is that the one life of the group, or tribe, extends continuously through its dead members as well as through the living; the dead are still part of the group, in the same sense as the living. This life, which is perpetually renewed, is reborn out of that opposite state, called 'death,' into which, at the other end of its arc, it passes again. In this idea of reincarnation, still widespread among savage races, we have the first conception of a cycle of existence, a Wheel of Life, divided into two hemicycles of light and darkness, through which the one life, or soul, continuously revolves.[2]

I don't like the reference to *savage races* either, but the point made by Cornford is an important one. Reincarnation theory does not trace its origins to sophisticated philosophical analysis. It does not necessarily represent an advanced state of development in a given religion; belief in reincarnation expresses a primal and commonplace impulse—emphatically pre-philosophical and pre-scientific—in emerging cultures. And Hinduism is no exception: as historian Klaus K. Klostermaier puts it, belief in reincarnation may be traced to the aboriginal dawn of Indian civilization:

> … some more or less universal Hindu beliefs like rebirth and transmigration of the *jiva* [soul] from animal to human existence probably originated among the autochthonous [indigenous] populations.[3]

But if it is not especially remarkable that reincarnation belief emerged in India—then why focus on India? The answer is simple: because what *is* remarkable about India is that the belief in reincarnation so powerfully and persistently conditioned the historical development of culture there. In ancient Greece, as we'll see in the next chapter, reincarnation remained largely a *theory*. In India, by contrast, reincarnation went beyond the realm of ideas and into history—documented history that can be studied and assessed.

The origins of a belief in reincarnation in India are likely rooted in agriculture. As Sukumari Bhattacharji says:

> There may be some truth in the idea that rebirth is a product of agriculture; a seed sown in the ground sprouts up as a plant after some time—this may have engendered the belief that death is not the final stage of life. The seed-plant regeneration may have been easily transferred to the human level and rebirth was formulated and accepted.[4]

India is an ancient culture, one of the most ancient *continuous* cultures on earth. And unlike the West, where belief in reincarnation has in the past remained a marginal phenomenon, reincarnation has been and remains a central feature of Indian culture. By looking at how belief in reincarnation has been historically manifested in India, we may be in a position to speculate about how that belief may, over time, find expression in Western culture. It is in the story of India that we are best able to see how theory translates into history; by studying India Americans can glimpse a possible future of American society.

2

The first civilization to emerge on the Indian subcontinent is named after the Indus River, which runs through the north-west quadrant of the area. The Indus culture was sophisticated and urban; its more spectacular remains are found in the ruins of huge urban centers at Mohenjo Daro and Harappa. Indus culture thrived for about a thousand years—from roughly 3000 BCE to 2000 BCE. By the time invaders from the north arrived, invaders who called themselves by the self-congratulatory name of *Aryan*—literally, "noble"—the Indus culture had fallen into a state of decline. This, of course, made them even more vulnerable to the warlike and less civilized Aryan tribes who, with their iron weapons and war chariots (advanced military technology of the day), already possessed significant advantages.

This history is relevant in that an important aspect of the belief in reincarnation is embodied in the confluence between the invaders and the invaded in subsequent Indian culture, a culture that we know as Vedic culture. A useful way to proceed here is to turn to some of the most ancient surviving literature of India, the hymns and chants collected in a vast body of literature called the *Rig Veda*.

The hymns that comprise the *Rig Veda* are thought to be composed between 1500-900 BCE. It is uncertain whether the values and assumptions inscribed in these extremely ancient hymns reflect the culture of the conquered indigenous peoples of the Indus culture—known as the Dravidians—or the invading conquerors, the Aryans. But Klostermaier, expressing what seems a consensus among historians, says this:

In contrast to the highly developed urban culture of the Harappan [Indus] civilization, the Aryans brought with them a relatively simple village culture and a patriarchal style of life. Though there is a strong probability that the institution of Brahmanism and the core of the *Rig-Veda* itself antedate the Aryan invasion of India, both were associated with them so closely and at such an early date that for all practical purposes, we may safely identify the Vedic religion with the early official worship of the Aryans.[5]

For our purposes, the important point is that we find in these ancient texts clear reference to a caste system. In a mythic hymn rooted, no doubt, in the dusky practice of human sacrifice, we read of a Primordial Man who is dismembered and whose parts are transformed into various aspects of the visible world, including the social world. This is from the *Purusha Sutra,* or "The Hymn of Man":

When they divided the Man, into how many parts did they apportion him? What do they call his mouth, his two arms and thighs and feet? His mouth became the Brahmin; his arms were made into the Warrior, his thighs the People, and from his feet the Servants were born.[6]

There are four categories mentioned: the Priests *(Brahmin)*, the Warriors *(Kshatriya)*, the People *(Vaishya)*, and the Servants *(Shudra)*. It is relevant that in the metaphor of the dismembered Man, we find a hierarchy that descends from the mouth, to the arms, to the thighs, and finally to the feet. This bodily descent mythically spells out a *social* hierarchy of descent. There are four castes. The *Brahmins* are the priest/scholars, and hold the highest social rank. Next are the *Kshatriyas,* the warrior/aristocrat caste. Then follow the *Vaishyas,* taken to be the mercantile and professional caste. Then, following as a distant fourth, the *Shudras,* the laborers—*servants* is far too polite a term. Typically, *Shudra* caste was ascribed to people of the more ancient, Dravidian culture that inhabited the Indus region before the Aryan invasions. We'll return to the *Shudras* later.

For now, as Americans we must be especially careful in thinking about social castes. When Americans think of social stratification, they think largely in terms of *class*, and they see class as a social station that is in principle mobile and transitory. Castes, by contrast, are social categories that are fixed by one's birth; they are taken in a caste-based society to be more *genetic* categories than social classes. Because of its superficial similarity to the idea of social classes, the very word *caste* is often misleading. In Sanskrit, the term is *varna,* which means literally *color.* Color as in *skin* color. Klostermaier again:

> From as far back as we know, the division of *varnas* ... *had multiple aspects: the very name varna,* "color" suggests a differentiation between fairer- and darker-skinned people. On the whole, Brahmins even today have a lighter skin color than *shudras* ... The *catuvarna* system [caste system] also embodied a religious hierarchy; combined with the universally accepted dogma of *karma,* it implied merit. Brahmins were born into the highest caste on account of *karma* accumulated over past lives. Lesser *karma* resulted in lower births. Birth as a *shudra* was designed to atone for sins past.[7]

Yet the list of four castes or *varnas* is in fact incomplete: Indian history is burdened with untold billions of people who were in none of the four castes designated in the *Purusha Sutra*—people who have no caste, who are *out-caste.* These people and their plight will be our focus later. For now, I return to a point made by Klostermaier at the end of the passage—that birth into this or that caste was taken to be guided by *karma.*

3

But how did the belief in karma come into the picture? Interesting speculation on this question is provided by Bruce R. Reichenbach. In his historical study, *The Law of Karma,* he points out that the law of karma was unknown to the ancient composers of the Vedas—such as the Rig Veda.[8] Even in later texts in the tradition, in ritualistic hymns and treatises known as the *Brahmanas,* the idea of an order guiding rebirth is mentioned, but not elaborated. Speaking of the probable origins of the law of karma, Reichenbach says:

> From the very character of the law, we might speculate that the reason for its [the law of karma] development had to do with a very pressing problem. The problem which confronted the Indian was how to account for the diversity of circumstances and situations into which sentient creatures were born, or for the natural events experienced during one's lifetime which affected one person propitiously and another adversely. There appeared to be no obvious, *prima-facie* connection between the good fortune of one individual and his personal worth, or between the ill fortune of another and his worth. Accordingly, it was postulated that there is a law which governs the kind of birth, qualities of character and temperament, and subsequent circumstances that a person experiences. Thus, it was in

the context of attempting to resolve a problem which was both theoretical and existential that the doctrine of karma had its inception.[9]

The suggestion is that there is a *psychological* basis for the emergence of the law of karma in India. Specifically, karma arose to meet a psychological problem generated by the experience of widely disparate social orders. It provided a theory that would, to repeat Reichenbach's words, "account for the diversity of circumstances and situations into which sentient creatures were born." While both rebirth and even the existence of castes are mentioned in the early Vedas, the idea of karma seems to have arisen later—and for reasons alluded to earlier in the previous chapter, namely to satisfy a human need for a sense of justice and rightness. It seems that even the most brutal of victors will, over time, become reflective; their rule, they come to believe, is not merely as assertion of *might*, but a manifestation of *right*. We will come back to this extremely important observation later. For now, let's look at how the doctrine of karma found expression in Indian culture.

4

In the previous chapter I cited Sarvepalli Radhakrishnan, who insisted that although karma is a doctrine of consequence, it is not thereby to be confused with *determinism*. And strictly speaking, that is so. But history seldom speaks strictly. And what we find when we look at the cultural manifestations of the doctrine of karma in India is very different from the formal terms of the theory. Radhakrishnan was uniquely placed to appreciate the social consequences of the doctrine of karma. In addition to being a prominent educator and scholar, Radhakrishnan was vice-president of India between 1952 and 1962, and from 1962 to 1967 he served as president of the nation. Of the social consequences of a belief in karma in India, he says:

> Unfortunately, the theory of Karma became confused with fatality in India when man himself grew feeble and was disinclined to do his best. It was made into an excuse for inertia and timidity, and was turned into a message of despair and not of hope. It said to the sinner, "Not only are you a wreck, but that is all you ever could have been. That was your preordained being from the beginning of time." But such a philosophy of despair is by no means the necessary outcome of the doctrine of Karma.[10]

Perhaps it is "by no means necessary" that karma be understood in terms of fatalism, but I suggest that there is a high *probability* that it will be so understood. An adequate understanding of the doctrine of karma, Radhakrishnan would agree, will require a careful and philosophically astute approach. But, as I argued earlier, when religious and philosophical doctrines find their way to the street, care and philosophical astuteness evaporate. It is to the details of that evaporation that we now turn.

5

We saw at the beginning of this chapter that a belief in *reincarnation* is pre-philosophical. But a belief in a law guiding that series of re-births—the law of karma—*is* the product of philosophical reflection. Why, for what reason, were some born in the various castes referred to in the *Purusha Sutra* from the Rig Veda? How is it that I am not a member of one of the despised castes? And how is it that I am not as successful and well-off as I wish myself to be? It was musing on such questions, scholars like Reichenbach suggest, which over time produced, and gradually refined, a belief in an orderly progression of rebirths, a belief in the law of karma.

The *Upanishads* represent a later development of the Vedic tradition—many say the very apex of Hindu philosophy and religion. They are thought to date between 900 BCE and 400 BCE. In the Upanishadic texts we find a general law of consequence applied directly to birth in regard to caste. In the famous *Chandogya Upanishad,* for example, we find this:

> Those whose conduct here has been good will quickly attain a good birth (literally womb), the birth of a Brahmin, the birth of a Kshatriya or the birth of a Vaishya. But those whose conduct here has been evil, will quickly attain an evil birth, the birth of a dog, the birth of a hog or the birth of a Chandala. *Chandogya Upanishad* V.10.7[11]

I say that this is a *general* law of consequence because, while the caste into which one is born into is of overwhelming importance, specific details in the reincarnated life are left unspecified—although we should note in passing that there is an implicit ranking of horrific births for those who have lived badly: a dog, a hog, and, lowest of all, a Chandala. The concept of the Chandala, the Outcaste, will be presented in detail later. For now, we turn to the theory of reality that underlies the caste system referred to in this passage.

6

With the emergence of the Upanishads, philosophical analysis became a central characteristic of the Hindu vision. The reflections of the early Upanishads are idiosyncratic and oracular, they are intellectually challenging. For all that, however, they embody a coherent philosophical outlook. They assert the primacy of a homogenous, unconditioned reality, called *Brahman*. Primordial *Brahman* was conceived as that out of which all particular things emerged, a divine Substance that is at once the essence and origin everything—emphatically including the human self. This ultimate reality, *Brahman*, was conceived as *divine*. *Brahman* was taken to constitute *perfection*, it was considered the source of all value and joy that are experienced, however fleetingly, in human life.

Another way to think of this is that all individual things—from molecules to gnats to suns to any gods or goddesses that may exist—are *manifestations* of *Brahman* under conditions of particularity, under conditions of space, time, and form. But of itself, considered as the ultimate reality, *Brahman* is without any qualities whatever. The impersonal nature of this primordial reality is evident: personality is based on qualities and distinctions. John's personality is manifested in terms of all the qualities he has and has not. Personality is a set of *conditions*. The ultimate reality, *Brahman*, in its most basic state, was thus rigorously impersonal. In the *Chandogya Upanishad*, the homogeneity and simplicity of *Brahman*, the substrate of all particular things, is likened to the pure clay which is the substrate of all things made of clay:

> Just as ... by one clod of clay all that is made of clay becomes known, the modification being only a name arising from speech while the truth is that it is just clay. *Chandogya Upanishad* VI.1.4

And because all particulars have as their essence that impersonal substrate likened to clay in the passage from the *Chandogya Upanishad,* as their *deep* reality, so also the human individual has as its *deep* reality that same impersonal substrate—*Brahman*. This deep and impersonal reality was taken to be the true self, the personality with all its qualities, a temporary manifestation of that deep self. The *deep* self persisted in existence; the personal self was a transient, ephemeral expression of that deep self. And thus a metaphysical basis of reincarnation was given rational presentation. There was, however, a problem.

The individual human being faces death, and at death the particularity and qualities that have defined the person are reabsorbed into the primordial reality of *Brahman*. But if the person is reabsorbed into the primordial basis of all things, how is it that karmic merit and demerit is freighted from one human life to the next? How, in other words, was karmic consequence brought from one life to another? At stake is an issue of enormous importance. If no plausible means for the transfer of karmic merit can be specified, then both the explanation and—more important—the *justification* of the caste system are lost. Theories about the dynamics of transition were plentiful, and they differed widely in their accounts. Here are some of them:

> The *jiva* has the form of a man the size of a thumb; this subtle body is taken on in order to experience the fruits of karma. That subtle body does not turn to ashes even in the blazing fire in hell; it is not destroyed in water, even after a long time ... *Brahmavaivarka Purana* 2.22-24.

This passage is cited by Wendy Doniger O'Flaherty, who adds "This subtle body, here called the *jiva,* is the carrier of the karmic deposit."[12] The problem, of course, is that the "man the size of a thumb," however subtle, is possessed of qualities and individuality. And how did these escape reabsorption into the primordial *Brahman* from whence they had emerged? Consider another version of the dynamics of transition:

> When the flawless semen is placed in the womb at the fertile season, it [the *jiva*] is blown by the wind and unites with the blood of the woman. At the time of the ejaculation of the semen, the *jiva* united with the cause and enveloped and joined with its own karmas enters the womb. The semen and blood in their united form become an embryo in one day. *Bhavishya Purana*[13]

Again the problem persists: *how* does the individual *jiva* survive death in order to freight karmic effect from one life to the other? Before assessing this inconsistency, I offer one more version of how karmic effect was transferred. This account comes from a later Buddhist tradition, but one that, like Hinduism, one based on the centrality of reincarnation. It was the early 5th century CE Buddhist philosopher Vasubandhu who proposed, according to the summary provided by James P. McDermott, that

> ... driven by karma, the intermediate-state being [*gandharva*] goes to the location where rebirth is to take place. Possessing the divine eye by virtue of which it is able to see the place of its birth, no matter how distant. There

it sees its father and mother to be, united in intercourse. Finding the scene hospitable, its passions are stirred. If male, it is smitten with desire for its mother; if female, it is seized with desire for its father. And inversely, it hates either mother or father, which it comes to regard as a rival.[14]

McDermott remarks of Vasubandhu's explanation that "The Oedipal character of his analysis would do justice to Freud." No doubt. But once again, the status of the carrier of karmic effect, "the intermediate-state being [*gandharva*]," is left unaddressed. For all that it is amusing, there is a dead-serious aspect of Vasubandhu's account of the dynamics of karmic transition, as well as the other two presented here. None of them seriously attempts to demonstrate a plausible mechanism for the transfer of karma across lives. Instead of arguing for such a mechanism, each account simply *assumes* it. The concern was not with establishing a philosophical consistency, the concern was to explain the acute disparities in social station in India—and further, to *justify* those disparities. But, to say it again, if no coherent explanation of *how* karmic effect is moved from life to life, then the attempt to explain and justify social disparities falls flat.

7

The mechanics of its operation aside, the general law of consequence underwent dramatic changes over the following centuries in India—individual deeds came to be understood as leading to very specific effects in future lives. The so-called *Manusmriti,* better known as the "Laws of Manu," are of significantly later composition. The *Laws of Manu* are thought to have been put into writing between 200 BCE and 100 CE. These laws are not innovations; they serve codify practices and beliefs that had existed for centuries. What is new about the *Laws of Manu* is their highly detailed pronouncements on karmic effect as it is transferred across lives. Consider the following:

> He who steals the gold of a Brahmana [a Brahmin] has diseased nails; a drinker of the spirituous liquor called Sura, black teeth; the slayer of a Brahmana, consumption; the violator of a Guru's bed, a diseased skin; an informer, a foul-smelling nose; a calumniator, a stinking breath; a stealer of grain, deficiency in limbs; he who adulterates (grain), redundant limbs; a stealer of (cooked) food, dyspepsia; ... a stealer of clothes, white leprosy; a horse-stealer, lameness. The stealer of a lamp will become blind ... *Laws of Manu* XI.49-52[15]

Using such assumptions as a guide, one might look at a person and find an indictment stated in her or his appearance. Before the advent of modern medicine and hygiene, many people walked around with a lot of questionable moral freight palpably manifested on their bodies. And such attitudes were not restricted to a philosophical elite.

Arguably the most popular work in the Hindu tradition is the epic titled *The Ramayana*. It dramatizes the wars between the Aryan invaders and the indigenous peoples, the darker skinned Dravidians, descendants of the Indus culture. At about 500-400 BCE, a sage known as Valmiki composed the Sanskrit version of the *Ramayana*. In his popular and highly readable rendering of the story, Chakravarti Rajagopalachari introduces one of the villains of the epic:

> Queen Kaikeyi has a woman companion and confidential servant. She was a hunch-back named Manthara ... Manthara is one of the best known characters in the *Raamaayana*. Every man, woman, and child in our land [modern India] knows and detests her, as the cause of Raama's exile, Dasaratha's death and all the sorrows which befell the royal family.[16]

Physical deformity, ugliness, is taken to be an outward sign of inner corruption. Deformity is the result of previous evil deeds, and also a signal of a propensity to future evil deeds. A parallel to Manthara in Greek myth is found in Homer's portrait in the *Iliad* of Thersites—both are ugly and hunchbacked, both are offered up as being ugly in personality as well as in body.

As India's most popular religious story, *The Ramayana* is not so much read as acted out: in towns and villages throughout India (and now, of course, on television) individual episodes of the great epic are performed as little plays—*Rama-lila,* they are called. One of the more popular *Rama-lila* is the one that enacts the seduction of Queen Kaikeyi's mind by her evil servant Manthara. If we go to the complete (and vast) translation of *The Ramayana* by K. M. K. Murthy, we find a scene not presented by Rajagopalachari, but one which is often dramatized in the local *Rama-lila.* Queen Kaikeyi is shown to be completely in the power of Manthara, and bereft of sound judgment and sensibility. In this mazed state, Kaikeyi lavishes praise on the very feature which, the audience watching knows very well, is the evidence of Manthara's moral corruption:

> Till now, I have not recognised you as this good. You are the best among the hunch-backed on this earth in making intellectual decisions. Oh, Manthara! You always show interest in my well being and wish for my

benefit ... In your long hunch, which looks like an apex of a chariot, are dwelling your various thoughts, royal arts and magic effects. Oh Manthara! When Rama goes to forest and Bharata gets kingdom, I shall adorn this hunch back with a golden garland. Oh, Manthara! After accomplishing the benefit desired by me, I shall, with delight, get your hunch back anointed with well refined gold of good quality.[17]

By 21st century standards, this is a cruel episode. We can almost hear snickers from the audience at a *Rama-lila*. But in the context of karma and reincarnation, Manthara's predicament, however unfortunate, is nonetheless *deserved*. We need only consult the *Laws of Manu* to understand her situation:

Thus in consequence of a remnant of the guilt of former crimes, are born idiots, dumb, blind, deaf, and deformed men, who are all to be despised by the virtuous. *Laws of Manu,* XI.53

And in a passage from the *Markandeya Purana,* we read of the etiological specifics of the physical condition of those whose appearance was like that of Manthara's. Speaking of the future reincarnation prospects of one who has done grievous wrong:

... he is born as a [hu]man, *a contemptible one like a hunchback* or a dwarf; among Candalas, Pulkasas, and so forth.[18]

Thus the episodes in *The Ramayana*—and by extension, of course, in Indian life—are not seen as incidents of cruelty or thoughtlessness, but as an illustration of justice served. They are cautionary tales: Don't behave badly or *you'll* be born a hunchback like Manthara in a later life.

8

One might suspect that more than religion is at work here. As stated earlier, religion is never just religion; religious ideas inevitably reflect and impact a social order. The caste system, the order of reincarnation—these clearly tilt in a particular direction. Specifically, these traditions privilege the Brahmin caste. Consider, for example:

A Brahmana [Brahmin] ... is born as the highest on earth, the lord of all created beings, for the protection of the treasury of the law. Whatever exists in the world is the property of the Brahmana, on account of the excellence of his origin. The Brahmana is, indeed, entitled to all. The Brahmana eats but his own food, wears but his own apparel, bestows but his own in alms; other mortals subsist through the benevolence of the Brahmana. *Laws of Manu* I.98-101

It needs no ghost of Karl Marx come from the grave to invoke a mistrust in regard to class privilege and oppression. An orthodox Hindu might reply that indeed it does mandate class privilege, but would add at once that such privilege is entirely *deserved*. Individuals are born into the Brahmin caste through accumulated merit from previous lives—they have *earned* their place in society. But let's take a closer look, now, at a particularly troubling aspect of the caste system as it evolved in India.

9

When we looked at the roots of the caste system in the "Hymn of Man," the *Purusha Sutra* from the *Rig Veda*, we saw reference to the four major castes (more accurately, recall, *varnas*). And I noted then that the list of four castes is in fact incomplete; what is left uncounted in the *Purusha Sutra* are the vast numbers of those who fall into none of the castes—those who are *Outcastes*. These human beings, designated as *Chandalas* in ancient Indian texts and referred to in the English speaking world as Outcastes or *Untouchables*, have in recent times organized politically. In doing so, they have given themselves the name *Dalit* which, taken from the Sanskrit root *dal* (to break, or destroy) means literally "broken people," or "the oppressed." And there are good reasons for the name. To dispel the notion that we are speaking of ancient history, dark and remote, it should be recognized that according to some estimates there are about 250 million *Dalits* living in India today.

But how could such an institution have evolved (and continue to exist into the 21st century) in a culture that is, in the history of human cultures on earth, unique in its philosophical orientation and its ethical sensitivity? Some suggest that the institutional oppression to which the *Dalits* were submitted has been based on a huge misunderstanding. In fact, so this view has it, the entire caste system—including the relegation of all-so-many to the status of *Dalit*—was originally based on reasoning that was both pragmatic and meritocratic. And indeed there are ancient Hindu texts that support that claim. The most famous of these is from the *Chandogya Upanishad*. The story is both engaging and short:

> Once upon a time Satyakama Jabala addressed his mother Jabala, "Mother, I desire to live the life of a student of sacred knowledge. Of what family am I?"
>
> Then she said to him: "I do not know, my child, of what family you are. In my youth, when I went about a great deal, as a maid servant, I got you. However, I am Jabala by name and you are Satyakama by name. So you may speak of yourself as Satyakama Jabala (the son of Jabala).
>
> Then he went to Gautama, the son of Haridrumat, and said, "I wish to become a student of sacred knowledge. May I become your student, Venerable Sir."
>
> He said to him "Of what family are you, my dear? He replied, "I do not know this, sir, of what family I am. I asked my mother. She answered me, 'In my youth, when I went about a great deal as a maid servant, I got you. So I do not know of what family your are. I am Jabala by name and you are Satyakama by name.' So I am Satyakama Jabala, Sir."
>
> He then said to him, "None but a Brahmana [Brahmin] could thus explain. Bring the fuel, my dear. I will receive you as a pupil. Thou hast not departed from the truth."[19]

A delightful story. Its thrust turns on the fact that, if Satyakama is an illegitimate son (and that is what his mother's accounting implies), then he is an outcaste, a *Chandala*. What Klaus K. Klostermaier says about individuals was also true for their offspring:

> People became casteless by violating the rules of their castes, either by marrying contrary to caste regulations, by following professions not allowed by caste rules, or by committing other acts that were punished by expulsion from the caste. Some books give them the appellation "fifth caste," but that may leave a wrong impression. They were cut off from all the rights and privileges that caste society offered its members, ritually impure and ostensibly the product of bad *karma* coming to fruition.[20]

But why, according to the orthodox Hindu way thinking, would the details of young Satyakama's begetting such an *issue?* Why is irregular childbirth—that is, childbirth outside the framework of legal marriage—taken to be of such momentous importance? In a culture based on caste, such a birth tends to subvert the entire body politic. The *Laws of Manu* say:

For by adultery is caused a mixture of the castes among men; thence follows sin, which cuts up even the roots [of society] and causes the destruction of everything. *Laws of Manu*, VIII, 352-3

Coming back, now, to the story of Satyakama Jabala, the delight of the tale is the teacher's recognition of the quality of the young man: a fearless telling of the truth, even if the truth was damaging to his prospects. That is, Gautama recognizes the quality of Satyakama's character, and on the basis of that recognition, he declares that Satyakama is in fact a *Brahmin*. Many modern commentators seize upon this as evidence that Hindu views on caste were originally rooted in the natural disparities in character and talent found among humans everywhere.

The appalling circumstances of the Dalits, an apologist for the caste system might claim, is a lamentable distortion of the theory of caste over time, a distortion fueled by greed and class chauvinism. And thereby, the defense goes, what was originally a meritocratic system degenerated into the brutal system of genetic categories that blights the history of one of the richest civilizations that ever developed on this planet. A typical apologist account is this commentary by Swami Shivanada:

A *Brahmana* (Brahmin or priest) is no *Brahmana* if he is not endowed with purity and good character, and if he leads a life of dissipation and immorality. A *Sudra* is a *Brahmana* if he leads a virtuous and pious life. What a great soul was [Gautama, the guru]! What a noble, candid, straightforward student was Satyakama Jabala!... Caste is a question of character. *Varna* is not the colour of the skin, but the colour of one's character or quality. Conduct and character count and not lineage alone.[21]

Shivanada's assessment is not an uncommon one, and perhaps it is an accurate characterization of the story.[22] But even so, his reading stands as compelling evidence that an idealistic theory about the implications of reincarnation can yield results that are horrific. The caste system, however stoutly it may be defended by Indian and even Western apologists, is never benevolent in practice. But it is time to look more carefully at the historical record and its all-too-concrete details.

The *Laws of Manu* were taken to be the Bible of social conduct. Consider these passages pertaining to *Chandalas*, or Outcastes, from Book 10:

... the dwellings of Kandalas ... shall be outside the village ... and their wealth shall be dogs and donkeys. (v.51)

Chandalas are emphatically *not* part of the community—they are outcastes in the double sense of belonging to no caste and, further, being *outcaste* as in something *cast out*—something discarded and treated as valueless. In Hindu society, dogs and donkeys were despised animals, and were thus deemed to be the appropriate companions and the "wealth" of *Chandalas*. There's more:

> By the king's order they shall [be the ones to] execute criminals, in accordance with the law, and they shall take for themselves the clothes, the beds, and the ornaments of such criminals. (v.56)

The *Chandalas* are to perform the function most loathed in society—that of the executioner. And the spoils of this grim employment, the property of the condemned criminals, is to be the source of their clothes, ornaments, and bedding. And more:

> Their food shall be given to them ... in a broken dish; at night they shall not walk about in villages and in towns. (v.54)

> By day they may go about for the purpose of their work, distinguished by marks at the king's command, and they shall carry out the corpses of persons who have no relatives ... (v.55)

Under curfew at night, by day doing their debasing tasks badged ("distinguished by marks") for easy recognition; their food dispensed to them on terms of calculated contempt—in broken crockery. In addition to all this, *Chandalas* were prohibited from using public wells. If they were allowed on public roads at all, they were required to flee at the sight of people in the recognized castes. The *Chandalas* were seen as embodying contamination; contact with them (even if their shadow crossed a caste Hindu) required extensive rituals to expiate pollution. Over generations, over centuries, such attitudes and practices became ossified into an institution of systematic dehumanization.

At this point, we should note a peculiarity of the caste system. For all its hateful treatment of Chandalas, the caste system embodied an attitude toward them that is highly unusual in circumstances of systematic social oppression. For all that the Chandalas are taken to be despicable, they are taken to be so only in their *present* incarnation. The circumstances of any one life are just that—circumstances. They are temporary encumbrances endured by the underlying soul, primordial *Brahman,* that is taken to have a divine status. From the standpoint of this ultimate reality, a reality evident to enlightened sages, Chandalas are a manifestation of the divine *Brahman* that underlies all existence. And so in one of the most important of Hindu scriptures, the *Bhagavad-Gita,* we read:

> Sages see with an equal eye a learned or a humble Brahmin; a cow, an elephant, or even a dog or an outcaste [Chandala]. Even here on earth [in this life], the created world is overcome by those whose mind is established in equality. God is flawless and the same in all. Therefore are these persons established in God. *Bhagavad-Gita* V:18-19[23]

So: Chandalas were taken to be permeated with the divine—with God, who is "the same in all." And at the same time, they were treated as objects of revulsion, as sources of pollution. An enigma? Yes, and it is an enigma to which we shall return. For now, however, we must ask a simple question, one that brings our focus back to the street, as it were. Was there no hope for the Chandalas? Yes, in fact there was. But not in the present life. Caste mobility was a possibility, but *only* through reincarnation. And for a low-caste or outcaste Hindu, to rise in the caste system by way of reincarnation requires complete resignation and obedience. In the *Laws of Manu* we read:

> A *Sudra* who is pure, the servant of his betters, gentle in his speech, and free from pride, and always seeks a refuge with Brahmanas, attains in his next life a higher caste. *Laws of Manu* IX. 335

In this view, the task of a *Shudra* or Chandala in any given life is to obey their "betters" and thereby secure happier circumstances in the next life. As one indignant Indian scholar wrote in irate assessment of this doctrine, "The unuttered lesson is: try and improve your lot through unquestioning service to the 'right' people, and [you] may enjoy a windfall in some future life."[24] Such a spirit of abdication toward the life one is presently living can only have detrimental effects—not only on the individual, but also on society.

10

I have been quoting ancient scriptures. But it is important to stress and stress again that the attitudes and social structures described above are not just artifacts from the mists of history. Here is an account from 19th century India by historian James Forbes:

> The Pooleahs [a sub-group of the *Chandala*] are not permitted to breathe the same air with the other castes nor to travel on the public road; if by accident they should be there and perceive a *Brahman* ... at a distance, they must instantly make a loud howling, to warn him from approaching until they have retired or climbed up the nearest tree ... [25]

Such incidents take the ideas under investigation out of the realm of abstract theory and, as it were, put flesh on them—human flesh. I invite the reader to consider a family member, a mother or a father, climbing a tree and howling a warning to avoid polluting the air of higher caste individuals who might be passing by. And such outrages were not restricted to Hinduism. In his magisterial study, *The Wonder That Was India*, A. L. Basham speaks of the extent to which Hindu attitudes on caste came to permeate all of Indian culture, including religions in which such practices are in theory entirely alien. He says:

> Caste was so strong that all attempts at breaking it down, until recent years, have ended in failure ... The Sikhs, despite the outspoken sentiments of their gurus and the adoption of rites deliberately intended to break down caste prejudice, such as the ritual meal eaten in common, did not overcome caste feeling. Even the Muslims, for all their equalitarian faith, formed caste groups. The Syrian Christians of Malabar early divided into sections which took on a caste character, and when in the 16th century Roman Catholic missionaries began to make converts in South India their flocks brought their caste prejudices with them, and high caste converts held themselves aloof from those of the lower orders.[26]

Basham's observation is corroborated in a recent report by author and journalist William Dalrymple, in his 2000 PBS documentary on Indian history and culture titled *Out of India*. He presents a moving portrait, augmented by the angry and articulate testimony of the novelist Arundhati Roy, of the persistence of caste consciousness among what he calls the "St. Thomas Christians" of southern India—the very group called by Basham the "Syrian Christians." Their community is one is which there are two churches, a community in which there are Christians, and there are Christians. That is, there are Christians descended from *Chandala* families, and Christians descended from *caste* families. Similarly, a colleague of mine from Pakistan, a Muslim, confided to me that in his home village—a village which, he said, had been Muslim for four centuries—there is a firmly intact caste system. The pattern is familiar: there are Muslims, and there are Muslims.

More than persisting among members of religions whose tenets reject it, the institution of a *pariah* category of people has persisted in the face of legal sanctions. The institution of "Untouchability" was declared illegal by the Indian constitution of 1949. But consider this report in *Newsweek* magazine that details the state of affairs at the beginning of the 21st century:

> The frailest assertions of a Dalit candidate's running for the local council, a Dalit boy's falling for an upper-caste girl, a Dalit's using water from an upper-caste well can spark violence. Upper-caste leaders and even police have reportedly raped Dalit women to teach their husbands and brothers "lessons" about the dangers of demanding the minimum wage or reclaiming lost land, according to a 1999 Human Rights Watch Report.[27]

And in a recent issue of *National Geographic,* we find disturbing confirmation of the continuing and savage dehumanization of *Dalits* in a report by Tom O'Neill—a report that is replete with horrific photographic illustrations. In what he characterizes as a commonplace during his stay in India, O'Neill says:

> During the winter I spent in India, hardly a day passed that I didn't hear or read of acid thrown in a boy's face, or a wife raped in front of her husband, or some other act whose provocation was simply that an Untouchable didn't know his or her place.[28]

It is of course troubling to read of such things. And for over a century, Hindu thinkers have expressed outrage at the appalling consequences of the institution of Chandala status, or Untouchability. Yet although Untouchability in particular has been attacked, the caste system itself is stoutly defended by leading modern figures in Hindu thought. The defense is in fact a variation of the interpretation we encountered earlier of the story of Satyakama Jabala. There, Swami Shivananda's claim was that the misunderstandings surrounding caste centered on whether birth was a matter of birth or of character. He asserted that the genetic basis of caste structure was a misunderstanding. I repeat his words: "Caste is a question of character. *Varna* is not the colour of the skin, but the colour of one's character or quality."

11

We turn now to three prominent Indian explicators of Hinduism, each of whom claims that the excesses of the caste system are rooted in a tragic misunderstanding. But for each of them, the misunderstanding is not centered on the idea that caste is determined by *birth,* as Shivananda claimed, but on the emergence of the tradition of Untouchability—of people being cruelly relegated to the social status variously designated as Dalit, or Chandala, or Untouchable.

My first example is Mohandas Gandhi (1869 1948). Many Westerners assume that the Mahatma's famous crusade against the institution of Untouchability entailed a rejection of the caste system. It did not:

> To destroy the caste system and adopt the Western European social system means that Hindus must give up the principle of hereditary occupation which is the soul of the caste system. The hereditary principle is an eternal principle. To change it is to create disorder ... It will be chaos if every day a Brahmin is to be changed into a Shudra and a Shudra is to be changed into a Brahmin. The caste system is a natural order of society ... I am opposed to all those who are out to destroy the caste system.[29]

The hereditary principle on which caste is based is, Gandhi tells us, "eternal." That is, it is operative for all time, it is natural, and thereby insusceptible to change; any attempt to change or discard it will yield disorder and chaos in society. To deny this is to resist both nature and Hinduism. Note that we do not hear from Gandhi what Swami Shivananda asserted—that the proper designation of caste centers on *character* rather than birth.

This emphasis on the *natural* basis of caste designation is also found in a source referred to earlier in this chapter, Sarvepalli Radhakrishnan. He was one of the most gifted and morally sensitive scholars of the 20th century, and Western students of Indian philosophy and religion have benefitted from his elegant translations and commentaries. And in his book *The Hindu View of Life,* he solidly endorses the rightness of the caste system in the history of Indian culture. I have a special interest in what Radhakrishnan says here because I take the views he presents to be representative of the very dangers that confront American society at the dawn of the 21st century. Consider his assessment:

> The Hindu thinkers, perhaps through a lucky intuition or an empirical generalization, assumed the fact of heredity and encouraged marriages among those who are of approximately the same type and quality ... If the parents are about the same class the child would be practically the equal of the parents. Blood tells. We cannot make genius out of mediocrity or good ability out of inborn stupidity by all the aids of the environment. It

does not, however, mean that nature is all and nurture is nothing. The kind of nurture depends on the group and its type. So long as we had the caste system, both nature and nurture co-operated ... If we want to prevent the suicide of the social order, some restrictions have to be observed with regard to marital relations. Marriages should be, not necessarily in one's own caste but among members of approximately the same level of culture and social development.[30]

What Radhakrishnan says here is an update, as it were, of Hindu thinking on caste, an update that serves to mesh traditional caste doctrine with an approach to society that was prominent in the world in which Radhakrishnan developed as a person and a thinker—Social Darwinism, a theory to be discussed in Chapter 8. Key phrases in what he says are "the fact of heredity," "blood tells," the inability to distill "genius out of mediocrity," and the necessity of restrictions on marriage if the "suicide of the social order" is to be avoided. Radhakrishnan wrote, as do we all, as a person situated in a specific historical context. I do not see him as either insensitive or unperceptive. In what follows I suggest that Radhakrishnan's well-intentioned endorsement of caste theory is not a grotesque museum piece in the history of ideas. Quite the contrary: his disposition to classify people into groups of "natural" qualities, groups of which it must be acknowledged (with however much regret) that "blood tells," represents a assessment that may find sympathetic attention in 21st century America. But for now, let's turn to another eminent Indian thinker.

Swami Vivekananda (1863-1902), at the turn of the last century, brought a subtle and profound understanding of Advaita Vedanta, a deeply philosophical form of Hinduism, to eager and receptive minds in America. Vivekananda was possessed of a keen intellect and a delightfully vibrant writing style. He made a point of avoiding extensive talk about caste to his American audiences. But to his Indian readers, he spoke of caste in pointed and urgent tones. On the one hand, as stridently as Gandhi ever did, Vivekananda heatedly denounces the institution of Untouchability. In an essay titled "The Caste Problem in India," he says:

The present religion of the Hindus is neither the path of Knowledge or Reason it is "Don't-touchism." "Don't touch me," "Don't touch me" that exhausts its description. "Don't touchism" is a form of mental disease. Beware! ... Just see, for want of sympathy from the Hindus, thousands of Pariahs [Untouchables] in Madras are turning Christians. Don't think that this is simply due to the pinch of hunger; it is because they do not get any sympathy from us. We are day and night calling out to them "Don't touch us! Don't touch us!" Is there any compassion or kindliness of heart in our country?[31]

Having said this, however, he goes on with equal intensity to endorse the caste system itself. And he does so by comparing the caste system in India to its absence in Europe:

> The means of European civilization is the sword; of the Aryans [Indians], the division into different varnas. This system of division into varnas is the stepping-stone to civilization, making one rise higher and higher in proportion to one's learning and culture. In Europe, it is everywhere victory to the strong and death to the weak. In the land of Bharata (India), every social rule is for the protection of the weak. Such is our ideal of caste, as meant for raising all humanity slowly and gently towards the realization of the great ideal of spiritual man ...[32]

The suggestion is that the caste system that developed in India has had the historical effect of both *including* and *protecting* the weak, whereas in Europe the weak were simply given over to death. History will not support Vivekananda's claim, neither in regard to Europe nor India. We have seen earlier that the *Shudra* caste is mythically represented in the ancient hymn from the *Rig Veda,* the *Purusha Sutra,* as having sprung from the *feet* of the Primordial Man, and that the prescribed activity of the lowly-originated caste is *labor.* These are the weak of whom Vivekananda speaks. But in fact, if being oppressed were somehow a grim contest, the *Shudras* have always been close runners-up to the Dalits. In a telling statement, Marc Galantner, a historian of the legal history of caste in India, says this:

> For purposes of applying Hindu personal law, the courts had never attempted to distinguish untouchables from Sudras; all Hindus other than the twice-born were lumped together as Sudras.[33]

The point is that, like the Chandalas, the condition of *Shudras* was a desperate one, and had they been consulted on the matter, they would have contested Vivekananda's claim that they were in any sense protected or meaningfully included in Hindu culture. Put otherwise, the view of the caste system as somehow "protective and humane," as it is characterized by both Gandhi and Vivekananda, lacks historical credibility: one need not have been an Outcaste, a Dalit, to experience the caste system as predatory and dehumanizing.

Such defenses of the caste system in India are by no means restricted to Indians. Western scholars, too, have endorsed the values of the system. For example, Alain Danielou, in his thought-provoking study on Dionysus and Shiva, offers an endorsement of Vivekananda's claim:

> The much-decried caste system has allowed the survival of the most diversified peoples, especially those who are least aggressive and least suited to an industrial civilization. In so-called democratic societies, the weakest are inevitably dispossessed, destroyed, or culturally annihilated.[34]

And historian Rhoades Murphey, in *A History of Asia,* concurs with the claims of both Gandhi and Radhakrishnan that caste is not of itself a bad thing:

> Caste provided a system of social organization which was otherwise largely lacking and gave each individual a sense of belonging in the form of membership in a larger group beyond the basic nexus of the family. Caste operated also as a mutual benefit society, helping caste members who were in material trouble, settling disputes, and working as a common interest group on behalf of the welfare of all members ... [35]

I do not deny that, in theory, the caste system may be committed to the protection of the less fortunate and to endorsing the sanctity of all life. But apologists for this system, whether Indian or non-Indian, must squarely face up to history as well as theory. They must look directly at how the system plays out in the street.

I have attempted to demonstrate that a cursory look at Indian history will stun the reader with glimpses of the lived reality of the caste system. Yet it is a history not unique to India, but is one that affirms a human tendency: when we see other humans exclusively as *group members,* and only afterward (if at all) as *individuals,* then those humans easily become "those people." From such a characterization, a dismissive and even contemptuous attitude follows as night follows day.

I certainly don't mean to impute either evasiveness or dishonorable intentions to thinkers like Swami Vivekananda—in fact his writings have been an inspiration to me since my student days. What then is amiss? A key is found, I think, in another of Vivekananda's statements in "The Caste Problem in India":

> Caste is a very good thing. Caste is the plan we want to follow. What caste really is, not one in a million understands.[36]

I accept that Vivekananda is entirely sincere in his claim. But if what he says is true, it stands as a point in the argument *against* caste. Here's why. Vivekananda speaks of an understanding of what caste "really is"—an understanding attained by "not one in a million." Reading him at some length over the years has instilled in me a great respect for his intellectual prowess. And so I allow that he may know what caste *really* is. But *I* don't. And apparently I have lots of company in that: obviously the Hindu officials and priests who historically have ruled India did not understand either, for they generated the institution of Untouchability that Vivekananda himself so hotly berates. To return to a methodological point I made in the Introduction: the concern in this book is not with *truth*, still less with a truth accessible to one in a million. My concern here is with the *consequences* of the ideas reincarnation, karma, and caste, not with their truth.

And in terms of that pragmatic concern, the importance of such profoundly influential doctrines is not rooted in the sophisticated understanding of an educated elite, not in what one in a million understands. On the contrary, the importance of a social doctrine like caste consists entirely in its broad social consequences—consequences that are wrought not upon the few, but precisely in the minds and lives of the teeming millions, however benighted they may be thought to be. It is those millions—those *billions,* if we think over historical generations—whose understanding brings the theories of caste into reality.

12

We've seen that some of the best Indian minds in the past hundred years—Gandhi, Radhakrishnan, and Vivekananda—have defended the perpetuation of the caste system. The injustices that have plagued Indian history in connection with the caste system, they claim, are problems not endemic to the system itself, but are regrettable perversions and misunderstandings. It won't come as a surprise that not all Indians have accepted this assessment of the disparity between theory and practice.

One of the most vigorous contenders against this defense of caste, and the very continuation of the caste system itself, was B. R. Ambedkar (1891 1956). Ambedkar's skepticism is understandable: he was born a *Dalit*, and throughout his life he championed the liberation of his people. In this he was an ally of Gandhi. His differences with Gandhi centered on Gandhi's insistence that the caste system be maintained. The problem, Ambedkar asserts, is not a lamentable corruption or misunderstanding of the caste system; the problem is the caste system *itself*. A caste system guarantees the existence and maintenance of evils like Untouchability:

> There will be outcastes as long as there are castes, and nothing can emancipate the outcaste except the destruction of the caste system. The mass of people in India have tolerated the social evils to which they have been subjected ... because they have been completely disabled for direct action on account of this wretched system of caste. They could not bear arms and without arms they could not rebel ... They could receive no education, so they could not think out or know the way to their salvation ... Not knowing the way of escape and not having the means of escape, they became reconciled to eternal servitude, which they accepted as their inescapable fate ... [37]

Recall that all three—Gandhi, Radhakrishnan, and Vivekananda—see caste as essential to Hinduism. Ambedkar is well aware of their concern, and he is resolutely deaf to it. Addressing himself in 1936 to Gandhi and other thinking Indians, he said:

> You must destroy the sacredness and divinity with which caste has become invested. In the last analysis, this means you must destroy the authority of the Shastras and the Vedas ... You must take the stand that Buddha took ... *You must have courage to tell the Hindus that what is wrong with them is their religion* —the religion which has produced in them this notion of the sacredness of caste.[38]

I repeat that Ambedkar was born a *Dalit*, an Untouchable. As such, he certainly saw his family and friends submitted to the debasement given pale account in the survey included in this chapter. It would be unrealistic to expect someone who had experienced such things to be inclined to spare the feelings of his Hindu interlocutors. "You must destroy the authority of the Hindu scriptures!" Yes, the Buddha said things like that—and in doing so he made it clear that he was *rejecting* Hinduism. "Have the courage to tell the Hindus that what is wrong with them is their religion!" This is not the language of negotiation; Ambedkar has no expectation that the Hindus he addresses will be amenable to a revamping of their religion to its very foundations. Indeed, in the last year of his life, Ambedkar made a highly public conversion to Buddhism.

13

The caste system as practiced in India is a toxic conflation of two very distinct realities: *individual* characteristics on the one hand, and socially defined *groups* on the other. Specifically, the caste system has taken the highly individualized qualities that constitute character—the varying degrees of intelligence, industriousness, impulse control, strength and dexterity, etc.—and ascribed them wholesale to *groups* of people.

Consider again Radhakrishnan's words quoted earlier: "If the parents are about the same class the child would be practically the equal of the parents. Blood tells. We cannot make genius out of mediocrity or good ability out of inborn stupidity by all the aids of the environment." Allowing that "blood" here refers to what we today call *genes,* his point is indisputably accurate—but only when applied to this *individual* or that one. However, such claims cannot be ascribed to *groups,* which is what apologists for the caste system like Radhakrishnan (and Gandhi and Vivekananda) do when they mount their defense. The Western tendency toward excessive individualism is often criticized, and not without reason. But the opposite tendency, to see people primarily in terms of group membership rather than as individuals, is equally problematic. When entire human groups are deemed to possess disparate capacities, as they are in the caste system, condescension is inevitable. And what begins as condescension has a powerful tendency, history shows us, to descend into dehumanization. No matter how loudly protested are ideals like the "protection of the weak" and "the sacred unity of all life"—inevitably groups on the lower end of the scale come to be seen as "those people." In the face of all the high ideals stands the brute reality of socially structured oppression that has, alas, characterized the history of the Indian subcontinent. In Hindu culture, this structured oppression becomes all the more intransigent because differences in group status are attributed to a *moral* etiology. Recall in this regard the observations of Klaus K. Klostermaier previously cited: "*Brahmins* were born into the highest caste on account of *karma* accumulated over past lives. Lesser *karma* resulted in lower births. Birth as a *Shudra* was designed to atone for sins past."

To review: human qualities of character vary among people; these qualities and their variance are indisputable, and have manifested themselves amply in the course of history. But these qualities of character pertain to, and vary among, *individuals:* to impute them to groups is to embrace a category error similar to that we encountered in regard to the doctrine of karma. Recall that in Chapter 2 we saw that the doctrine of karma, taken as a doctrine of consequence, becomes pernicious only when it is placed in the category of *mechanistic* law rather than in the category of *statistical* law. And as the error of placing a doctrine of consequence in the wrong category is entirely misguided, so also the error of placing qualities of character into the category of *groups* rather than individuals is misguided. And not only misguided, but outrageous and heartbreaking in its applications.

14

Finally, it is time to face a blunt question. Is the caste system operative in Hindu culture just old-fashioned bigotry? And if so, should that allegation not be stated right out loud? Indeed, the imputation of character qualities to groups rather than to individuals has, historically, been the mark of bigotry. However, my response to the question "Is it bigotry?" is *no*. And I am aware that my *no* would be stoutly rejected by people like B. R. Ambedkar and other Indians who have suffered bitterly as *Dalits* and *Shudras*. But what is at work here is *not* bigotry, at least not bigotry as we think of it in America. And the fact that the Hindu caste system is not "bigotry as usual" is one of the most disturbing things about it.

Yes, there are lofty ideals brought forward in defense of the caste system. But such ideals do not redeem it; idealism tends to be tiresomely characteristic of most forms of bigotry—National Socialism is only the most glaring example. Nor is the caste system redeemed by its claim that *Dalits* and *Shudras* have somehow *earned* their despised status: the claim that "they've got it coming" has been the monotone over which bigots have asserted their doctrines throughout the ages. The great irony here is that what redeems the caste system from the charge of bigotry are the very ideological assumptions on which it is based—*reincarnation and karma.*

In light of the theory of reincarnation, the situation of the *Dalit* or *Shudra* is *temporary,* yes, but even this is not the important point. The important point, and what sets the caste system off from other forms of "bigotry as usual," is that the *Dalit* or *Shudra* is a *passing phase* undergone by an incarnated (and reincarnated) essence that is taken to be *divine* and possessed of supreme value.

Yes, the *Dalit* before you is utterly wretched, but what's really unfolding is a drama in which a divine essence is working through processes of purification, processes that will culminate in a reunification with the Absolute. Just this is the basis of the assurance we found in the passage quoted from the *Bhagavad-Gita* that when seen with the eye of a sage, the *Brahmin* and the Chandala are no different. They just have different karma to work out in this life.

Again, it is this belief in the essential divinity of the oppressed castes that decisively sets off caste theory from "bigotry as usual." It surely distinguishes Hindu caste theory from the bigotry with which most Americans are familiar. It strains credibility to the breaking point to think of a Nazi or Ku Klux Klan member as seeing a Jew or a Black as a divine essence undergoing a temporary process of purification. Entirely to the contrary, these familiar bigots see their targets as vermin, as something to simply be eradicated.

That the Hindu caste system is not "bigotry as usual" is what makes it, seemingly, so impervious to change in Indian culture. At least as an ideal, the system is not maintained by mean-spiritedness: it is not without reason that Gandhi came to be called the *Mahatma*—the great soul. A thoroughly disarming generosity of spirit is evident throughout the writings of Vivekananda; a broad humanitarian wisdom and erudition informs the voluminous work of Radhakrishnan. It would be outrageous to class such men, all vigorous supporters of the caste system, with the likes of Heinrich Himmler or some Kleagle of the Klan.

Recall the eloquent protest of B. R. Ambedkar. He insisted that Hinduism as a religion was the problem; that if Indians want to do right they should abandon their incurably corrupt religion—"the religion which has produced in them this notion of the sacredness of caste." A radical proposal, one not likely to gain support in India. His bitter experiences are no doubt the root of his anger and impatience. And since radical proposals are on the table, let me go further than Ambedkar. My proposal cuts even deeper to the heart of traditional Hinduism. It is this: so long as there is a generally accepted belief in reincarnation and karma, there will be castes; so long as there are castes, there will be hateful and dehumanizing social structures that reflect those castes. Just as Ambedkar sees Gandhi's proposal to eliminate Untouchability as not being sufficiently radical, so I suggest that his own proposal to eliminate castes does not attack the problem of dehumanization at its root. I contend, again, that traditional beliefs in reincarnation and karma will *inevitably* produce a caste system with all its monstrous injustices.

Can Hinduism evolve and change? Clearly, Ambedkar thinks not. Perhaps because I've been socialized in America and not India, I'm more optimistic. I consider that ugly concepts like perpetual damnation, along with Hell itself, have been gently let go by all but the most committed of Fundamentalist Christians. And the doctrine of the Chosen People, along with mandates for lethal enforcement of select points of the Torah have been gently let go by all but the most Fundamentalist of Jews. And later in this study we'll see that traditional Buddhism, as it arrives in the West, is gently letting go of much of its historical freight.

Will Hinduism ever be able, will it ever be willing, to leave behind its ancient traditions that involve reincarnation, karma, and caste? No one can say for certain, but most sources I've read are deeply pessimistic about the prospects of such an outcome. In addition, informal conversations with Indians living in the San Francisco Bay Area, including naturalized citizens, long-term residents, and recent immigrants, have yielded a monolithic consensus. With courtesy, I'm gently informed that the prospect of Hinduism leaving behind reincarnation and caste theory is—laughable. Reincarnation, karma, and caste, they say, are in the very bones of Hinduism.

But my concern here is not with the fate of India or Hinduism, but with the future of American society, and the role that a belief in reincarnation might play in that future. My intention in this chapter has been to briefly trace the effects that belief in reincarnation has produced in Indian society, and to emphasize how intractable that belief has proven to be. Once adopted, the lens of *caste* is difficult to remove; once the cultural habit of looking at "those people" becomes installed, it quickly gains an imperviousness to change. As of now in America, belief in reincarnation is not, as the Indians I spoke to put it, "in our bones." For now, it is merely *chic*. But America is changing, and changing fast: what took centuries in India could be realized here in a generation or three.

Notes

1. Dalrymple, W. *Out of India,* PBS Documentary, 2000.
2. Cornford, F. M. *From Religion to Philosophy: a Study in the Origins of Western Speculation.* New York: Harper Torchbooks, 1957 (1912), p.161.
3. Klostermaier, K.K. *A Survey of Hinduism.* Albany: State Univ. of New York Press, 1989, p.35.
4. Bhattacharji, S. *Fatalism in India.* Calcutta: Sarmistha Roy, 1995, p.viii.
5. Klostermaier, 1989, p.37-8.
6. O'Flaherty, W. D., translator. *The Rig Veda* 10.90, *Purusha Sutra,* 11-12. New York: Penguin Books, 1981, p.31.
7. Klostermaier, 1989, p.317.
8. Reichenbach, B.R. *The Law of Karma: a Philosophical Study.* Honolulu: Univ. of Hawaii Press, 1990, p.10.
9. Reichenbach, 1990, p.13.

10. Radhakrishnan, 1965, p.55.
11. Radhakrishnan, S., translator. *The Principal Upanishads.* New York: Humanities Press, 1969, p.433. All passages from the Upanishads will be from this edition.
12. O'Flaherty, W. D. "Karma and Rebirth in the Vedas and Puranas," in O'Flaherty, W. D. *Karma and Rebirth in Classical Indian Traditions.* Berkeley: University of California Press, 1980, p.16.
13. O'Flaherty, 1980, p.20.
14. McDermott, J. P. "Karma and Rebirth in Early Buddhism," in O'Flaherty, 1980, p.171.
15. Bühler, G., translator. *The Laws of Manu. Sacred Books of the East,* v.25. http://www.sacred-texts.com/hin/manu.htm All citations from *The Laws of Manu* will be from this edition.
16. Rajagopalachari, C., translator and editor. *Ramayana.* Bombay: Bharatiya Vidya Bhavan, 1968, p.51.
17. Murthy, K. M. K., Translator. *The Ramayana,* Bk. II, Ch. 9, vv. 38-48. http://www.valmikiramayan.net/ayodhya/sarga9/ayodhya_9_frame.htm.
18. O'Flaherty, W.D. "Karma and Rebirth in the Vedas and Puranas" in O'Flaherty, 1980, p.18. Emphasis added.
19. *Chandogya Upanishad IV.4.1-5,* in Radhakrishnan, 1969, p.406-7.
20. Klostermaier, 1989, p.326.
21. Shivanada, Swami. The Divine Life Society. http://www.hinduism.co.za/dharma.htm.
22. Yet a close look at the delightful story suggests otherwise. The careful and detailed repetition of what in Hindu culture was a manifestly questionable begetting centers our attention and our expectations on *parentage;* the dramatic tension of the episode turns on an assumption that the teacher Gautama will be thinking in *genetic* terms. The refreshing surprise in the story—contrary to expectations—is that Gautama brushes aside Satyakama's parentage and focuses on his *character.* Since the expectations addressed in the story are rooted in parentage, not character, I suggest that the story does not embody an old way of doing thing which alas has gone corrupt through later misunderstandings, but is instead a critique of *established* practice.
23. Radhakrishnan, S., translator. *The Bhagavadgita.* New York: Harper & Row, 1973, p.181-2.
24. Bhattacharji, S. *Fatalism in India.* Calcutta: Sarmistha Roy, 1995, p.xviii.
25. Cited in Griffiths, P. *Modern India.* New York: Frederick A. Praeger, 1957, p.33
26. Basham, A. L. *The Wonder That Was India.* Calcutta: Rupa and Co., 1967, p.151.
27. Power, C. *Plight of the "Untouchables" Newsweek,* 25 June, 2000.
28. O'Neill, T. "Untouchable." *National Geographic,* June 2003, pp.14-15.
29. Gandhi, M. K. *Collected Works of Mahatma Gandhi, Vol.9.* Delhi: Ministry of Information, Govt. Of India, 1958, p.275.

30. Radhakrishnan, 1965, pp.73-4.
31. Vivekananda, S. "The Caste Problem in India" from *Swami Vivekananda on India and Her Problems*. Online at http://www.sivanandadlshq.org/messages/caste.htm.
32. Vivekananda, "The Caste Problem in India."
33. Galanter, M. *Competing Equalities : Law and the Backward Classes in India*. Berkeley: University of California Press, 1984, p.145. Note that the concept of "twice born," as used here, does not refer to reincarnation, but to the fact that membership in the top three castes—*Brahmin, Kshatriya*, and *Vaishya*—made a person eligible for religious initiation, an initiation which was taken to be a second birth in *this* life.
34. Danielou, A. *Gods of Love and Ecstasy: the Traditions of Shiva and Dionysus*. Rochester, Vermont: Inner Traditions Press, 1992, p.19.
35. Murphey, R. *A History of Asia*. New York: HarperCollins Publishers, 1992, p.190.
36. Vivekananda, "The Caste Problem in India."
37. Cited in: Singh, S. "A Cosmetic Approach To Malignancy: Gandhi and Casteism" http://www.sikhe.com/gsdno/articles/opinion/11212001_sundeep singh_gandhiandcasteism.htm
38. In *The Hindu*: April 9, 2002 (Online edition), at http://www.hinduonnet.com/2002/04/09/stories/2002040900791000.html. My emphasis.

4

CANNIBALS & CAVEMEN: REINCARNATION IN ANCIENT GREECE

> The safest general characterization of the European philosophical tradition is that it consists of a series of footnotes to Plato ... I allude to the wealth of general ideas scattered through [his writings]. His personal endowments, his wide opportunities for experience at a great period of civilization, his inheritance of an intellectual tradition not yet stiffened by excessive systematization, have made his writings an inexhaustible mine of suggestion.
>
> —Alfred North Whitehead[1]

1

Whitehead's claim is one of the more famous generalizations in the history of philosophy. And most who are familiar with the development of Western civilization agree with him, although many feel that the trend he describes is a mixed blessing at best. The most significant aspect of Plato's philosophy for our present concerns is his doctrine of reincarnation. The whole of Plato's philosophy—his understanding of the self, his religious agenda, his theory of knowledge, and his political theory—all these hinge in one way or another on his theories on reincarnation. That's a large claim, and I won't attempt to defend it in full in what follows. Instead, I will bring to focus those aspects of Plato's views on reincarnation that are germane to the central concerns of this book—specifically, how such views constitute a very real danger in 21st century American culture. I will proceed by setting Plato's views on reincarnation into historical context. To do that, our discussion will move backward in time from Plato—tracing the doctrine of reincarnation back from Plato to speculations about the earliest origins of the doctrine in Greek culture. Having reached those ancient origins, I will then return to Plato, and present the specifics of his theories of reincarnation.

2

In ancient Greek, the word was *palingenesía,* and later, *metempsychosis.* Both terms refer to rebirth, transmigration, or reincarnation. Plato (428/7 348/7 BCE) is indisputably the most important proponent of reincarnation theory in ancient Greece, but he was not the first. The historian Herodotus, who lived in the middle of the 5th century BCE, claimed that the doctrine originated not in Greece at all, but in Egypt:

> They [=the Egyptians] were also the first to broach the opinion that the soul of man is immortal and that, when the body dies, it enters into the form of an animal which is born at the moment, thence passing on from one animal into another, until it has circled through the forms of all the creatures which tenant the earth, the water, and the air, after which it enters again into a human frame, and is born anew. The whole period of the transmigration is (they say) three thousand years. There are Greek writers, some of an earlier, some of a later date, who have borrowed this doctrine from the Egyptians, and put it forward as their own. I could mention their names, but I abstain from doing so.[2]

Most modern scholars do not accept this account. For example, the historian W. K. C. Guthrie dismisses Herodotus' story, saying that "One may simply [note] that the doctrine was certainly a Greek one, since in fact Egyptian religion knew nothing of transmigration."[3] Egyptian religion did not incorporate reincarnation theory, but it may nonetheless be hasty to assume that Egyptian religion did not exert an influence on the emergence of Greek views on the topic. We find a perceptive suggestion in the classic work of the early 20th century historian of religion, Jane Harrison. In her *Prolegomena to the Study of Greek Religion* she notes this:

> A people who saw in a chance snake the soul of a hero would have no difficulty in formulating a doctrine of metempsychosis. They need not have borrowed it from Egypt, and yet it is probable that the influence of

Egypt, the home of animal worship, helped out the doctrine by emphasizing the sanctity of animal life. The almost ceremonial tenderness shown to animals by the Pythagorean Orphics is an Egyptian rather than a Greek characteristic.[4]

Nothing—or *few* things—are purely harmful or purely beneficial. Harrison points out one of the aspects of reincarnation theory that is salutary: no matter that the theory of reincarnation did not arise in Egypt, her emphasis on the resonance between reincarnation and the Egyptian appreciation of the sanctity of animal life—and, further, the profound connectedness of human life with non-human life—are insightful.

But let's turn back for a moment to Herodotus. Herodotus intimates less than honorable behavior on the part of certain Greeks in their appropriation of ideas that originated in Egypt—and he tactfully declines to name names. But in fact the names are no secret, and the most famous among them are those of Pythagoras (580 500 BCE), and his later advocate, the philosopher Empedocles (490 - 430 BCE).

3

Empedocles lived closest in time to Plato, who was born some two or three years after his death. Ancient accounts of Empedocles suggest that he was a colorful character, a self-promoter and religious impresario. He was handsomely opinionated; his writing gives no evidence of his being distracted by doubts. Consistent with his dramatic writing style, a popular legend holds that, in order to demonstrate his divinity to his followers, he threw himself into the volcanic crater at Mt. Etna. Legends aside, Empedocles was no mere showman: he was a incisive thinker who posited, among other interesting views, a theory that the world was driven by two contrary forces, Eros and Strife—a distant prequel to Freudian theories of Eros and *Thanatos*. But at present we are concerned with his thought on reincarnation. It is assumed that Empedocles derived his views on reincarnation from Pythagoras: he is said by Diogenes Laertius to have studied with Pythagoras' son, Telauges. Empedocles' acceptance of the belief in reincarnation led him (again following Pythagoras) to a forceful rejection of meat eating, and a corresponding diagnosis of the lamentable state of human existence:

> Alas that the pitiless day of death did not destroy me before I devised that abominable act, the eating of flesh! (8.3, p.152)[5]

Meat eating is taken to be *the* primal sin by Empedocles. Through his commitment to reincarnation, he saw meat eating as nothing less than *cannibalism,* and therefore as the root cause of all human misery. The animal sacrifice and meat banquets that were commonplace features of the Greek culture of his day were to Empedocles' eyes a ghastly spectacle:

> The father lifts up his own dear son in a changed form, an with a prayer slays him in his great folly. Some of those sacrificing hesitate, hearing the entreaties of the victim; but he, deaf to its outcries, slaughters it and makes ready in his halls the evil feast. In like manner the son seized upon his father and the children their mother, and tearing their lives from them, devour the flesh of their own kin. (8.12, p.154)

Parents unwittingly sacrifice and devour their own children; children in turn feast on the reincarnated flesh of their parents. This dreadful behavior, Empedocles asserted, had consequences. And the consequences came to fruition in later lives of the people who engaged in it:

> Alas, wretched breed of mortals, sore unblessed; such are the strifes and groanings from which you have been born! For this reason are you distraught with dire evils, and shall never ease your heart of grievous sorrows. (8.14-15, p.154)

The life we experience is retribution for offenses in previous lives—but especially for the offense of *cannibalism.* Again we encounter the view that we found so prominent in India, that the cause of human misery is traceable to misdeeds in previous lives. This tendency to find explanations of present conditions in behaviors in previous lives, is, as discussed in Chapter 1, a consistent feature of reincarnation theory wherever it arises. We found it in India; we find it in Empedocles; we shall find it again when we turn to Plato—and we shall encounter it again when we look at 21st century American views of reincarnation. Before leaving Empedocles, however, let us examine two more of his sayings that bear upon his understanding of reincarnation:

> For by now I have been born as a boy, a girl, a plant, a bird, and a dumb fish in the sea. (8.11, p.154)

> Wretches, utter wretches, keep your hands from beans! (8.18, p.155)

Empedocles claims (8.11) to have recalled his previous lives: some male, some female, some as a bird, some as a fish. But also—and this is different from most Indian views on reincarnation—he recalls his previous life as a *plant*. Interesting. And our interest is further provoked by his admonition, as enigmatic as it is forceful, to keep our hands from *beans*. To understand what's going on, we must now move further back in time, to an earlier phase in the development of reincarnation theory in ancient Greece—to the thought of Pythagoras.

4

Pythagoras is rightly famous as a geometer: every schoolchild knows his theorem for calculating the hypotenuse of a right triangle. In addition, however, Pythagoras was committed to a mysticism of numbers—of numerical ratios that are found in arithmetic and geometry, and also in the harmonics of music. Finally, and to the point of our investigation, Pythagoras was deeply committed to the doctrine of reincarnation. Like Empedocles after him, Pythagoras claimed to recall previous lives. In Diogenes Laertius' *Lives of Eminent Philosophers,* we read:

> ... he used to say about himself that he had once been Aethalides and was accounted to be Hermes' son, and Hermes told him he might choose any gift he liked except immortality; so he asked to retain through life and through death a memory of his experiences. Hence in [this] life he could recall everything, and when he died he still kept the same memories.[6]

In fact, many proponents of reincarnation theory claim to recall past lives. And the capacity to *recall* is, we'll see, an essential aspect of Plato's theory of learning. This ties in with the observations of Buddhist scholar Edward Conze presented in Chapter 1, observations regarding some unflattering motives for embracing reincarnation theory: that it offers the prospect of exalted past lives, and that it offers the consolation that the "precious self" will not be lost at death. Pythagoras' claims clearly exemplify both: he was once the son of the god Hermes, and the god's gift to him of reincarnation is clearly a variant of personal immortality—a gift of "me forever" through a recollection that persists throughout a succession of lives.

But let's look at other aspects of Pythagoras' view of reincarnation. Again like Empedocles after him, Pythagoras believed that reincarnation could proceed not only through human and nonhuman animal lives, but also through incarnations as a *plant*. In a passage closely following the one just cited, it is reported that "he told of the wanderings of his soul, how it migrated hither and thither, into how many plants and animals it had come ... " (DL VIII.4, p.325)

What might the significance be of Pythagoras and Empedocles including plants among potential incarnations for the migrating soul? We know that Greek philosophers prided themselves on being "scientific"—on claiming that their theories were grounded in experimentation. Such speculations are always tentative, of course, but we can follow some clues. The soul, or *psyche* in Greek, is typically identified with *breath* in ancient Greek thought. In the entry under *psyche,* in *Greek Philosophical Terms: A Historical Lexicon,* F. E. Peters tells us that the term refers to "breath of life," ghost, or vital principle, that in Homer it is the breath that leaves the mouth of the dying hero at the moment of death; he tells us that the connection between *psyche* and breath varies among the pre-Socratics, and that for some it was of an "airy" quality.[7]

Both Empedocles and Pythagoras speak of incarnations as plants, but not as *all* kinds of plants. We find a key in Empedocles' irascible outburst, quoted above, "Wretches, utter wretches, keep your hands from beans!" Diogenes Laertius tells us that the followers of Pythagoras were enjoined "To abstain from beans because they are flatulent and partake most of the breath of life." (DL VIII.24, p.341)

As scientists, as experimentalists, it's clear that Pythagoras and his circle were impressed by a phenomenon that, millennia later, was to provide crude and childish delight to American boys sitting around campfires:

Beans, beans, they're good for your heart—
The more you eat, the more ... etc.

It is easy to smile at this aspect of Pythagoras' teaching. Even Plato, who was deeply influenced by Pythagoras' philosophy, especially on the point of reincarnation, pokes fun at this "gaseous" conception of the psyche. In his account of Socrates' death, Plato depicts him as chiding his Pythagorean students, Simmias and Cebes:

... you are afraid, as children are, that when the soul emerges from the body the wind may really puff it away and scatter it, especially when a person does not die on a calm day but with a gale blowing. *Phaedo* 77d[8]

Amusing as it may seem by later standards, Pythagoras clearly took the destruction of beans, whether by eating them or by any other means, to be as egregious an offense as cannibalism. This is not easy for a modern person to take seriously, but Pythagoras' sincerity about this belief is evident in two different accounts of his death recorded in Diogenes Laertius. In one account, the aged Pythagoras and his friends were attacked by political enemies:

> Pythagoras was caught as he tried to escape; he got as far as a certain field of beans, where he stopped, saying he would be captured rather than cross it, and be killed rather than prate about his doctrines; and so his pursuers cut his throat. (DL VIII.39, p.355)

Diogenes further cites an epigraph that recounts the master's death, but with a sense of dismay and incredulousness:

> Woe! Woe! Whence, Pythagoras, this deep reverence for beans? Why did he fall in the midst of his disciples? A bean field was there he durst not cross; sooner than trample on it, he endured to be slain at the cross-roads by the men of Acragas. (DL VIII.45, p.361)

We've traced the history of reincarnation theory in Greek thought back from Plato through Empedocles and Pythagoras. But our quest for beginnings does not stop here, for neither Empedocles nor Pythagoras originated reincarnation doctrine. Those origins trace back to still more ancient roots—to the cult of Orphism.

In what remains the foremost work on Orphism, W. K. C. Guthrie's *Orpheus and Greek Religion*, the author laments "the scantiness of direct evidence for Orphism."[9] Based on his study of the fragmentary allusions to Orphism in antiquity, Guthrie speculates on what is known to have been a strict prohibition against meat eating:

> The reasoning was this. If the soul of a man may be reborn in a beast, and rise again from beast to man, it follows that soul is one, and all life akin. Hence the most important Orphic commandment, the commandment to abstain from meat, since all meat-eating is virtually cannibalism.[10]

But more than just cannibalism is at issue in our relations with animals, according to the Orphic view. Not only were Orphics forbidden to eat, for example, sheep—they further were forbidden to wear wool. Of this, Guthrie says:

Probably this prohibition was closely connected with the former, the use of animal products being forbidden in general. To be sure, it was possible to obtain wool without committing the crime of murdering a kinsman, which was involved in eating mutton, but perhaps to rob him was considered unworthy of the pure.[11]

The Orphic understanding of human destiny constituted a major point of transition from the traditional Greek view, especially in regard to death. The traditional view was codified in the epics of Homer. In this view, life was to be seized with vigor, because death began a gloomy underworld existence in Hades, a fate that could be avoided by none. All mortals, from Achilles to the anonymous sweaty spearman, faced an afterlife that was a grey, shadow existence—interminable and with no prospect of relief. By contrast, Guthrie tells us:

> Orphism was a religion with a belief in immortality and in posthumous rewards and punishments. So far so good. But it had a more individual doctrine than that. Hades ... was not the end. There was also the doctrine of the circle of birth, or cycle of births, and the possibility of ultimate escape from reincarnation to the state of perfected divinity.[12]

We see here that the notion of moral consequence was associated with Greek views of reincarnation from its earliest expressions. Commenting on this, the classicist F. M. Cornford says:

> How did the doctrine of rebirth come to be moralized? Among the Orphics and Pythagoreans, we find it associated with the fall of the soul from its original state, a purification of the soul's sins in this life ...[13]

That the concepts of *offense* and *retribution* are at the core of early Greek reincarnation theory is evident, as we've seen, in the fragments of the philosopher Empedocles. And Empedocles, like Pythagoras, took the idea from the Orphic religion. Speaking of this tendency within Orphism, Guthrie tells us:

> The Orphic was an ascetic, that is to say, he believed that the source of evil lay in the body with its appetites and passions, which must therefore be subdued if we are to rise to the heights which it is in us to attain. This is precept, but like all Orphic precept it is based on dogma. The belief behind it is that this present life is for the soul a punishment for previous sin, and the punishment consists precisely in this, that it is fettered to a body.[14]

The business at hand, in the cycle of reincarnations, is a process of *purification*. Concern for the self was paramount; society was seen as a mere stage setting for the drama of personal release from enmeshment in the body. In regard to this centrality of the self, what Guthrie says of Orpheus and his religion is relevant to the concerns of this book:

> His religion was the height of individualism. Any religion which involves the doctrine of transmigration, with its absorption if "soul-history," is almost bound to be, a truth which is amply borne out in Hindu countries to-day. It is this, incidentally, which may largely account for its obscure position when Athens was at the height of her power. Everything then was for the state, and to the glories of the state the state religion ministered. With the decay of the city-state and the growth of individualism from the fourth century onwards, the religions of this type had much freer play.[15]

Guthrie here seems to refer to the psychological basis for popular belief in reincarnation—the very reason suggested by Edward Conze—that an attraction to the doctrine is often fueled by a psychological clinging to the notion of the individual self, or ego. Belief in reincarnation, in other words, tends to put concern with the self before a concern for the welfare of society. Belief in reincarnation centers concern on the expiation of primordial guilt, the purification, and the eventual liberation of the individual soul that incarnates and reincarnates. And this, Guthrie suggests, is why reincarnation theory remained marginal in the heyday of Athenian culture—this despite the fact that, as we'll see, one of the leading figures in that culture, Plato, had made the doctrine the linchpin of his philosophy.

Before turning to Plato, however, we can move back further into Greek history toward the origins of reincarnation theory in Greek thought. And to do so, we turn again to Guthrie, who speculates about the origins of Orphic religion:

> Orpheus was not regarded as a god, but as a hero, in the sense of some one who could claim close kinship with the gods, in virtue of which he had certain superhuman powers, but who had to live the ordinary span of life and die like any other mortal ... To the question "who was the god of the Orphic religion?" there can be but one answer—Dionysos. Orpheus was a religious founder, and the religion he founded was a species of the Bacchic.[16]

Now here is an unexpected turn. For those with even a cursory acquaintance with the history of Dionysian rites, their mention evokes images of drunken debauch and orgy, attended by terrifying acts of human sacrifice, dismemberment, and cannibalism. How could such conditions be the source of the Orphic religion? We've already noted the lament of Guthrie that solid evidence about these events is *scant*. We are therefore left to rely only on informed speculation. Historian of ideas Arthur Koestler provides an interesting and plausible account. He speculates about the psychological dynamics involved in both the *emergence* of Dionysian religion in Greece and its *transformation* from husky rites into the more ascetic dispositions of Orphism. Of the rise of the Dionysian cult, he says:

> At an unknown date, but probably not much before the sixth century, the cult of Dionysus-Bacchus, the "raging" goat-god of fertility and wine, spread from barbaric Thracia into Greece. The initial success of Bacchism was probably due to [the fact that the] ... Olympian Pantheon had come to resemble an assembly of wax-works, whose formalized worship could no more satisfy truly religious needs than the pantheism—this "polite atheism" as it has been called—of the Ionian sages. A spiritual void tends to create emotional outbreaks; the Bacchae of Euripides, frenzied worshipers of the horned god, appear as the forerunners of the mediaeval tarantula dancers, the bright young things of the roaring 'twenties, the maenads of the Hitler youth.[17]

On the emergence of the Orphic disposition out of all this dusky festivity, Koestler continues:

> ... and the pendulum now began to swing in the opposite direction: from carnal ecstasy to other-worldliness. In the most telling variant of the legend, Orpheus appears as a victim of Bacchic fury: when, having finally lost his wife, he decides to turn his back on sex, the women of Thrace tear him to pieces ... The Orphic cult was thus in almost every respect a reversal of the Dionysian ... The Bacchic technique of obtaining emotional release by furiously clutching at the Now and Here, is replaced by renunciation with an eye on after-life. Physical intoxication is superseded by mental intoxication ... "orgy" no longer means Bacchic revelry, but religious ecstasy leading to liberation from the wheel of rebirth.[18]

Koestler's story is provocative, psychologically perceptive and at least plausible historically. And with this telling, it would seem that we are finally at the source of reincarnation theory in Greece. But there is also a line of inquiry, one gaining credence among academics, that presses the investigation further, one that proposes that the roots of reincarnation theory in Greece can be traced to an even more remote past than the emergence of the Dionysus cult.

But what are the origins of the god Dionysus? Where did this god come from? Ancient sources are unanimous that Dionysus is not indigenous to Greek culture, but that he arrived from "the East." A leading scholar in this inquiry is Alain Danielou. In his book *Gods of Love, Gods of Ecstasy: the Traditions of Shiva and Dionysus*, he argues that the ancient Greek god Dionysus is in fact a persona of an even more ancient god—the Hindu god Shiva. He traces the emergence of the Dionysian cult with the arrival of wine cultivation:

> The invention of wine and its diffusion among men are an essential theme of Dionysiac legend. It appears that the vine is a plant of Indian origin and was imported into the Mediterranean area together with the Bacchus cult well before the Aryan invasions. [The ancient Greek historian] Megasthenes mentions the importance of the Indian vineyards. Wine became the sacred drink of the Mediterranean peoples.[19]

Danielou takes as evidence that the worship of the god Shiva moved West under a new name for the deity—Dionysus—the existence of certain key cognates in Greek and Sanskrit languages. For example, he points out, "The god's followers are called *bacchoi* (bacchants) in Greece and *bhaktas* (participants) in India." Further, for both the Indian and the Greek versions of the cult (the same cult, as Danielou would have it), the ecstasy and intoxication of the erotic is the basis of true wisdom, a wisdom deeper than reason: the Sanskrit term for this wisdom is *jñana*, its Greek cognate, *gnosis*.[20]

In fact the Indian connection, even should it be historically sound, is not of great relevance to the thesis of this book. But in a discussion that traces the roots and consequences of reincarnation theory in the West, the prospect of an ancient connection between India and Greece is of irresistible interest. More to the point for my concerns here, however, is the fact that, as presented in the previous chapter, the doctrine of reincarnation took deep and baleful root in India. It did not do so in ancient Greece. But that failure to take root was not because of a lack of trying: one of humanity's most gifted minds gave it his best effort. I speak, of course, of Plato, to whom we now return.

5

Plato is well known for his metaphysical theory, for his view of an ideal realm of unchanging realities that transcends the more coarse and unstable realities of nature. But Plato's concerns were not restricted to abstract theory: he also cherished eminently practical aspirations—*social* applications of his understanding of reality. He is famous for saying:

> Unless ... either philosophers become kings in our states or those whom we now call our kings and rulers take to the pursuit of philosophy seriously and adequately, and there is a conjunction of these two things, political power and philosophical intelligence ... there can be no cessation of troubles ... for our states, nor, I fancy, for the human race either. *Republic V,* 743d

How does the wisdom that characterizes the philosopher kings come to be developed? In Plato's view, what is required cannot be distilled from sense experience. This is because for him, the realm of sense experience is like a cave existence. In one of the most famous non-Biblical myths in the Western tradition, we read:

> Picture men dwelling in a sort of subterranean cavern with a long entrance open to the light on its entire width. Conceive them as having their legs and necks fettered from childhood, so that they remain in the same spot, able to look forward only, and prevented by the fetters from turning their heads. Picture further the light from a fire burning higher up and at a distance behind them, and between the fire and the prisoners and above them a road along which a low wall has been built, as the exhibitors of puppet shows have partitions before the men themselves, above which they show the puppets ... See also, then, men carrying past the wall implements of all kinds that rise above the wall, and human images and shapes of animals as well, wrought in stone and wood and every material, some of these bearers presumably speaking and others silent ...

> If then they were able to talk to one another, do you not think that they would suppose that in naming the things that they saw they were naming the passing objects? ... And if their prison had an echo from the wall opposite them, when one of the passers-by uttered a sound, do you think that they would suppose anything else than the passing shadow to be the speaker? [No.] Then in every way such prisoners would deem reality to be nothing else than the shadows of the artificial objects. *Republic VII,* 514a - 515c

That is the stage setting; what then is the drama? The drama is an archetypal one—the quest for freedom. The prisoners sit locked in place, as Plato tells us, "their legs and necks fettered from childhood, so that they remain in the same spot, able to look forward only, and prevented by the fetters from turning their heads." Recall the aversion conditioning against violence given to the character Alex in the film *A Clockwork Orange:* his head is locked in place and he's forced to look at the flickering shadows of films. That's the idea; that's how things are at the bottom of the cave. The cave prisoners never see realities, but erratic, flickering shadows cast onto the cave wall in front of them by the dancing, unsteady light of a fire. An undignified and dismal situation.

But again: under such circumstances, how is the development of wisdom possible? All that we know in life is rooted in sense experience, but sense experience, for Plato, is unreliable—it is no more than a series flickering shadows. And so, the development of wisdom will not involve the mind looking outward, into the sense perceived world—the cave—but will instead be attained through the mind looking *inward.* While knowledge is not possible through sense experience, sense experience is not the only source of human cognition. Through *anamnesis*—recollection, memory—the individual human can recall what was seen *between lives.* Here's how Plato puts it:

> They say that the soul of man is immortal. At one time it comes to an end—that which is called death—and at another is born again, but is never finally exterminated ... Thus the soul, since it has been born many times, and has seen all things both here and in the other world, has learned everything that is. So we need not be surprised if it can recall the knowledge of virtue or anything else which, as we see, it once possessed.
> *Meno* 81b-c

Under the guidance of a *midwife,* as Plato's teacher Socrates is said to have styled himself, the individual psyche is brought to give birth, as it were, to the wisdom latent within itself—wisdom attained prior to the psyche's taking on human form. Here, then, is one use of the doctrine of reincarnation in Plato's philosophy. Reincarnation allowed him to solve a major philosophical problem generated by his metaphysics—how the embodied psyche could come to know an unchanging reality while imprisoned in a cave of flickering change.

The ascent from imprisonment in the cave begins with recollection, recollection of what the psyche had experienced between lives. As Plato has Socrates say on the day of his execution: "Then our souls had a previous existence, Simmias, before they took on this human shape." (*Phaedo* 76c) But of course, there's more. How is it that the psyche came to find itself in the wretched condition described in the Myth of the Cave?

Heir to the asceticism of Orphism and Pythagoras and Empedocles, Plato believed that the proper task of the psyche was liberation from the drives and impulses of the body. For Plato, the body was emphatically not the self but was instead the *prison* of the self. The true self, the psyche alone, was believed by him to be *contaminated* by its unfortunate association with the body. To be embodied was a source of pollution; the cleansing of that pollution was dissociation from its source:

> And purification ... consists in separating the soul as much as possible from the body, and accustoming it to withdraw from all contact with the body and concentrate itself by itself, and to have its dwelling, so far as it can, both now and in the future, alone by itself, freed from the shackles of the body. *Phaedo* 67c-d

Nothing less, Plato asserted, was the business of philosophy. That is why, for the true philosopher, death is not to be dreaded; death is no more than a culmination of the practice of philosophy, which is the discrimination between the true self (the psyche) and its prison (the body). Again Plato puts his words into the mouth of Socrates: "Those who rightly practice philosophy are directly and of their own accord preparing themselves for dying and death." (*Phaedo* 64a)

For those who did *not* rightly practice philosophy in life, the penalty was—reincarnation. As did Empedocles, Plato held that to be born into nature is a *failure*. But where Empedocles took human life and its vicissitudes as punishment for the primordial crime of cannibalism, Plato sees rebirth as a consequence of being an insufficiently diligent student of philosophy—of not adequately discriminating the true self, the psyche, from the body. And as we saw to be the case in India, individual faults would find expression in the specific conditions of future rebirth:

> ... if at the time of its release the soul is tainted and impure, because it has always associated with the body and cared for it and loved it, and has been so beguiled by the body and its passions and pleasures that nothing seems real to it but those physical things which can be touched and seen and eaten and drunk and used for sexual enjoyment, and if it is accustomed to hate and fear and avoids what is invisible and hidden from our eyes but is intelligible and comprehensible by philosophy—if the soul is in this state, do you think it will escape independent and uncontaminated? ... those who

have cultivated gluttony of selfishness or drunkenness, instead of taking pains to avoid them, are likely to assume [when reincarnated] the form of donkeys and other perverse animals. *Phaedo* 81b-e

But donkeys and perverse animals are not our concern here. The undisciplined and unphilosophical were also reborn as humans, and their human incarnations stood as evidence of past behaviors. The most complete account of how this occurs is presented in another myth—this time the myth of Er, which is found in the Book X of the *Republic*. The myth tells of a warrior named Er, who was killed on the battlefield. Twelve days after the battle, as he was laid on a funeral pyre, Er suddenly revived and offered an account of what happens after death. There is a lot of detail in Er's account, but I will discuss only those aspects which pertain to reincarnation. According to Er, the souls of the dead were assembled and told:

"Souls that live for a day, now is the beginning of another cycle of mortal generation where birth is the beacon of death. No divinity shall cast lots for you, but you shall choose your own deity. Let him to whom falls the first lot first select a life to which he shall cleave of necessity. But virtue has no master over her, and each shall have more or less of her as he honors her or does her despite. The blame is his who chooses. God is blameless." So saying, the prophet flung the lots out among them all, and each took up the lot that fell by his side ... And whoever took up a lot saw plainly what number he had drawn. *Republic X,* 617e - 618a

The gathered souls of the dead had lots assigned to them—thrown to them. These lots determined the order of choosing new lives: number 1 would go first, number 2 second, and so on. And the story proceeds:

And after this again the prophet placed the patterns of lives before them on the ground, far more numerous than the assembly. They were of every variety, for there were lives of all kinds of animals and all sorts of human lives, for there were tyrannies among them, some uninterrupted till the end and others destroyed midway and issuing in penuries and exiles and beggaries, and there were lives of men of repute for their forms and beauty and bodily strength otherwise and prowess and the high birth and the virtues of their ancestors, and others of ill repute in the same things, and similarly of women. *Republic X,* 618b

Now "patterns of lives"—that is, specific lives that could be chosen— were set before the assembled souls. Note that there were more lives to be chosen than there were souls choosing, so the order of choice set by the first casting of lots was not of decisive importance. Indeed, it is announced to the souls that

> Even for him who comes forward last, if he make his choice wisely and live strenuously, there is reserved an acceptable life, no evil one. Let not the foremost in the choice be heedless nor the last be discouraged. *Republic X,* 619b

Many lives to choose from. But now comes the dangerous part. As the scenario unfolds, we find that each soul chooses an incarnation on the basis of the habits developed in previous lives. Unreflective and impulsive habits of life were a particular liability. And the fate of the soul to which lot number 1 had fallen, the soul that got to choose first, was a cautionary tale. For that undisciplined soul grabbed a life that, at first sight, seemed desirable—the life of a king. But he grabbed rashly, before reading the fine print, as it were. And this unhappy soul learned too late that the king's life it had chosen was that of King Thyestes:

> When the prophet had thus spoken he said that the drawer of the first lot at once sprang to seize the greatest tyranny, and that in his folly and greed he chose it without sufficient examination, and failed to observe that it involved the fate of eating his own children, and other horrors, and that when he inspected it at leisure he beat his breast and bewailed his choice, not abiding by the forewarning of the prophet. For he did not blame himself for his woes, but fortune and the gods and anything except himself. *Republic X,* 619c

On realizing the bad news, the intemperate soul behaved in characteristic fashion: it blamed fortune, it blamed the gods, it rashly ascribed blame everywhere except where it actually belonged—to itself. And as we saw in the Indian beliefs in karma and reincarnation, in Plato too the individual is entirely responsible for her or his own predicament. But now the drama of the myth moves from general dispositions to more specific qualities of character. The more reflective souls choose their lives with care, but their choices still express their previous experiences. Plato has Er say:

> … it was a sight worth seeing to observe how the several souls selected their lives. He said it was a strange, pitiful, and ridiculous spectacle, as the choice was determined for the most part by the habits of their former lives … The soul that drew the twentieth lot chose the life of a lion; it was the soul of Ajax, the son of Telamon, which, because it remembered the adjudication of the arms of Achilles, was unwilling to become a man. The

next, the soul of Agamemnon, likewise from hatred of the human race because of its sufferings, substituted the life of an eagle ... he saw the soul of Epeus, the son of Panopeus, entering into the nature of an arts and crafts woman. Far off in the rear he saw the soul of the buffoon Thersites clothing itself in the body of an ape. *Republic X,* 619e - 620c

The incarnations chosen by the famous souls reflect the various proclivities for which they were renowned. There is, we are given to understand, a rightness to the process. And the process is not over yet; there is a final test for each soul, a test that again exposes the strengths and weaknesses of previous lives. After specific lives are chosen and locked in, as it were, the souls were again gathered together. Now began an ordeal:

... they all journeyed to the Plain of Oblivion, through a terrible and stifling heat, for it was bare of trees and all plants, and there they camped at eventide by the River of Forgetfulness, whose waters no vessel can contain. They were all required to drink a measure of the water, and those who were not saved by their good sense drank more than the measure, and each one as he drank forgot all things. And after they had fallen asleep and it was the middle of the night, there was a sound of thunder and a quaking of the earth, and they were suddenly wafted thence, one this way, one that, upward to their birth like shooting stars. *Republic X,* 621a-b

And that's how we all got here. And in fact, we didn't do too badly—we, that is, who earned incarnation as humans instead of animal incarnations like Ajax, Agamemnon, and Thersites. And between lives, between incarnations, we all got to apprehend reality directly: as we saw earlier, in the passage from *Meno* 81c, the individual soul "has seen all things both here and in the other world, has learned everything that is." This is *very* valuable knowledge because, as we'll soon see, it is what determines a human's station in life. But to return to the story, an ordeal is underway—an ordeal that is the final test before incarnation. The soon-to-be-reincarnated psyches are made to walk across the Plain of Oblivion, a plain that is very hot. Along the way, they are tormented by a terrible thirst. (Never mind that is the *body* that gets thirsty—let's walk with Plato's myth.) They come at last to a river, the River Lethe, the River of Forgetfulness. They arrive at the riverbank with their precious cargo of knowledge. There they are told that they all must drink a "measure" from the River of Forgetfulness. If in previous lives an individual psyche developed the habit of controlling bodily appetites, it will take the smallest of sips, and depart with much of its hard-won wisdom intact. Those capable of such self-control are rare, in

Plato's view. For the great majority of us at the banks of the River of Forgetfulness: gub, gub, gub ...

Plato's reincarnation myth, the Myth of Er, serves the same purpose as the several Indian myths examined in Chapter 3. It provides an explanation for the varying circumstances in which humans find themselves. How did we come to find ourselves imprisoned at the bottom of a cave? Simply stated, through ignorance and indiscipline. It is because we failed to sufficiently perfect ourselves in the discipline of philosophy that we find ourselves abjectly identified with our body and its appetites, utterly committed to the delusion that our highest hope is to feel good.

We are not equally situated in that cave, and for Plato there are good reasons for that. A person's station in the cave is determined through the capacity to grasp wisdom. Wisdom, as we've seen in the passages from the *Meno,* is gained through the capacity to turn inward—through the capacity to *recollect* what had been seen between lives. The learning that matters for Plato is not the acquisition of facts in the world, but access to what lies latent (and forgotten) within the psyche.

The rightness of the differences in social station among people is taken to be a direct result choices made by individual psyches in their *between lives* pilgrimages. Discrimination and judgment are needed in the choice of a life; self-control is needed at the banks of the River Lethe. And since the gains of a wise choice of life can be negated through an intemperate gulping down of the waters of the River of Forgetfulness, it is clear the self-control is even more important than discrimination. We can say, then, that social station is determined by the capacity to rule and govern, most particularly, on the capacity to rule and govern *oneself.* To cite again the claim made by Plato as to the basis of a well-ordered society—either philosophers must become kings or kings must become philosophers. And the philosopher-kings in this ideal society will tell the citizens the following story about their social stations:

> While all of you in the city are brothers ... yet God in fashioning those of you who are fitted to hold rule mingled gold in their generation, for which reason they are the most precious—but in the helpers silver, and iron and brass in the farmers and other craftsmen. And as you are all akin, though for the most part you will breed after your kinds, it may sometimes happen that a golden father would beget a silver son and that a golden offspring would come from a silver sire and that the rest would in like manner be born of one another. So that the first and chief injunction that the god lays upon the rulers is that of nothing else are they to be such careful guardians and so intently observant as of the intermixture of these metals in the souls

of their offspring, and if sons are born to them with an infusion of brass or iron they shall by no means give way to pity in their treatment of them, but shall assign to each the status due to his nature and thrust them out among the artisans or the farmers. And again, if from these there are born sons with unexpected gold or silver in their composition they shall honor such and bid them go up higher, some to the office of guardian, some to the assistantship, alleging that there is an oracle that the state shall then be overthrown when the man of iron or brass is its guardian. *Republic* 415a-c

The people of the society envisioned by Plato will be of a common general stock, but through admixture of this common stock with four different kinds of metals—so the tale goes—there will be four distinct social groups. The rulers are those with gold mixed in; their helpers (typically called *Auxiliaries*, a military/police class) are those with silver mixed in. Those with admixtures of baser metals, brass and iron, really are a single group in Plato's scheme—they are those who make things work. Before going further, it is important to note a peculiar feature of this tale, as Plato presents it. It is, he says just before he introduces it, a "noble lie."

How, then, said I, might we contrive one of those opportune falsehoods of which were just now speaking, so as by one noble lie to persuade if possible the rulers themselves, but failing that the rest of the city? *Republic* 414b-c

Why a lie, however "noble"? Did Plato simply invoke the idea of social groups as a political ruse? One might understandably suspect so. But in fact his motives are not so sinister. The noble lie about social groups was needed as a device for persuading people of the urgent need for *meritocracy*, for leadership by the most able. And this attempt to persuade would be addressed for the most part to people whose memory had been dulled by the waters of Lethe before they were born—people who lacked the philosophical acumen required to understand their predicament, people who know only what they want and nothing of what they need. Thus the tale incorporates a dire prophecy that warns of the demise of the state should any of Brass or Iron constitution come to rule: a regular testing and sorting-out of children was necessary. Such regular testing is necessary because in general like breeds like—but not always. Sometimes a Brass or Iron child was born to rulers; sometimes a Gold or Silver child to workers. Vigilance is necessary. Membership in a social group is not strictly determined by birth, but by individual ability, ability that can be ascertained through testing.

Sentimentality had no role here: the survival of the state was at stake. So the tale was told.

It is important to note that the social groups spoken of by Plato are not castes, at least not as found in modern India. This point is made forcibly by Plato scholar A. E. Taylor:

> ... we must be clear, in the first place, on the point that there is no system of "caste" in the *Republic.* The characteristic of "caste" is that one is born into it, and that once born into a caste it is impossible to rise above it. You may forfeit your caste in various ways, as a Brahmin does by crossing the seas, but no one can become a Brahmin if he is not born one.[21]

Taylor's point that Plato's social groups are not castes is accurate: in India, an infant born a *Shudra* or a *Dalit* can never test out of that abject circumstance. And this point must be supplemented with another insight—neither are these groups *economic* classes, as classes are conceived in contemporary America. In Plato's ideal republic, the Rulers and their Auxiliaries (those mixed with gold and silver) are mandated to live a Spartan existence which, from the standpoint of 21st century American aspirations, would be profoundly repugnant and would simply not make sense in terms of a class analysis. Here's how he puts it:

> In the first place, none [of the two higher groups] must possess any private property save the indispensable. Secondly, none must have any habitation or treasure house which is not open for all to enter at will. Their food, in such quantities as are needful for athletes of war sober and brave, they must receive as an agreed stipend from the other citizens as the wages of their guardianship, so measured that there shall be neither superfluity at the end of the year nor any lack. And resorting to a common mess like soldiers on campaign they will live together. Gold and silver, we will tell them, they have of the divine quality from the gods always in their souls, and they have no need of the metal of men ... for these only of all the dwellers in the city it is not lawful to handle gold and silver and to touch them nor yet to come under the same roof with them, nor to hang them as ornaments on their limbs nor to drink from silver and gold. *Republic* 416d - 417a

Hardly *la dolce vita.* This austere regimen for the Rulers and Auxiliaries was deemed necessary by Plato, for should the Gold and Silver groups become wealthy and acquisitive, they would become corrupt and incapable of ruling through wisdom. Wealth has its place, but only among the Brass and Iron groups. It is not individual wealth, but the political influence of wealth in society—the emergence of a *plutocracy*—that Plato deplored. There is, to the modern mind, an interesting twist here. To quote Taylor:

> ... the whole "capital" of the State is in the hands of the *demiourgoi* [the people of Brass and Iron]. A "merchant prince," under such a classification, is just as much one of the "industrials" as his clerks and office-boys.[22]

And in fact, from the standpoint of contemporary assessments, the situation is even more—shall we say—peculiar. But first, a brighter moment. Plato was one of the earliest thinkers in the Western tradition to demand that women be treated equally in all ways to men. That meant that women were to be included among both the Rulers and the Auxiliaries. By extension, that also meant that the person of Gold who was the ruling philosopher might be the philosopher-queen as well as the philosopher-king. But whether queen or king, these Gold folk did not have lives of their own. Of the women of Gold stock, we read—

> That these women shall all be common to all these men, and that none shall cohabit with any privately, and that the children shall be common, and that no parent shall know its own offspring nor any child its parent. *Republic* 457d

But this commonality of sexual access does not have a Dionysian dimension to it. Quite the contrary. Romance and passion are firmly set aside in favor of reason and utility. The plan, as Plato spells it out, is twofold: on the one hand it is designed to keep the Rulers' loyalties and concern for the state undistracted by the favoritism that family life inevitably generates, on the other hand the plan is designed to facilitate the production of more and better Gold people. My interest here centers on the latter concern, the concern to produce more and better Gold people. The plan to implement this concern is an enterprise known today (with no small notoriety) as *eugenics*. The hope is to "improve the breed" of humanity by enhancing, through selective breeding, both the *quantity* and the *quality* of the most promising among us. It is worth noting that the core of Plato's argument, as presented in the following passage from the *Republic,* was extremely attractive in Europe and America a hundred years ago. But for now, here's how Plato puts it:

> Tell me this, Glaucon. I see that you have in your house hunting dogs and a number of pedigreed cocks. Have you ever considered something about their unions and procreations? [What? he said.]

> In the first place, I said, among these themselves, although they are a select breed, do not some prove better than the rest? [They do.]
>
> Do you then breed from all indiscriminately, or are you careful to breed from the best? [From the best.]
>
> And. again, do you breed from the youngest or the oldest, or, so far as may be, from those in their prime? [From those in their prime.]
>
> And if they are not thus bred, you expect, do you not, that your birds' breed and hounds will greatly degenerate? [I do, he said.]
>
> And what of horses and other animals? Is it otherwise with them? [It would be strange if it were.]
>
> ... how imperative, then, is our need of the highest skill in our rulers, if the principle holds also for mankind ... It follows from our former admissions, I said, that the best men must cohabit with the best women in as many cases as possible and the worst with the worst in the fewest, and that the offspring of the one must be reared and that of the other not, if the flock is to be as perfect as possible. And the way in which all this is brought to pass must be unknown to any but the rulers, if, again, the herd of guardians is to be as free as possible from dissension. *Republic* 459a-e

The guardians, the Rulers, those of Gold admixture, are to be treated no differently than animal breeders treat their livestock. The goal, again, is to enhance both the quantity and the quality of the highest group in the state—the Gold people from which the philosopher-queens and philosopher-kings may emerge. And we are not yet finished with "noble lies." The Rulers are superior by virtue of their bravery and philosophical acumen, yes—but even among them there are degrees of excellence. And to even further enhance good breeding among the them, Plato proposes that the following ruse be foisted on the younger, breeding age Rulers:

> Certain ingenious lots, then, I suppose, must be devised so that the inferior man at each conjugation may blame chance and not the rulers ... And on the young men, surely, who excel in war and other pursuits we must bestow honors and prizes, and, in particular, the opportunity of more frequent intercourse with the women, which will at the same time be a plausible pretext for having them beget as many of the children as possible. *Republic* 460a-b

Time, now, to take stock of where we are. Plato is committed to the attainment of wisdom. That attainment is best facilitated in a well-ordered state, and such a state can be brought about only by the rule of philosophers. Philosopher-kings or queens are born to be such; their birth is in fact a rebirth, a reincarnation, that reflects the qualities accrued in previous lives—as we've seen in the Myth of Er. Politics and religion are not separate enterprises for Plato; politics for him is ultimately a religious enterprise, an enterprise based on the practice of philosophy. And for that enterprise to succeed, it is imperative that the state be ruled by philosophers, by those possessed not of opinion, but of true knowledge. Meritocracy, rule by those of merit, is indispensable. Plato's eugenic proposals, his insistence that Rulers were to have no traffic in wealth, his noble lies—all these are in the service of one thing, meritocracy. The lie of social groups, metaphorically identified with various metals, is intended to strike fear into the populace should any of the inferior types, the Brass or Iron, presume to rule the state. The lie of a fair lottery of mating among young Rulers—a lottery which is in fact carefully *rigged*—serves the purpose of continually improving the quality of the stock among Rulers. Again, meritocracy and eugenics will be served, and enhanced.

Plato is important to our discussion because his philosophy provides a full-dress elaboration of the theory of reincarnation, complete with its social implications. It is true that, in the West, Plato's version of the doctrine remains pages of theory in the history of philosophy, yet his presentation is elaborated in more detail than any account found in the earlier Greek thinkers on reincarnation that have been examined in this chapter.

6

In concluding our discussion of Plato, we will assess his theories on reincarnation through a consideration of two questions. First, in light of the towering influence attributed to him, how is it that Plato's views on reincarnation did *not* find a prominent place in place in the nearly two and a half succeeding millennia of Western culture? Second, could the doctrine of reincarnation *as Plato conceived it*—that is, in his conception of it as a strict *meritocracy*—could that conception of the doctrine of reincarnation have survived and become institutionalized in Western culture?

Why didn't Plato's views on reincarnation prevail in the West? This question cannot be answered simply, "And along came Christianity." Yes, Plato's school, his Academy, which survived for almost 900 years, was finally closed in 526 CE, as an act of Christian piety, by the Roman emperor Justinian. And before that, a number of the early so-called Church Fathers—including Justin Martyr, Origen, Irenaeus, and Tertullian rejected the doctrines of the so-called pagan philosophers. Yet Plato's thought was not rejected whole cloth; many aspects of his philosophy were incorporated into the official Christian outlook through the efforts of powerful figures like St. Augustine of Hippo and others. Many aspects, but not all—and specifically not his views on reincarnation. There is a reason for this. Christianity, from its inception some two thousand years ago until the present, has been based upon a specific promise. The great promise of Christianity was that of *personal immortality*—the perpetual existence of *this* person or *that* one, not just the persistence of an impersonal essence that took on this person now and that one later.

Love him or hate him, Paul of Tarsus, known in the Christian tradition as St. Paul, was a key architect in the formulation of the traditional vision of Christianity. Love him or hate him, Paul was also a keen observer of the human predicament. The integral, reciprocal existence of the body and the personality did not escape him; he took personal identity to be bound up with the destiny of the body. And it was not an abstract sense of selfhood, but individual persons that were the central concern in his speculations about immortality, persons like those that Paul knew—persons like Silvanus, Timothy, Crispus, Gaius, and Phoebe—persons whose life was lived in terms of the body.

We've seen that in Plato's philosophy, the body is viewed as the prison of the self. In Paul's view, by contrast, the body and the personality have a reciprocal existence, that the body is *essential* to the self, not its prison. This is evident in his repeated insistence on the future resurrection of the *body*—the continuation of the body was taken by Paul as a necessary condition of the personal immortality that was the central promise of Christianity.

And so, it may be fairly stated that Paul took the *body* to be the foundation of his unique understanding of personal immortality. The immortality promised by Christianity, according to Paul, is not the immortality of a disembodied "ghost," but immortality rooted in the *resurrection of the body* after death. His first letter to the Corinthians provides some of the most striking images of his hopes for immortality. Likening the human body to a seed that is "planted" at death, he says:

> It is sown [=buried] a physical body, it is raised a spiritual body. If there is a physical body, there is also a spiritual body. I. Cor. 15:44

Death is averted, and it is averted on terms that *count* for the vast majority of humans who have ever lived—I, the personality who knows myself and who knows you, I do not have to die; what *looks* like death is really only sleep, a sleep from which I will be awakened:

> For since we believe that Jesus died and rose again, even so, through Jesus, God will bring with him those who have fallen asleep. I. Thessalonians 4:14

> For this perishable nature must put on the imperishable, and this mortal nature must put on immortality. When the perishable puts on the imperishable, and the mortal puts on immortality, then shall come to pass the saying that is written: "Death is swallowed up in victory." "O death, where is thy victory? O death, where is thy sting?" I. Cor. 15:53-55

It is clear from Paul's writings that the resurrected body will be a *transformed* body, but a body nonetheless. The importance of the individual body reflects a commitment as to the importance of the individual person. In reincarnation theory, the person is transient and disposable. Thus a belief in reincarnation is incompatible with the great promise of Christianity: the promise of *personal* immortality.

In summary: it was not the ascendancy of Christianity, it was not the closure of the Academy in the year 536—the reason why reincarnation theory was not institutionalized in the West was its incompatibility of with the bedrock hope of Christianity: personal immortality. As we saw, reincarnation theory has its consolations. But the consolations of reincarnation pale in contrast to those offered by the model of personal immortality. Whatever its consolations, reincarnation still asserts the transitoriness and disposability of the personality that I think of as "me." The promise of *personal* immortality, the promise that has been the core doctrine of the vast majority of Christian believers throughout the centuries, is a far more heady one. "Me" forever; "me" without end. Yes, yes—transformed, purified, resurrected, and sanctified; but in the last analysis, "me." Against this promise, reincarnation theory could not successfully compete. At least not until recently.

7

We turn now to assess Plato's views on reincarnation on their own terms. Setting aside for the moment the tidal wave of Christianity that swept the ancient world, could Plato's singular understanding of reincarnation—with its strident commitment to meritocracy intact—have survived? Not a chance—no way, no how.

We must remember what Plato was: he was *the* preeminent philosopher—of his own time and, if we are to take Whitehead's assessment seriously, of all subsequent Western philosophy. But a philosopher is first and foremost a *theoretician*, and that is something we need to bear in mind. Theoreticians think in terms of ideals; experiment for them tends to be *thought* experiment. Plato's disposition in this regard is evident not only in his proposals to ensure a meritocracy in his ideal republic, it is also nicely exemplified in his proposals about the appropriate way to approach the study of *astronomy:*

> It is by means of problems [theoretical models] ... as in the study of geometry, that we will pursue astronomy too, and we will let be [ignore] the things in the heavens, if we are to have a part in the true science of astronomy ... *Republic VII,* 530c

The modern mind is astonished and bemused by Plato's recommendation that the science of astronomy will best proceed through the study of theoretical models rather than direct observation of the heavens. And as with his astronomy, so Plato's political thinking privileges the study of rational models over direct observation of flesh-and-blood humans. To a philosopher who dismissed the realm of sense experience as a "cave," who defined the human self through a rejection of the body in favor of a rational psyche, this might be deemed consistent. But just as such an astronomy committed to setting aside direct observation could never have produced the sophisticated cosmologies of the present, so his eminently rational aspirations for a meritocracy grounded in reincarnation theory could never have borne fruit. Had Plato's theories been given the chance to become embodied in the sweaty realities of history, it is all but impossible that his blueprint for grouping people according to their capacity for wisdom—which to say, according to their histories in previous lives—would have lasted more than a generation after his death. And there is a simple reason for this.

Plato seems to have actually believed that people, and in particular those gifted people of high intelligence and philosophical acumen, could be persuaded or snookered or hoodwinked into a blithe concession in regard to one of the most compelling evolutionary imperatives within the human psyche. I don't refer here to an imperative (if such it is) to choose one's mate and to maintain with that mate a sexually exclusive relationship. I speak now of something even more primordial: the drive to know and cherish and provide advantages to one's offspring. Certainly there are individual exceptions, but this drive is generally endemic to the human psyche; its pervasiveness is rooted not in culture but in nature, in an evolutionary imperative designed to secure the future existence not of intellectuals, but of the human species. Plato, the archetypal philosopher, brought himself to think in terms of pat solutions to the knotty issues surrounding the social implications of reincarnation theory. He came to believe that the primal mainsprings of human nature are susceptible to the eminently reasonable solutions that he proposes in the *Republic*. Only a professor could think this way. And that is why Mark Lilla, in a perceptive book titled *The Reckless Mind: Intellectuals in Politics*, says

> One practical lesson that is often drawn from the *Republic* is that when philosophers try to become kings either their philosophy is corrupted, politics is corrupted, or both are. Therefore the only sensible thing is to separate them, leaving philosophers to cultivate their gardens with all the passion they have, but keeping them quarantined there so they can cause no harm.[23]

Nor is this assessment of the dangers of philosophers in politics a recent one. At the dawn of Modernism, the controversial political thinker Nicolo Machiavelli clearly had Plato in mind when he wrote:

> A great many men have imagined states and princedoms such as nobody ever saw or knew in the real world, for there's such a difference between the way we really live and the way we ought to live that the man who neglects the real to study the ideal will learn how to accomplish his ruin, not his salvation.[24]

Certainly the evolutionary imperative to know and nurture and privilege one's own offspring operates in the deep psyche of intellectuals, too. But not in all of them. Not, apparently, in the case of Plato. Consider, for example, his discussion of progeny in the *Symposium*.

A youthful Socrates is depicted as receiving his relating his spiritual education at the hands of a wise woman named Diotima. She speaks to the young Socrates first of those who seek progeny in biological terms—through children. This, of course, is exactly what is to be strictly controlled in the ideal state described in the *Republic*. This is for Plato clearly an inferior mode of progeny, and he has Diotima speak dismissively of—

> ... those whose procreancy is of the body turn to woman as the object of their love, and raise a family, in the blessed hope that by doing so they will keep their memory green, through time and through eternity. *Symposium* 208e

We are told in the sentence immediately following of another form of progeny: "But those whose procreancy is of the spirit rather than of the flesh—and they are not unknown, Socrates—conceive and bear the things of the spirit." Plato elaborates on this theme, claiming that the friendship resulting from the pursuit of philosophy will produce a far nobler offspring than mere family-making. Speaking of this philosophical issue, or progeny, he says:

> And what is more, he and his friend will help each other rear the issue of their friendship—and so the bond between them will be more binding, and their communion even more complete, than that which comes of bringing children up, because they have created something lovelier and less mortal than human seed. *Symposium* 209c

Diotima is right, I think, when she tells her young student of such offspring and enjoins him "and they are not unknown, Socrates." Certainly not unknown, but exceptionally rare. And had Plato's combination of political and reincarnation theories survived, we can be certain that they would yielded not the meritocracy he envisioned, but a caste system such as emerged in India.

I conclude with a final point of clarification. I am not suggesting that reincarnation could not have taken root in the West. Absent the powerful consolatory promises of Christianity, it may well have. My contention is that reincarnation *as envisioned by Plato* could not possibly have succeeded. As reincarnation *per se* could not have succeeded in the West because it is inconsistent with the central promise of the Christianity that came to dominate the West, so Plato's uniquely meritocratic vision of a social implementation of reincarnation theory could not have succeeded *anywhere* because it is fundamentally inconsistent with primordial elements of human motivation.

Notes

1. Whitehead, A. N. *Process and Reality.* New York: The Free Press, 1978, p.39.
2. Herodotus, *The Histories, II, 123.* Translated by George Rawlinson. http://www.herodotuswebsite.co.uk/Text/Book2.htm
3. Guthrie, W. K. C. *A History of Greek Philosophy, v.1-2.* New York: Cambridge Univ. Press, 1978, p.160.
4. Harrison, J. *Prolegomena to the Study of Greek Religion.* New York: Meridian Books, 1966, p.589.
5. Robinson, J. M., ed. and transl., *An Introduction to Early Greek Philosophy: The Chief Fragments and Ancient Testimony.* Boston: Houghton Mifflin Co., 1968, p.152. All citations from Empedocles are from this edition, and are referenced by both Robinson's designation number and page number. For example, this passage is referenced as 8.3, p.152.
6. Diogenes Laertius *Live of Eminent Philosophers, v.2,* translated by R. D. Hicks. Cambridge, Mass.: Harvard Univ. Press, 1979. Book VIII.4, p.323, 325. All quotations from Diogenes Laertius (hereafter, DL) will be from this edition.
7. Peters, F. E. *Greek Philosophical Terms: a Historical Lexicon.* New York: New York University Press, 1967, p.166-7.
8. All quotations from Plato are from *Plato: The Collected Dialogues.* Hamilton, E. and H. Cairns, eds. Princeton: Princeton Univ. Press, 1961.
9. Guthrie, W. K. C. *Orpheus and Greek Religion.* Princeton: Princeton Univ. Press, 1993, p.9.
10. Guthrie, 1993, p.196.
11. Guthrie, 1993, p.198.
12. Guthrie, 1993, p.164.
13. Cornford, F. M. *From Religion to Philosophy: a Study in the Origins of Western Speculation.* New York: Harper Torchbooks, 1957, p.162.
14. Guthrie, 1993, p.156.
15. Guthrie, 1993, p.201.
16. Guthrie, 1993, p.41.
17. Koestler, A. *The Sleep Walkers: A History of Man's Changing Vision of the Universe.* New York: Macmillan, 1959, p.33-4.
18. Koestler, 1959, p.34-5.
19. Danielou, A. *Gods of Love and Ecstasy: the Traditions of Shiva and Dionysus.* Rochester, Vermont: Inner Traditions Press, 1992, p.154-5.
20. Danielou, 1992, p.16ff.
21. Taylor, A. E. *Plato: the Man and His Work.* New York: Meridian Books, 1964, p.275.
22. Taylor, 1964, p.276
23. Lilla, M. *The Reckless Mind: Intellectuals in Politics.* New York: New York Review Book, 2001, p.44.

24. Machiavelli, N. *The Prince,* ch.xv, in Adams, R. M., editor and translator. *The Prince: a new translation.* New York: W. W. Norton and Co., 1977, p.44.

5

AN INDIAN BREEZE IN MODERN EUROPE

> In India our religions will never at any time take root; the ancient wisdom of the human race will not be supplanted by the events in Galilee. On the contrary, Indian wisdom flows back to Europe, and will produce a fundamental change in our knowledge and thought.
>
> —Arthur Schopenhauer[1]

1

We leap forward over two millennia to modern Europe, to the German philosopher Arthur Schopenhauer (1788-1860) and his philosophical world. Schopenhauer is acknowledged as a landmark figure in the story of the emerging European passion for Indian religion and philosophy. He is relevant to this study for two reasons. First, Schopenhauer not only studied the Indian ideas arriving in Europe in the late 18th century, he enthusiastically *embraced* them. But as we'll see, he embraced Indian ideas critically, not unquestioningly. The second reason for including Schopenhauer centers on his resolutely dark disposition. Oddly, this disposition invested his philosophy with a plausibility for the Europeans who read him. Life, said Schopenhauer, is *bad news*. And this bleak message sounded hauntingly realistic, and therefore compelling, to European intelligentsia. In this crucial sense, Schopenhauer's philosophy may be seen to darkly foreshadow a scientific theory that was to sweep the Western world—Darwin's theory of evolution by means of natural selection.

But let's return to Schopenhauer's role as a pivotal figure in the presentation of Indian philosophy and religion into Europe. His eminence in this historic development is endorsed by the prominent German Indologist Paul Deussen, who dedicated his monumental translation of the Upanishads, *Sixty Upanishads of the Veda*, "To the spiritual ancestors of Arthur Schopenhauer."[2] Indeed, Schopenhauer's importance is indisputable—but for all his importance, he is not the origin of Indian studies in Europe.

A French linguist, Abraham Anquetil-Duperron (1731-1805), mastered the ancient Asian languages of Persian, Sanskrit, and Pahlavi. He had come across a translation of the Upanishads, a translation from Sanskrit to ancient Persian. From that text he produced a Latin translation that he titled the *Oupnek'hat*. As early as 1776 Anquetil-Duperron published excerpts from his translations of the *Oupnek'hat*, and in 1801 the entire text was published as a monograph. It was a notoriously turgid and difficult translation, yet it deeply impressed Schopenhauer, who offered the following breathless encomium:

> For how thoroughly redolent of the holy spirit of the *Vedas* is the *Oupnek'hat*! How deeply stirred is he who, by diligent and careful reading, is now conversant with the Persian-Latin rendering of the incomparable book! How imbued is every line with firm, definite, and harmonious significance! From every page we come across profound, original, and sublime thoughts, whilst a lofty and sacred earnestness pervades the whole. Here everything breathes the air of India and radiates an existence that is original and akin to nature.[3]

2

In addition to Anquetil-Duperron's work, Schopenhauer was also influenced by the work of the German thinker Johann Gottfried von Herder (1744-1803). In 1784, Herder wrote *Outlines of a Philosophy of the History of Man*, in which he raises a critical concern, one that is central to the present study:

> It [reincarnation theory] excited a false compassion towards every living creature, it diminished real sympathy for the miseries of our fellows; the

unhappy among whom it held as criminals suffering under the burden of former misdeeds ... [4]

Herder's concern was that reincarnation theory can all too easily breed indifference to human misery—a misery glossed over by breezy references to the sacredness of *all* life. His suspicions establish the fact that the major concern of this book—that reincarnation theory is anything but harmless—is not a recent one. Speaking of the caste system and its relation to karma and reincarnation, he says:

> Now what could be more natural, than to consider it at length as a punishment from Heaven, to be born a *pariar* [pariah, Chandala], and, conformably to the doctrine of the metempsychosis, as a fate merited by crimes in a former state of life? This hypothesis of the transmigration of souls, grand as it was in the mind of him, by whom it was first imagined, and greatly as it may have benefitted mankind, must necessarily occasioned much evil also ... [5]

Herder's critique is perceptive; his fears that selfishness, self-deception, and social apathy are likely to attend reincarnation doctrine, anticipate by almost two centuries the concerns articulated by Buddhist scholar Edward Conze as discussed in Chapter 1 of this study.

Still another precursor of Schopenhauer was Friedrich Schlegel (1772-1829), another pioneer in Indian studies in Europe. In 1808, Schlegel published an influential study titled *On the Language and Wisdom of the Indians*. This work proved to be even more influential than the *Oupnek'hat* in bringing Indian thought to the European reading public. For all the effectiveness of Schlegel's presentation, European reception of the new outlook from India was conflicted from the outset. The early 19th century in Europe embodied an intellectual milieu quite different from that of the Enlightenment a century earlier. Many Enlightenment thinkers were deeply suspicious, if not outright hostile, not just to the Christian religion, but to religion itself. By contrast, 19th century thinkers were typically deeply religious, yet they were beset by serious misgivings about the religious traditions of their culture. In this state of ambivalence, European intellectuals saw not only what was attractive about Indian religion, but also what they took to be *wrong* about the European Judaic and Christian tradition to which they were born. Buddhist scholar Stephen Batchelor characterizes the situation this way:

> Many of the [19th century] Romantics boldly rejected much of traditional Christianity. But having denounced the standard European framework of meaning, they found themselves desperately yearning for meaning. The secular alternative of scientific progress being equally anathema, many of them plunged into nihilistic despair.[6]

Caught between what they took to be a dilemma between a sterile rationalism and materialistic science on the one side, and empty ritual and outdated dogma on the part of Christian Churches on the other, many early 19th century thinkers found themselves in a predicament entirely familiar to thinking people living at the beginning of the 21st century. Specifically, they were quite certain about what was *unsatisfactory,* but at the same time they were haunted by uncertainty as to what might *replace* the outlooks with which they were dissatisfied. Such ambivalence, however, did not disquiet Arthur Schopenhauer. His rejection of the Western religious traditions was vigorous and utterly unconflicted.

Schopenhauer's major work, a two-volume edition titled *The World as Will and Representation,* was published in 1819. In 1851 he published a large collection of aphorisms and essays under the title *Parerga and Paralipomena,* which, like *The World as Will and Representation,* were widely read throughout Europe. As stated, Schopenhauer rejected Christianity without regret. But by today's scholarly standards, his understanding of Indian religion was limited; in his writings he regularly refers to "Brahminism and Buddhism"—an amalgam that would now be seen as a *confusion* of Hinduism and Buddhism. Scholarly objections aside, Schopenhauer fervently embraced the ideas from India and was convinced that their arrival was of momentous historical importance—comparable to an earlier influx of non-Christian texts that nourished the genius of Thomas Aquinas and provided Scholastic Christianity with a rigorous philosophical basis:

> ... I surmise that the influence of Sanskrit literature will penetrate no less deeply than did the revival of Greek literature in the fifteenth century.[7]

In his study of Schopenhauer's life and work, Patrick Gardiner tells us that in late life, when he had become famous, Schopenhauer's living quarters "were furnished very simply, with little in the way of ornament except a statue of Buddha and a bust of Kant that stood on his writing desk."[8] It is worth repeating that Indian philosophy and religion were more than an intellectual pursuit for Schopenhauer. From 1815 to 1817, while he lived in Dresden and was formulating his philosophy, Schopenhauer had regular contact with a neighbor named Karl Friedrich Krause. Krause was a scholar of Indian religion, had learned Sanskrit, and had made his own translations from the Upanishads. Schopenhauer consulted him regularly, and in addition to receiving scholarly instruction, he learned from him the basic techniques of meditation.[9]

Precisely because he took Indian thought so seriously, Schopenhauer was pressed to squarely face the issue of reincarnation—an issue he found as objectionable as Herder did, but for different reasons. Schopenhauer's reservations about reincarnation are not based, as were Herder's, on concerns about the social consequences of the idea. He was concerned instead about the doctrine's philosophical cogency. Schopenhauer candidly faced questions about the consistency of the dynamics of reincarnation that we saw were so scrupulously avoided in the Indian tradition.

3

Schopenhauer insists that reincarnation, which he refers to in its Greek locution as *metempsychosis*, is a kind of religious pablum provided to the masses in India. His view is that the doctrine of reincarnation is an accommodation to the general run of humanity who lack the philosophical acumen to understand—or perhaps the emotional resources to face up to—the reality of humanity's relation to the phenomenon of death. He sets forth his own view against reincarnation in *Parerga and Paralipomena* as follows:

> We might very well distinguish between *metempsychosis* as the transition of the entire so-called soul into another body, and *palingenesis* as the disintegration and new formation of the individual, since his *will* alone persists and, assuming the shape of a new being, receives a new intellect. The individual, therefore, decomposes like a neutral salt whose base then combines with another acid to form a new salt.[10]

And in *The World as Will and Representation,* we find his views on why this confusion of the doctrines of *metempsychosis* and *palingenesis* arose in ancient India. Speaking of Buddhism, he says:

> The proper and, so to speak, esoteric doctrine of Buddhism, as we have come to know it through the most recent researches, also agrees with this view, since it teaches not metempsychosis, but a peculiar palingenesis resting on a moral basis, and it expounds and explains this with great depth of thought ... Yet for the great mass of Buddhists this doctrine is too

subtle; and so plain metempsychosis is preached to them as a comprehensible substitute.[11]

Schopenhauer confidently asserts that "real" Buddhism was in line with his own preference for *palingenesis,* as he understood it, over against a popularized version of the doctrine that was taught to the masses. Like Conze over a century later, he clearly suspects that reincarnation provides most people with a hope to evade or indefinitely defer personal annihilation. No matter that both Hinduism and Indian Buddhism maintain a commitment to the view that reincarnation is a kind of *hell*—the prospect of being reborn in "hell" provides at least *something* to hold on to. That "something," of course, is the hope for a persisting identity that gets recycled in the round of *samsara*, in the circle of reincarnation. Better that than nothing.

Schopenhauer avoids tangled and improbable theories about how karmic effect might be transferred across lives: he flatly denies the possibility. He throws cold water on the entire hope. All individual things, including any spiritual essence, is emphatically bound up with particular *bodies.* He says:

> An *individual consciousness* and thus a consciousness in general is not conceivable in an *immaterial or incorporeal being,* since the condition of every consciousness, knowledge, is necessarily a brain-function because the intellect manifests itself objectively as brain.[12]

Note that Schopenhauer doesn't say that the body is the whole story of the self; he does insist, however, that any and all *particularity* on the level of spirit or consciousness would be bound up with *physical* particularity—in the case of humans, with the human body. There is nothing—literally, no *thing,* no particular essence—that can survive the death of the body and serve as vehicle for the transport of karmic effect. At death, all particularity is dissolved back into the primordial Will out of which particularity continually emerges.

This outlook mirrors that of Hinduism: unmanifest Brahman is the source out of which all particular things emerge. But where Indian religion, in order to account for karmic transition between lives, had mounted the desperate explanations typified by those presented in Chapter 3, Schopenhauer insisted on a rigorous consistency. In *Parerga and Paralipomena,* he presents his position in this puckish dialogue:

> **Thrasymachos:** To be brief, what am I after my death? Now, be clear and precise!

Philalethes: Everything and nothing.[13]

"Everything" in that one would be resolved into the primordial substance that is the essence of each and every particular thing. "Nothing" in that—in regard to any *particular* existence—one would not exist at all. In Schopenhauer's view, reincarnation (understood by him, we've seen, as *palingenesis*) carries no significance for the *individual*. And given his deeply pessimistic outlook, this is not at all a bad thing.

We see, then, that for all he embraced Indian religion and philosophy, Schopenhauer firmly rejected the Indian doctrine of reincarnation. In his view, the persistence of an essential self through the sequences of rebirth was inconsistent with the belief in the ultimately *impermanent* nature of all particular realities. He therefore insisted that the *real* teaching—the *esoteric* teaching—of "Brahminism and Buddhism" did not entail a commitment to reincarnation as understood by mundane Indian religion. In fact he was wrong on this point, as we saw in Chapter 3. Hinduism, in both its exoteric and esoteric expressions, was and remains stoutly committed to reincarnation theory. And the same is true of Indian Buddhism.

That Schopenhauer rejected reincarnation establishes that it is possible to embrace Asian religions like Buddhism without accepting every aspect of those religions. More important however, is *why* Schopenhauer rejected reincarnation. For him, the problem with the doctrine was not what Herder centered on—that the doctrine was morally questionable in that it might license social indifference. Moral decency, if we may call it that, will not serve as a criterion for legitimacy, not for a tough-minded thinker like Schopenhauer. For Schopenhauer, the doctrine of reincarnation was indefensible because it is philosophically incoherent.

4

Understanding the relation of Schopenhauer's philosophy to Indian thought requires a bit of background. He held a theory of reality broadly similar to that of Hinduism. The primordial reality out of which all particulars emerge he called "Will." The domain of individual things, particularizations of that primordial Will, he called "Representation." Hence the title of his most important work, *The World as Will and Representation*. But given that he so admired Indian thought, why didn't Schopenhauer simply call his reality *Brahman*? One reason, no doubt, is the variance he saw between his own understanding of the ultimate reality as unmitigated evil and the bliss and sanctity associated with Brahman in the Upanishads.

But there is another reason why Schopenhauer chose a term from German rather than Sanskrit to name the ultimate reality as he understood it:

> I called the thing in itself, the inner essence of the world, by the word for what we are most familiar with: the will. Admittedly this is a subjective term, chosen out of consideration for the subject of knowledge: yet such consideration, as we are communicating knowledge, is essential. It is therefore infinitely better than if I had called it, say, *Brahm* or *Brahma* or world soul or whatever.[14]

Intending to communicate a powerful yet unfamiliar outlook to Europeans—and to a broader segment of the population than either Schlegel or Anquetil-Duperon addressed—Schopenhauer chose to avoid using an arcane, foreign term to designate the central concept of his philosophy. His agenda was a large one, for he intended to bring about a revolution in religious consciousness in the West more significant than the one instituted by Martin Luther.

5

We return, now, to an aspect of Schopenhauer's thought emphasized earlier—its deeply pessimistic outlook. One scholar of Western Buddhism, P. Abelsen, makes a relevant observation about the difference between Schopenhauer's philosophy and the Indian tradition that so inspired it:

> As a matter of fact, it can be disputed if Schopenhauer's philosophy and Buddhism do indeed breathe the same atmosphere. Schopenhauer often put emphasis on Buddhism's pessimistic outlook on earthly existence, but compared to his world view, which is very severe, Buddhism seems almost cheerful ... it lacks the sheer disgust of life that is characteristic of his doctrine.[15]

Central to Schopenhauer's philosophy is his dour outlook on life. He did not blush at being a pessimist; on the contrary he took it to be the only mature disposition toward life; the alternatives were, in his mind, ignorance or naivete. Whether one shares his views or not, Schopenhauer's advocacy of pessimism throughout his work is typically entertaining. His observations on the human predicament are often psychologically penetrating and eminently readable. He presents his pessimism as "scientific"—as grounded not only in philosophical analysis, but also in a careful observation of nature. I set aside for the moment the fact that his purportedly "objective" observations are often glaringly inaccurate and unscientific—sometimes hilariously so. Yet Schopenhauer's reports are important to our study because they give voice to a view that served as something of an underground suspicion in the European collective psyche in the 19th century. Specifically, if the details the traditional Western religions have become untenable, then how can we know that Schopenhauer's disposition toward life is not as realistic as he claims? But let's take some time to savor his pessimism:

> Whoever wants summarily to test the assertion that the pleasure in the world outweighs the pain, or at any rate that the two balance each other, should compare the feelings of an animal that is devouring another with those of that other.[16]

For the animal eating, a quick lunch; for the animal being eaten, a moment of ultimate horror. It is important to note that Schopenhauer's pessimism is not restricted to life—that is, our human existence within nature. His dark assessment extends to reality itself; human life is bad because the reality out of which has emerged is bad—bad to the very core. Again, this is a point on which he differs profoundly from Indian religion, in particular from the Hinduism of the Upanishads that he so admired. As we saw in Chapter 3, the Hindu view is that pain and evil indeed exist, but that their scope is restricted to nature, to the realm of particular things. The primordial source of particularity, *Brahman,* is taken to be a reality of perfection, of supreme value and joy. Not so at all in Schopenhauer's view. As we've seen, he designates the ultimate reality not as *Brahman,* but as "Will," or the *will-to-live.* And evil goes straight to the core of this primordial reality. For Schopenhauer, the Will is neither blissful nor pure—it is unmitigated *evil.* The reason why life in the world is so horrific is not due directly to separation or particularity itself, it is because individual things, according to Schopenhauer, are particularizations of a thoroughly *evil* reality.

The Indian scholar Sarvepalli Radhakrishnan, whose views we encountered in Chapter 3, accurately characterizes Schopenhauer's pessimism in relation to Indian philosophy:

> Schopenhauer's pessimism ... was not derived from his study of Indian thought. What he owed to Indian thought was his love of the idea, of the peace and tranquillity that come from contemplation ... It is a pity that Schopenhauer failed to give that which was nearest to his heart a leading position in the ontological world. On the contrary, he had to give it a back

seat ... due to his lack of faith, to the absence of that buoyant optimism which characterized the ancient sages of India.[17]

Entirely unlike the Hindu concept of *Brahman*, the Will is understood by Schopenhauer to be an unstable, restless, driving force. And it is important enough to repeat that this turbulence is innate to the Will itself, not just the domain of nature—or Representation—produced by the Will. It is the nature of the Will to surge and thrust itself into ever more complex and misery-drenched manifestations:

> ... the *will-to-live*, far from being an arbitrary hypostasis or even an empty expression, is the only true description of the world's innermost nature. Everything presses and pushes towards *existence*, if possible towards *organic* existence, i.e., *life*, and then to the highest possible degree thereof. In animal nature, it then becomes obvious that *will-to-live* is the keynote of its being, its only unchangeable and unconditioned quality ... the will-to-live presses impetuously into existence under millions of forms everywhere and at every moment ... seizing every opportunity, greedily grasping for itself every material capable of life.[18]

For the Upanishads evil is conditional; for Schopenhauer it is *unconditional*. The disquiet he found to be inherent in the essence of reality does not yield an appealing ambience: the world we experience—nature, or, in Schopenhauer's technical terminology, Representation—may be accurately described as a food chain in which life eats life, voraciously and cruelly:

> ... every animal can maintain its own existence only by the incessant elimination of another's. Thus the will-to-live generally feasts on itself, and is in different forms its own nourishment, till finally the human race, because it subdues all the others, regards nature as manufactured for its own use. Yet ... this same human race reveals in itself with terrible clearness that conflict, that variance of the will with itself, and we get *homo homini lupus* [humanity is a wolf to humanity].[19]

We behave like wolves to each other—and not the way in which it has become fashionable to see wolves as our quadruped brothers and sisters, after the manner depicted in the film *Dances with Wolves*. The animal world in Schopenhauer's view is utterly pitiless and rapacious, and we humans are emphatically *part* of it. The prospects for humanity in such a scenario are not likely to be sunny. And Schopenhauer takes exquisite pains to assure us that they are *not*. While the Indian thought he so admired was pessimistic about nature, the domain of particularity, it was also optimistic—even ecstatic—in its attitude toward the primordial reality out of which nature emanates. Schopenhauer, again, is an unqualified pessimist. Again, for him reality is *bad*, bad to its deepest levels—bad, *period*. He illustrates this belief with great relish throughout his writings. And while his illustrations are often silly, the historical or scientific accuracy of his examples is not the issue here; what is of interest to us is the attitude toward reality that Schopenhauer's tales generate. In a fanciful and plainly inaccurate description of an incident wherein a mother squirrel, hypnotized by a snake, was then eaten—he offers lurid evidence of the nature of the Will:

> In this example we see what spirit animates nature ... That an animal is attacked and devoured by another is bad, yet we can reconcile ourselves to this; but that such a poor innocent squirrel, sitting by its nest with its young, is compelled, step by step, reluctantly, struggling with itself and lamenting, to approach the snake's wide, open jaws and hurl itself consciously into these, is so revolting and atrocious, that we fell ... how frightful is this nature to which we belong![20]

6

There is a reason why I press Schopenhauer's grim visions onto the attention of the reader. The Indian thought that Schopenhauer so proselytized did not, in fact, take Europe by storm. But Schopenhauer's deeply pessimistic disposition took root as a baseline suspicion throughout European culture. This suspicion was generated by a crisis in religion, a crisis fomented by emerging insights in both philosophy and science. Traditional religious assumptions were being put in doubt; and if those assumptions were hollow—so it was feared—then the horrors lavishly articulated by Schopenhauer were perhaps plausible. If God is not in his heaven, as traditional religion situated Him, then we are confronted with the uneasy task of saying why Schopenhauer is *wrong*.

That Schopenhauer embraced Indian philosophy and religion yet rejected reincarnation is important to my discussion. But this aspect of his philosophy did not have great impact in the history of ideas in Europe. As we'll see, by the end of the 19th century interest in Indian religion was renewed with fervor, and in this renewal the theory of reincarnation was fully intact. The primary vehicle of this resurgence in interest in Indian thought was the Theosophical Society. But between the pessimistic visions of Schopenhauer and the emergence of Theosophy, there was an historical development that served as a bridge between the two. That bridge was evolutionary theory. But the impetus that so powerfully stimulated the rise of Theosophy was not evolutionary theory in the abstract, but evolutionary theory as presented in the writings of Charles Darwin. Darwin's evolutionary outlook was taken by many to be a scientific way of saying "Schopenhauer." And it is to the specifics of Darwin's theories that we now turn.

Notes

1. Schopenhauer, A. *The World as Will and Representation,* 2 volumes, translated by E. F. J. Payne. New York: Dover Publications, 1969, v.I:63, p.357. All quotations from *The World as Will and Representation* will be from this edition.
2. Deussen, P. *Sixty Upanishads of the Veda.* Delhi: Motilal Banarsidass, 1980.
3. Schopenhauer, A. *Parerga and Paralipomena, 2 vols.,* v.II:184, translated by E. F. J. Payne. New York: Oxford University Press, 1974, pp.396-7. All quotations from *Parerga and Paralipomena* are from this edition.
4. Herder, J. G. *Outlines of a Philosophy of the History of Man (1784).* Translated by T. Churchill. New York: Bergman Publishers, 1800, p.309.
5. Herder, 1800, p.309.
6. Batchelor, S. *The Awakening of the West: The Encounter of Buddhism and Western Culture.* Berkeley: Parallax Press, 1994, p.251.
7. *The World as Will and Representation,* v.I: *Preface,* p.xv.
8. Gardiner, P. *Schopenhauer.* Baltimore: Penguin Books, 1971, p.21.
9. Safranski, R. *Schopenhauer and the Wild Years of Philosophy.* Cambridge: Harvard Univ. Press, 1991, p.202.
10. *Parerga and Paralipomena,* v.II, ch.10, aph.140, p.276.
11. *The World as Will and Representation,* Vol. II, ch.41, p.502-3.
12. *Parerga and Paralipomena,* v.II, ch.10, aph.139, p.273.
13. *Parerga and Paralipomena,* v.II, ch.10, aph.141, p.279.
14. Cited in Safransky, 1991, p.203.
15. Abelsen, P. "Schopenhauer and Buddhism." *Philosophy East and West,* 43: Ap. 1993. Internet version. http://ccbs.ntu.edu.tw/FULLTEXT/JR-PHIL/peter 2.htm
16. *Parerga and Paralipomena,* v.II, ch.12, aph.149, p.292.
17. Radhakrishnan, S. *History of Philosophy: Eastern and Western, Vol. 2.* London: Allen & Unwin, 1952, p.290.
18. *The World as Will and Representation,* v.II, Ch. 28, p.350.
19. *The World as Will and Representation,* v.I, Ch. 27, p.147.
20. *The World as Will and Representation,* v.II, ch.28, fn, p.356.

6

EVOLUTION AND ITS DISCONTENTS

> But a season of mental anguish is at hand, and through this we must pass in order that our posterity may rise. The soul must be sacrificed; the hope in immortality must die. A sweet and charming illusion must be taken from the human race, as youth and beauty vanish never to return.
>
> —Winwood Reade, *The Martyrdom of Man.* 1872[1]

1

What is the place of evolutionary theory in a discussion of reincarnation? To state it simply: evolutionary theory, and in particular Darwin's version of that theory, was a catalyst for the emergence of an important school of thought, Theosophy, in which reincarnation was a central doctrine. The relevance of evolutionary theory to my concerns in this book turns on three points. (1) Darwin's formulations of that theory generated cultural anxieties that demanded resolution. (2) Reincarnation was proposed by leading figures in the Theosophical Society as a corrective to Darwin's view—not evolution by means of natural selection, but evolution by means of *reincarnation.* Finally, (3) we'll see in the final chapter of this study that evolutionary theory is used by some contemporary Western Buddhists, in a reversal of the Theosophists' proposals, as a replacement for reincarnation. My focus in this chapter is on the first of these points—on the crisis generated by evolutionary theory in the 19th century.

The 19th century in Europe was a time of rethinking, and of *troubled* rethinking. Traditional religion was under siege from a number of directions: from a growing sophistication in historical analysis of church institutions and of sacred texts, and from a general industrialization and consequent secularization of society. But the greatest challenge came from *science,* and no scientific challenge was more potent than that raised by the theories of Charles Darwin (18091882). The publication of *The Origin of Species by Means of Natural Selection* in 1859, followed by *The Descent of Man* in 1871, brought to a head tensions that were building in the Western religious consciousness since the strident critiques of the Enlightenment a century earlier. Darwin's revolution forcefully called into question traditional assumptions not only about human origins, but more profoundly, about human nature. The epigraph of this chapter, the passage by Winwood Reade, gives voice to the anxieties that were developing.

2

Speaking very simply, the doctrine of evolution holds that all living species, emphatically including humanity, are in transition. Species transform into other species: every life form is transitional. The idea challenges the assumption, as old as Aristotle, that species are *fixed*—that a rose is a rose is a rose. In Darwin's view, by contrast, a rose and a cabbage are but two different adaptations of a single botanical model. But the crisis precipitated by Darwin's 1859 book did not center on classifying vegetation. Far more pressing was the reclassification of human beings—the inclusion of humanity squarely within the family of animals. This inclusion entailed a pre-human, non-human ancestry: for all humans, for all Europeans, even for Queen Victoria.

The challenge was to more than traditional scientific views. Traditional religious values were called into question, so also were assumptions about the social order. Worse, human self-esteem was significantly put at risk. A human being, according to a literal reading of the *Genesis* account (and among the general population of Europe and America in the 19th century, most readings of that account *were* literal), was created by God and in God's image. Humanity thus created was a finished product, a direct consequence of God's will. More, humanity was set apart from the brutes of the animal kingdom: animals panted and heaved beast-breath, whereas humans had the breath of God in them. Humanity was given *dominion* over all of nature; we are depicted as nature's overlords, not as part of nature.

Darwin's theories potently suggested a very different view. And for all that his view electrified many scientists and philosophers, and also some theologians, it struck a sizeable majority of the population exposed to it with horror. To get a sense of why that was so, it will be helpful to spell out Darwin's position in more detail.

In contrast to the *Genesis* account, Darwin's view holds that neither the human species nor any other species is a finished, once-and-done product, but a work in progress. Life forms from amoebas to humanity were not, in this view, created by God, but were generated by nature. Darwin was not so imprudent as to explicitly reject God in his account, but his theories render God utterly unnecessary. Not a divine plan on the part of God, but a dynamic inherent in nature brought about the human species. Darwin's name is associated, appropriately enough, with the word *evolution,* but the *punch* of his revolution is stated in the last half of his most famous book's title: *The Origin of Species by Means of Natural Selection.* Natural selection is the engine of evolution according to Darwin; natural selection describes the "how" of evolution—it describes how evolution *works.* Here's how Darwin presents it:

> I have called this principle, by which each slight variation, if useful, is preserved, by the term Natural Selection, in order to mark its relation to man's power of selection. But the expression often used by Mr. Herbert Spencer of the Survival of the Fittest is more accurate, and is sometimes equally convenient. We have seen that man by selection can certainly produce great results, and can adapt organic beings to his own uses, through the accumulation of slight but useful variations, given to him by the hand of Nature. But Natural Selection, as we shall hereafter see, is a power incessantly ready for action, and is as immeasurably superior to man's feeble efforts, as the works of Nature are to those of Art.[2]

Through the process of natural selection, nature does something similar, Darwin tells us, to the human enterprise of selective breeding. The crucial difference is that selective breeding is dedicated to human benefit: we breed more edible pigs and friendlier and cuter dogs, and all to human taste. Nature's criteria, by contrast, are indifferent to human benefit—or even to human survival. The criterion of natural selection is starkly simple: nature "selects" in favor of those life forms that are best adapted to their local environment. In Darwin's view, life forms are what they are *relationally,* rather than *essentially.* That is, an individual or a species does not have an intrinsic or *atomistic* existence; a species does not have an innate essence independent of circumstances. A life form is not inherently what it is, striding, for its moment, across a neutral and passive stage-set. What an organism is, literally, is the *relation* between itself and its environment, a relation in which the environment is emphatically *active*. Darwin calls this ongoing relation *adaptation;* it is the process of adaptation that defines—always provisionally—what that organism is. Here's how Darwin puts it:

> It may metaphorically be said that natural selection is daily and hourly scrutinising, throughout the world, the slightest variations; rejecting those that are bad, preserving and adding up all that are good; silently and insensibly working, whenever and wherever opportunity offers, at the improvement of each organic being in relation to its organic and inorganic conditions of life. We see nothing of these slow changes in progress, until the hand of time has marked the lapse of ages, and then so imperfect is our view into long-past geological ages, that we see only that the forms of life are now different from what they formerly were.[3]

Darwin's use of the term "metaphorically" is important: in the process of natural selection, there is no super-entity called "Nature" that engages in a conscious process of selection. The process is impersonal; it is blind to the needs or even the survival of this or that species. The environment changes, and those individuals that find themselves fortunate enough to have inherited from their parents the means to effectively adapt to those changes survive at a disproportionate rate—and because they survive, they also *reproduce* at a disproportionate rate. And thus some life forms survive and thrive through reproduction, others are marginalized or brought to extinction.

To fully appreciate the impact of his views, we must return to Darwin's characterization of natural selection as "the survival of the fittest." Struggle and conflict are at the very heart of the theory. This is brought home in Darwin's insistence that *time,* of itself, will not bring about evolution. He says:

> The mere lapse of time by itself does nothing, either for or against natural selection. I state this because it has been erroneously asserted that the element of time has been assumed by me to play an all-important part in modifying species, as if all the forms of life were necessarily undergoing change through some innate law. Lapse of time is only so far important, and its importance in this respect is great, that it gives a better chance of

beneficial variations arising and of their being selected, accumulated, and fixed.[4]

Not the passage of time, but the bloody business of competition and strife, a contest that yields "the survival of the fittest," is what serves as the engine of evolution. The process is not a pretty one, and Darwin is fully aware of the human tendency to look away from the grim realities embodied in it:

> Nothing is easier than to admit in words the truth of the universal struggle for life, or more difficult at least I have found it so than constantly to bear this conclusion in mind. Yet unless it be thoroughly ingrained in the mind, I am convinced that the whole economy of nature, with every fact on distribution, rarity, abundance, extinction, and variation, will be dimly seen or quite misunderstood. We behold the face of nature bright with gladness, we often see superabundance of food; we do not see, or we forget, that the birds which are idly singing round us mostly live on insects or seeds, and are thus constantly destroying life; or we forget how largely these songsters, or their eggs, or their nestlings are destroyed by birds and beasts of prey; we do not always bear in mind, that though food may be now superabundant, it is not so at all seasons of each recurring year.[5]

But for Darwin, the savagery and extinction of the natural selection process told only a part of the story. For however rough the details were, the results of natural selection were evident for all to see: nature in all its variety and glory. In the famous concluding words of *The Origin of Species,* Darwin expresses wonder at nature's magnificence, while shrewdly bringing to a single focus the Biblical sense of value with the Newtonian paragon of science:

> There is grandeur in this view of life, with its several powers, having been originally breathed by the Creator into a few forms or into one; and that, whilst this planet has gone cycling on according to the fixed law of gravity, from so simple a beginning endless forms most beautiful and most wonderful have been, and are being evolved.[6]

Darwin is optimistic not only over the "grandeur in this view of life," but also over his hope that religious tradition and science are not irrevocably at odds. This optimism and hope were not shared by all. It is well known that parsons and preachers on both sides of the Atlantic—not all of them, but most of them—took to their pulpits to denounce the savagery implicit in Darwin's views, and to warn darkly about the effects that those views would wreak on society and on individual lives. The perceived problem with Darwin's ideas, it should be noted, is not merely "that isn't what it says in *Genesis.*" That may well be an objection for Biblical literalists, but the problem posed by Darwin's view of life goes far deeper. The challenge raised by the theory of evolution by means of natural selection goes straight to the heart of almost all religions: it poses an affront to the human sense of dignity, it mocks the assumption that there is meaning to human life that runs deeper than animal instinct.

It was not only the uneducated that were disquieted. Nor, interestingly, was Darwin himself immune from misgivings. According to the account in his *Autobiography,* the idea of natural selection occurred to him in October of 1838. For over twenty years Darwin sat on what he knew to be one of the most important breakthrough insights in the history of science. It has been speculated that only a concern that he would be scooped by his fellow naturalist Alfred Russel Wallace prompted him to publish his great work in 1859. But even if this supposition is accurate, other details from Darwin's life suggest that there is more to the story. Speculating on the psychological basis of Darwin's hesitation, his recent biographers Adrian Desmond and James Moore say:

> He sat on his theory of evolution for twenty years, scarcely mooting his innermost thoughts about 'monkey-men' and apes evolving morality, castigating himself as a 'Devil's Chaplain.' Even in 1859 he had to be prodded into publishing the *Origin of the Species,* and even then he let it go with barely a hint about human origins ... When Darwin did come out of his closet and bare his soul to a friend, he used a telling expression. He said it was 'like confessing a murder.' Nothing better captures the idea of evolution as a social crime in early Victorian Britain. Anglicans damned it as false, foul, French, atheistic, materialistic, and immoral. It was dangerous knowledge, and tempting. Darwin had known this for years, hence his ruminations were confined to secret notebooks.[7]

And so the master himself, the very "Devil's Chaplain," was subject to the same forebodings as was Parson Brown regarding the potential consequences of his theories.

3

Evolutionary theory was a hot topic in 19th century Europe—and interest in the idea was not restricted to scientists and academics. Its pros and cons were avidly discussed by clergy and in newspapers, on the streets and no doubt in taverns. As the prominent evolutionary scientist and historian of ideas Stephen Jay Gould says:

> ... contrary to popular belief, evolution was a very common heresy during the first half of the nineteenth century. It was widely and openly discussed, opposed, to be sure, by a large majority, but admitted or at least considered by most the great naturalists.[8]

When they were finally published in 1859, Darwin's ideas were immediately taken to have disquieting overtones—even, as we've seen, by Darwin himself. It was suspected that there was an underside to these ideas that went beyond what was explicitly stated. To his 19th century readers, there was a sense of menace implicit in Darwin's theories. At issue was a set of forebodings—not a coherent system that might be refuted, but a nexus of anxieties that generated what might be called a spiritual disquiet. Hand in hand with the dissemination of Darwin's ideas was the suspicion that the traditional belief in God, and in a divine ordering and governance of the world, might be nothing more than a comforting illusion. The fear was that Darwin's version of evolution, along with the harsh realities with which it was freighted, was the last word.

In the previous chapter we saw that in the early to mid-19th century Arthur Schopenhauer issued a call to realism, a challenge to face up to the fact that, given the savage realities that serve as context to human life, *pessimism* is the most plausible disposition. The point to be noted now is that Darwin's theory of evolution by means of natural selection seemed to be a scientific *confirmation* of Schopenhauer's dark vision. Consider closely the phrasing in this characterization of nature presented in *The World as Will and Representation:*

> ... the futility and fruitlessness of the struggle of the whole phenomenon are readily grasped in the simple and easily observable life of animals. The variety and multiplicity of the organizations, the ingenuity of the means by which each is adapted to its element and to its prey ... [shows us] only momentary gratification, fleeting pleasure conditioned by wants, much and long suffering, constant struggle, *bellum omnium,* everything a hunter and everything hunted, pressure, want, need, and anxiety, shrieking and howling ... Junghuhn relates that in Java he saw an immense field entirely covered with skeletons, and took it to be a battle-field. However they were nothing but skeletons of large turtles five feet long, three feet broad, and of equal height. These turtles come this way from the sea in order to lay their eggs, and are then seized by wild dogs *(Canis rutilans);* with their united strength, these dogs lay them on their backs, tear open their lower

armor, the small scales of the belly, and devour them alive. But then a tiger often pounces on the dogs. Now all this misery is repeated thousands and thousands of times, year in year out. For this, then, are these turtles born. For what offense must they suffer this agony? What is the point of this whole scene of horror? The only answer is that the *will-to-live* thus objectifies itself.[9]

Schopenhauer's phrasing is important here, because many found Darwin's concepts and terminology grimly prefigured in it: variety and multiplicity of organisms, ingenuity of adaptation to environment, constant struggle, everything a hunter and a hunted, predator and prey. For many, and not just religious fundamentalists, evolution by means of natural selection looked like Schopenhauer dressed in scientific theory. We are descended from beasts, and, the implication was, we remain beasts. Indisputably rational beasts, but beasts nonetheless. Indeed, our mode of evolution betokens our nature: a constant struggle that produces the survival of the fittest. And again, this disturbing suspicion was in the cultural atmosphere of Europe and America well before the publication of *Origin of the Species* in 1859. Clear evidence of this is found among the verses of the British Poet Laureate Alfred Lord Tennyson's long poem cycle, *In Memoriam*. Consider these lines, written in the 1840's, from stanzas LV and LVI, which read like a literary anticipation of Darwin's theories:

LV

… Are God and Nature then at strife,
That Nature lends such evil dreams?
So careful of the type she seems,
So careless of the single life;

That I, considering everywhere
Her secret meaning in her deeds,
And finding that of fifty seeds
She often brings but one to bear …

LVI

"So careful of the type?" but no.
From scarped cliff and quarried stone
She cries, "A thousand types are gone:
I care for nothing, all shall go.

"Thou makest thine appeal to me:
I bring to life, I bring to death:
The spirit does but mean the breath:
I know no more." And he, shall he,

Man, her last work, who seem'd so fair,
Such splendid purpose in his eyes,
Who roll'd the psalm to wintry skies,
Who built him fanes of fruitless prayer,

Who trusted God was love indeed
And love Creation's final law—
Tho' Nature, red in tooth and claw
With ravine, shriek'd against his creed—

Who loved, who suffer'd countless ills,
Who battled for the True, the Just,
Be blown about the desert dust,
Or seal'd within the iron hills?

No more? A monster then, a dream,
A discord. Dragons of the prime,
That tare each other in their slime,
Were mellow music match'd with him.[10]

Tennyson's verses give eloquent expression to a deep motif within the mid-19th century psyche in the West. It is a motif of *anxiety*—the very successes of science had become a threat, a threat to the human sense of dignity and self-worth. Where Schopenhauer might nod with grim satisfaction, the psychological well-being of most people was tipped into crisis. Let's review Tennyson's words, written in the 1840s, over a decade before Darwin's publication of his explosive theories in 1859.

Evolutionary theory in Darwin's formulation centers attention on *species*—the survival and reproduction of individuals is important only so far as it promotes the continuance of the species, whether butterfly, badger, or human. "Careful of the type [species]; careless of the single life." By contrast, traditional Christianity makes strong promises to each *individual*. The scientific emphasis on the species over the individual would seem to pit science against religion—to put "God and Nature at strife." But in the 19th century it was evident from the developing fossil record that even species were entirely dispensable. And that includes, so the fear arose, the human species. *Homo sapiens* was one life form among others, no more. The traditional Western religious view is rooted in *Genesis,* where we read that the human race is, metaphorically, distinguished from the rest of the animal kingdom by virtue of being possessed of the breath of God; humans, unlike animals, are possessed of *spirit*. Evolutionary theory seemed to relentlessly and rudely insist that we are animals among animals. Nature now speaks instead of God: "I bring to life, I bring to death: The spirit does mean but the breath: I know no more." Spirit, when scientifically understood, is mere breath. And worse: in the strife between God and science, God seemed decisively shoved aside by a force that is not so much God's creation as God's ultimate *adversary*—nature. In the face of all our faith and hopes in God, Tennyson intoned in what are today among the most famous of his words, the voice of science, the voice of nature, in a shriek: "Nature, red in tooth and claw with ravine, shriek'd against his creed." With *ravine,* a word derived from "rapine" and "ravish"—a brute and ghastly reality shrieked into the face, into the traditional myth, of God. The implication, the dread suspicion, was that the progress of science would unveil the human predicament as no more than this: "A monster then, a dream, a discord. Dragons of the prime, that tare each other in their slime, were mellow music match'd with him." The fear was that human life—the scope of the entire human enterprise—was, in the big picture, of no more significance that any species of toothy reptile that strutted and fretted its hour upon the stage, and was heard no more.

In Darwin's view, evolution does not tend toward "us," it does not find culmination in the human species. Adaptation, winning in the competition to survive and reproduce in a constantly changing local environment, tells the whole story. Returning to Stephen Jay Gould:

> In a famous epigram, Darwin reminded himself never to say "higher" or "lower" in describing the structure of organisms—for if an amoeba is as well adapted to its environment as we are to ours, who is to say that we are higher creatures?[11]

Tennyson's fears precisely. Under scientific analysis, the sacred is exposed as little more than muscle and impulse. Spirit, inspiration?—so much breath and panting, and nothing besides. Humans are just another animal species among myriad other species that have struggled to hold their moment in history through a single virtue, if such it could be called: *adaptation.* Continual adaptation to ever-changing environmental circumstances was the be-all and end-all of the human agenda; it was the ultimate *purpose* of the species, the motive underlying all other motives that masqueraded as aspiration and ideal. That, it was assumed, was the "scientific" story—and too bad for those who felt let down by it.

4

And many people felt let down indeed. There were those, the great majority of people in the 19th century, who simply refused to accept Darwin's view of evolution. But for many educated people, such a refusal did not sit comfortably—for rejecting Darwin's theories seemed a rejection of the Enlightenment value of reason, the very reason that held a torch of light to the face of abject medieval superstition. To reject Darwin seemed further to be a rejection of *science itself*—the very science that was since Newton the pride of Western culture. No doubt to many educated people troubled by Darwin's theories, a rejection of those theories was attended by specters of irrationality. The specter, for example, of Captain R. Fitzroy of the Royal Navy. Fitzroy was the captain of H.M.S. *Beagle,* the ship on which Darwin had served as naturalist for some five years, a voyage that had brought him to conceive his theories on evolution. A conservative fundamentalist Christian, Fitzroy apparently felt some responsibility for what he took to be Darwin's appallingly wicked ideas. In the building in which a prominent debate on evolutionary theory was held, Fitzroy engaged in a somewhat grotesque gesture of protest. In Gould's telling of the incident:

> At the famous British Association Meeting of 1860 ... the unbalanced Fitzroy stalked about, holding a Bible above his head and shouting, "The Book, The Book." Five years later, he slit his throat.[12]

While it would be inappropriate to take Fitzroy's distraught exhibitionism as representative of traditional religious resistance to Darwin's ideas, the extreme and, in Gould's words, *unbalanced* features of his protest suggested a disquieting resonance to all religiously grounded rejections of Darwin's theories. Those who could smoothly and without conflict embrace the Biblical accounts as literally true were, in a certain way, the fortunate ones. To them, the apparent disjunction between science and religion was not problematic. To others, however, it was not so easy. Darwin's revolution brought home forcefully the realization that traditional assumptions about human nature and the role of God in the world were more than questionable—they were dubious. And this was a crisis most acutely felt among intellectuals—among people, for example, like Tennyson. Even Darwin, we've seen, was not immune from a sense of impending crisis.

In historical retrospect, religious transitions may seem an adventure; in immediate experience they typically constitute a grave psychological crisis. Indeed, even one of the most strident 19th century critics of the Western religious tradition was aware of how momentous the incipient crises were. Friedrich Nietzsche, having announced the "death of God," immediately afterward presses an urgent series of questions:

> Whither are we moving? Away from all suns? Are we not plunging continually? Backward, sideward, forward, in all directions? Is there still any up or down? Are we not straying through an infinite nothing? Do we not feel the breath of empty space? Has it not become colder? Is not night continually closing in on us?[13]

And thus was generated for many a sense of impending despair—suppose all of Nietzsche's questions were answered in the affirmative? What then? Was Schopenhauer's pessimistic assessment of life the last word? It was in this atmosphere of acute spiritual discontent that a unique religious movement arose. That movement was Theosophy.

Notes

1. Reade, W. *The Martyrdom of Man.* 1872. Online edition. http://www.exclassics.com/martyrdom/martcnts.htm
2. Darwin, C. *The Origin of Species by Means of Natural Selection of the Preservation of Favored Races in the Struggle for Life.* Chapter 3. New York: Signet Classic, 2003, p.75.
3. Darwin, 2003, p.91-2.
4. Darwin, 2003, p.108.
5. Darwin, 2003, p.75.
6. Darwin, 2003, p.459.
7. Desmond, A. and J. Moore, *Darwin.* New York: W. W. Norton and Co., 1994, p.xviii.
8. Gould, S. J. *Ever Since Darwin: Reflections in Natural History.* New York: W. W. Norton & Co., 1977, p.23.
9. Schopenhauer, *The World as Will and Representation,* Vol. II, ch.28, p.354.
10. Tennyson, A. "In Memoriam: A. H. H." Published 1850. Online edition: http://charon.sfsu.edu/tennyson/inmemoriam.html.
11. Gould, 1977, p.36
12. Gould, 1977, p.33.

13. Nietzsche, F. *The Gay Science*, translated by W. Kaufmann. New York: Vintage Books, 1974, aphorism 125, p.181.

7

THEOSOPHY & THE REVOLT AGAINST DARWIN

> If the Pythagorean metempsychosis should be thoroughly explained and compared with the modern theory of evolution, it would be found to supply every "missing link" in the chain of the latter. But who of our scientists would consent to lose his precious time over the vagaries of the ancients?
>
> —Helena Petrovna Blavatsky[1]

1

Its origins are complex, of course, but it may be fairly said that the movement called Theosophy began in America, in Vermont, near the town of Chittenden, at a farm belonging to William Eddy, on October 14th, 1874. The Eddy farm was famous for wonders: there were seances, spirits appeared, ghostly music of no apparent earthly source was heard. Not surprisingly, this supernatural setting attracted visitors, visitors urgently seeking a new grounding for religious experience. One visitor was a veteran of the American Civil War—Colonel Henry Steele Olcott. Another was an extraordinary woman from Russia.

Helena Petrovna Hahn was born in 1831 in the Ukraine. At the age of 17 she married a minor Russian official, Nikifor V. Blavatsky. The marriage lasted only a few months, but she kept her husband's name. Thus Helena Petrovna Blavatsky—Madame Blavatsky—was launched into the world. She is reported to have traveled throughout Asia and Europe. There is a story that in 1867 she fought along with Garibaldi in Italy. It is known with certainty that she came to the United States in 1873 and that, in October of 1874, she met Colonel Olcott at the Eddy farm in Vermont. They quickly developed a deep spiritual alliance, and by the following year, in 1875, they formed the Theosophical Society in New York City.

My focus in this chapter is on the Theosophical movement—its origins, the basis of its extraordinary popularity, and the causes of its eclipse. Because she was so potent in the emergence of the Theosophical movement, Helena Blavatsky gets a lot of attention in what follows. But my concern remains centered on karma and reincarnation, and on the way in which those doctrines, so powerfully asserted by Theosophy and its variant movements, underwent a predictable trajectory—a trajectory that is both the topic and the concern of this book.

But let's go back, now, to that rural area in 19th century Vermont. It is significant that Blavatsky and Olcott were drawn together by their mutual interest in the extraordinary events at the Eddy farm. The wonders on exhibit there were part of a cultural phenomenon that enjoyed great popularity throughout America and Europe—spiritualism. Spiritualism arose as an antidote to the cultural crisis discussed in the previous chapter. It arose in response to the desiccation of Western religious traditions. Spiritualism met the human need for active and direct experience in matters religious. Instead of tepid church services, spiritualism offered—*contact*. Contact with spirits of dead loved ones, contact with angelic (or perhaps demonic) spirits of power, contact with spirits of higher beings of wisdom who were willing to *teach* those they deemed worthy of instruction. Such contact was the *raison d'etre* of spiritualism; it was the goal of the individual spiritualist.

And this brings us back to Theosophy. In the year that the Theosophical Society was founded, 1875, a charter member, Mrs. Emma Britten, published a book titled *Art Magic*. A well-known spiritualist writer, Britten took her new book to be a breakthrough. Historian Bruce F. Campbell gives this account:

> Mrs. Britten claimed that the new work was different from her earlier writings because it had been written by an Adept of her acquaintance, Chevalier Louis, for whom she was but acting as translator and secretary ... Mentioned in this connection were belief in an ancient occult science and in the existence of Adepts, the distinction between white and black magic, and the belief in the astral light and in elemental races or nature spirits.[2]

And we might say—the rest is history. Not Mrs. Britten's history, but, at least in the short run, Madame Blavatsky's. The idea of discarnate spirit guides who served as a *contact,* who constituted an unimpeachable authority, proved irresistible to the religiously discontented in the 19th century. And there was a reason for this. Institutional religion had, in the view of many, compromised its credibility through its war with science. We tend to be dismissive of spiritualism today, but the basis of its appeal in the 19th century was that it held out the prospect that the religious life could be described and understood on *scientific* bases. Science and spirituality could meet, it was hoped. What was wanted was *authority.* And authority is what spiritualism promised. As the historian Peter Washington puts it in *Madam Blavatsky's Baboon:*

> Spirituality [that is, religion] itself was not in question, so much as a secure source of spiritual authority. It was the need for authority that made disciples so very vulnerable to charismatic teachers.[3]

The primary figures in Theosophy were nothing if not charismatic. And their charisma was potently endorsed by their—*connections.* In 1877, two years after Emma Britten published *Art Magic,* Blavatsky published her first major work, *Isis Unveiled.* In that work, as in *The Secret Doctrine* (1888), she claimed to be in contact with Hidden Masters, spirit guides that she had met during her travels in Tibet. These Masters, named Koot Hoomi and Morya, were taken by her to be the source of her revelation—revelation that served as the basis of the esoteric tradition that bears the name Theosophy. Significant here is that, like the traditional religions of the West, Theosophy is not based on human reason or even human wisdom. A familiar "Ascended Spirit" was clearly taken as *comme il faut.* Such a spirit, whatever else it may do, confers *authority.* How was this authority manifested to the Theosophist? An example is found in what Blavatsky reports of a particular Hidden Master, one of many which, she claimed, were her close communicants. She presents a channeled pronouncement on the role of karma in nature. The capitalization and boldface are in the original text:

> Such is the course of Nature under the sway of **KARMIC LAW**: of the ever present and the ever-becoming Nature. For, in the words of a Sage, known only to a few Occultists:—"**THE PRESENT IS THE CHILD OF THE PAST; THE FUTURE, THE BEGOTTEN OF THE PRESENT. AND YET, O PRESENT MOMENT! KNOWEST THOU NOT THAT THOU HAST NO PARENT, NOR CANST THOU HAVE A CHILD; THAT THOU ART EVER BEGETTING BUT THYSELF? BEFORE**

THOU HAST EVEN BEGUN TO SAY 'I AM THE PROGENY OF THE DEPARTED MOMENT, THE CHILD OF THE PAST,' THOU HAST BECOME THAT PAST ITSELF. BEFORE THOU UTTEREST THE LAST SYLLABLE, BEHOLD! THOU ART NO MORE THE PRESENT BUT VERILY THAT FUTURE. THUS, ARE THE PAST, THE PRESENT, AND THE FUTURE, THE EVER-LIVING TRINITY IN ONE—THE MAHAMAYA OF THE ABSOLUTE IS."[4]

It's easy to smile at such hyper-dramatic pronouncements and to dismiss them as so much shenanigans. Yet just such thundering certainties about an alternative to Darwin's theories on evolution served to assuage terrors that beset the 19th century mind—terrors not so much of death, but of meaninglessness. Science on its traditional course had come to be *feared*. As we saw Tennyson poetically state it, the fear invoked by science centered on the perceived threat of science to negate and mock all human values and aspirations. Nature was being portrayed with increasing insistence as a domain void of purpose, meaning, or spiritual value. And in particular, Darwin's version of evolutionary theory, with its pitiless engine of natural selection driving the process of evolution, seemed to confirm all the worst of those fears. Little wonder, then, that the certainties professed by Theosophy were focused on evolutionary theory.

Further, it is clear from his communique that Blavatsky's sage in the passage just cited is not inviting us to dialogue. And in a way, that was just the point. Dialogue implies an exchange of ideas, a process of turn-taking between two or more parties. At issue was *authority*. The Ascended Masters like Morya and Koot Hoomi did not speak in the language of hypotheses; they spoke the language of certainty—eternal truth, truth presented as *revelation*. Here, instead of dialogue, was *authority*. And the oracular Authority proclaims, in an antiquated English peculiarly reminiscent of the King James version of the Bible, that nature is woven into a unity of past, present, and future through the operation of karma. Theosophy, then, is based on *divine revelation*—it purports to be a revealed religion in the same way in which Judaism or Hinduism present a vision that is spoken *through* a human medium, but which originates *from* a trans-human source.

But let's return now to the issue that may be said to have contributed powerfully to the rise of Theosophy—evolutionary theory and the discontents it inflicted on 19th century culture. Blavatsky cites from *The Book of Dzyan,* a work she claims to have channeled from an ascended master, on matters touching on evolution:

Men are made complete only during their third, toward the fourth cycle (race). They are made "gods" for good and evil, and responsible only when the two arcs meet (after 3½ rounds towards the fifth Race). They are made so by the Nirmânakaya (spiritual or astral remains) of the Rudra-Kumâras, "cursed to be reborn on earth again; meaning-doomed in their natural turn to reincarnation in the higher ascending arc of the terrestrial cycle."[5]

Setting aside the arcane terminology and conceptual *mysterium* that drench the paragraph, the message in this passage is that reincarnation traces a progressive ascent, an ascent that is centered not only on the career of the individual psyche, but an "ascending arc of the terrestrial cycle." It was not the scientific method with its rigorous (and often bothersome) techniques of testing and falsification that brought Theosophy its wisdom, it was *contact*. Typical of the attitude toward science found in Theosophical writers is that science itself is not rejected—on the contrary, it is embraced. But the science embraced is what might be called "deep science." The science accepted in 19th century culture—Darwinian science, for example—was concerned only with surfaces, with what is relatively of little significance.

Admittedly, a lot in the history of Theosophy has the character of farce. Peter Washington's study of the movement, *Madame Blavatsky's Baboon*, is both informative and entertaining. And unfortunately, the capers presented by Washington are a verifiable, documented part of the record of Theosophy. Was it charlatanism or just silliness? Blavatsky and Olcott very quickly formed a team, and as Washington suggests, each had something the other needed:

Olcott needed someone to convince him of the spirit world's existence, Blavatsky someone to convince. Whether Olcott was Blavatsky's fellow-conspirator or her dupe, it is hard to say. The colonel was a classic case of someone whose desire to believe is hard to distinguish from belief itself.[6]

Such observations must not tempt us to take Theosophy lightly. Indeed, we dismiss the story of Theosophy at our peril, for it shows us, at relatively close hand, a trajectory of the development of the idea of reincarnation in a context that is eminently Western and relatively modern. It is for that reason that the appeals of Theosophy are reviewed here. To say it again, it is the *ideas* of Theosophy, not the theatrical and troubled personalities that are the source of those ideas, that are of primary interest in this chapter. The focus of attention in what follows will be on two ideas, integrally connected in Theosophical thought—reincarnation and evolution.

2

Theosophy, as Blavatsky presents it, could only have emerged in a European culture in which ideas from India were in vogue. The vocabulary of Theosophy, its conceptual heritage, its publicly proclaimed allegiances—almost all of these point to India. And as we've seen, the doctrine of reincarnation was rejected by the ablest promoter of Indian philosophy in 19th century Europe, Arthur Schopenhauer. In contrast to Schopenhauer, Blavatsky embraced reincarnation with a fervor. And with a difference. Here is a succinct summary of Theosophical position from a study friendly to that position:

> Theosophists have an approach to the reincarnation theory that is manifestly different from that commonly found in the East ... In the Orient the great hope has been to escape as quickly as possible from the wheel of rebirth, and to attain Moksha or Nirvana ... The Theosophists, however, regard re-embodiment as the universal law of evolutionary progress, holding that in an infinite universe there must be infinite possibilities for growth and development. Hence one would never outgrow the need for fresh experience and new cycles of incarnations ...[7]

We've seen that Indian traditions see reincarnation as eminently *undesirable;* liberation in Indian religion is liberation from being reborn. Theosophy, by contrast, views reincarnation as entirely *desirable*—a never-ending adventure, an ongoing quest for higher and higher growth and development.

Another important difference in the Theosophical understanding of reincarnation turns on its view that reincarnation and evolution are in fact two aspects of a single agenda. Not only is reincarnation re-construed, so also is evolutionary theory. For in this view, evolution is not at all what Darwin proposed. In rejecting Darwin's theories, however, Theosophy vigorously asserted that it did not reject science. In fact, its proponents insisted that Theosophy was grounded in rigorous science, but a *deeper* science than that of Darwin. Let's take a closer look at that claim. In *Isis Unveiled,* Blavatsky says:

> But what lies back of the Darwinian line of descent? So far as he is concerned nothing but "unverifiable hypotheses." For, as he puts it, he

views all beings "as the lineal descendants of some few beings which lived long before the first bed of the Silurian system was deposited." He does not attempt to show us who these "few beings" were. But it answers our purpose quite as well, for in the admission of their existence at all, resort to the ancients for corroboration and elaboration of the idea receives the stamp of scientific approbation.[8]

Darwin spoke of human evolution exclusively in terms of the development of animal species. In the view of Theosophy, Darwin's account was not only incomplete, but also *misdirected*—it focused on the least important aspect of evolution. Darwin's theory of natural selection centered on the *outer* dimensions of evolution—on the dusky and violent processes that yielded species, body-types, survival strategies, etc. Theosophy, by contrast, centers attention on what might be called "deep evolution," the evolution of the Spirit. And the mechanism of that evolution is not natural selection, but *reincarnation*. Unlike Darwin's theory of evolution by way of natural selection, evolution by way reincarnation turns on the *inner* world of consciousness and intention. In her essay "Spiritual Progress," Blavatsky brings together the painful realities attendant on evolution according to Darwin's combative vision with her own commitment to the primacy of the inner realm of the spirit:

> The true Adept, the developed man, must, we are always told, *become*—he cannot be made. The process is therefore one of growth through evolution, and this must necessarily involve a certain amount of pain ... Again, the idea of growth involves also the idea of disruption: the inner being must continually burst through its confining shell or encasement, and such a disruption must also be accompanied by pain, not physical but mental and intellectual.[9]

Evolution, in this view, was not focused on the species; evolution centered on the *individual* and involved the individual's capacity to "burst through its confining shell"—the physical body that constituted its membership in the species of humanity. That Darwin's theories addressed only the external, physical organism was their primary limitation. In *The Secret Doctrine,* Blavatsky says:

> It is the Spiritual evolution of the *inner*, immortal man that forms the fundamental tenet in the Occult Sciences. To realize even distantly such a process, the student has to believe (*a*) in the ONE Universal Life, independent of matter (or what Science regards as matter); and (*b*) in the

individual intelligences that animate the various manifestations of this Principle.[10]

In Darwinian theory, the individual is emphatically *mortal*—if it were otherwise, evolution could not take place. Natural selection only works if individuals, that is *specimens,* are constantly replaced through death and the sexual reproduction that results in the ongoing adaptation of the species. By contrast, Theosophy offers the hope of *individual* immortality, the hope that was discussed in Chapter 1. On this point its broader appeal is understandable. And there is another point that made the Theosophical view more attractive than the Darwinian: the human need, discussed in Chapter 2, for a sense of justice and control. Natural selection, unlike the law of karma, is relentlessly blind to intention. Further, natural selection is indifferent to morality: there is the brute competition to survive, there are winners in that competition, and those winners leave behind more offspring. Competition and triumph. Red in tooth and claw. To this menace, Theosophy offered a hope that was eagerly seized upon. In the words of Blavatsky:

> It is only the knowledge of the constant re-births of one and the same individuality throughout the life-cycle; the assurance that the same MONADS [=individual psyches] ... have to pass through the "Circle of Necessity," rewarded or punished by such rebirth for the suffering endured or crimes committed in the former life ... it is only this doctrine, we say, that can explain to us the mysterious problem of Good and Evil, and reconcile man to the terrible and *apparent* injustice of life.[11]

She says all the right things—all the aspects of karma and reincarnation that constitute the sunny surface of the doctrines as they are embraced by 21st century folk. The menace evoked philosophically by Schopenhauer, poetically by Tennyson, and scientifically by Darwin is disarmed by Theosophy. And the menace is disarmed precisely through the doctrines of karma and reincarnation. No longer is the individual a dispensable pawn in an indifferent selection process centered only on local and immediate adaptation to whatever environmental circumstances happen to prevail. The individual is, at least in principle, *in control*—present acts have consequences, consequences that extend beyond the present into future lives. For Theosophy, in other words, the dynamics of karma and reincarnation that we encountered in India and ancient Greece are fully operative. And, unlike the perceived evasions of fundamentalist religion, Theosophy claimed to be entirely scientific. Relief from the horrors posed by evolutionary theory was to be gained not through a rejection of science, but through the embracement of a more profound science. Blavatsky's primary informant—the Hidden Master named Koot Hoomi with whom she was in telepathic contact—also came to hold discourse with some of Blavatsky's followers. One of those followers, A. O. Hume, received a communication from Koot Hoomi on November 1, 1880, in which Hume was instructed on the distinctions between physical science and metaphysical science:

> But will you permit me to sketch for you still more clearly the difference between the modes of—physical, called exact—often out of mere politeness—and metaphysical sciences? The latter, as you know, being incapable of verification before mixed audiences, is classed by Mr. Tyndall with the fictions of poetry. The realistic science of fact, on the other hand, is utterly prosaic ... And what, in its proud isolation, can be more utterly indifferent to every one and everything, or more bound to nothing, but the selfish requisites for its advancement than this materialistic and realistic science of fact?[12]

A crucial aspect of Koot Hoomi's distinction is that physical, or "exact" science is prosaically committed to the very enterprise of which the higher, metaphysical science is incapable—"verification before mixed audiences." And by mixed audiences, we are to understand, Koot Hoomi means a group of people comprised of those who are confirmed believers in metaphysical science and those who still, regrettably, remain mired in physical science and demand experimental confirmation (or disconfirmation) of any and all hypotheses. One can sense here a 19th century anticipation of the position espoused in the late 20th century by advocates of reincarnation like Stanislav Grof, whose position was reviewed in Chapter 1. The tiresome insistence on empirical verification which is at the heart of the scientific method—the method of *physical* science, if you will—is nothing other than a stubbornness that restricts their capacity to apprehend reality in its fullness. It is (to cite Grof's words again) to "ignore all the available evidence and rigidly adhere to the established ways of thinking." Such physical scientists make a virtue of *doubt*. And what is needed, in this view, is not doubt, but *trust*. As Koot Hoomi says in another letter, this one communicated to A. P. Sinnett, it is precisely *doubt* that is the great enemy of the spiritual aspirant:

> My good friend—Shakespeare said truly that "our doubts are traitors." Why should you doubt or create in your mind ever growing monsters? A little more knowledge in occult laws would have set your mind at rest long ago, avoided many a tear to your gentle lady and pang to yourself ... When shall you trust *implicitly,* in my heart if not in my wisdom for which

I claim no recognition on your part? It is extremely painful to see you wandering about in a dark labyrinth created by your own doubts every issue of which, moreover, you close with your own hands.[13]

Doubt, monstrous and painful, is the way of ignorance; trust in the Hidden Master, in occult laws, is the way of wisdom. This is the basis of metaphysical science—a science that dwarfs in both significance and scope the realistic science of facts. And again, the basis of this higher science is not experimentation and verification, but *revelation*. The method of metaphysical science involves recourse to what had become confirmed practice in Theosophy, the establishment of *contact*—contact with a source of higher wisdom, a Hidden Master. In the face of an institutional Christianity that had compromised its credibility by setting itself against science, on the one hand, and the scientific juggernaut of *bad news* presented by Darwin's theories on the other, Koot Hoomi's pronouncements were welcome relief. Here was science, deep science, that conferred certainty and consolation; here was science grounded not in the icy doubt and rigor of verification, but in warm and trustworthy *authority*—the authority of the Hidden Master.

3

Theosophy drew heavily on Indian religious and philosophical views in its advocacy of karma and reincarnation. Its appeal, considered in the abstract, is quite similar to that which we found in India. The individual essence, if not the personality, survives the death of the body; the consequences accrued in one life are freighted to another life through the law of karma, a universal law that guarantees a justness and rightness throughout nature. The reference to India is important here, for as we found that bias and group prejudice became incorporated into the social expressions of the doctrines of karma and reincarnation there, so we find similar dynamics at work in Blavatsky's thinking. Her thinking was typical, and lamentably so, of 19th century European attitudes toward Jews. And as she had taken reincarnation and karma from India, so also she appropriated Indian attitudes toward a despised class of people, the Chandalas, and directed them toward those she herself despised—the Jews:

> The Semites, especially the Arabs, are later Aryans—degenerate in spirituality and perfected in materiality. To these belong all the Jews and the Arabs. The former are a tribe descended from the Tchandalas of India,

the outcasts, many of them ex-Brahmins, who sought refuge in Chaldea, in Scinde, and Aria (Iran), and were truly born from their father A-bram (No Brahmin) some 8,000 years B.C.[14]

Laughable history and gimcrack etymology—the Jews as latter-day Chandalas, the father of the Jews was named A-bram, meaning "no Brahmin." At this point we must pause to ask, How could the reading public have taken this sort of thing seriously? And it must be remembered that such pronouncements were presumed to be beyond question, emanating from a source of unimpeachable authority, the Hidden Masters. In *Madam Blavatsky's Baboon,* Peter Washington observes that Blavatsky's intention

> ... was not to please reviewers and scholars. [Her work] appeals instead to passionate amateurs and spiritual autodidacts: readers too concerned with answers to important questions to be bothered with academic quibbles about authenticity and internal coherence. Blavatsky's book answered to deep needs at a time when religious doubt was fueled by the first great age of mass education. The late nineteenth century produced a large, semi-educated readership with the appetite, the aspirations and the lack of intellectual sophistication necessary to consume such texts.[15]

The ideas presented by Blavatsky appealed powerfully to a sense of wounded self-esteem on the part of a *thinking* public that was not a sufficiently *educated* public. The rise of Theosophy in the 19th century coincided with the rise of mass industrial society and the wide dissemination of scientific breakthroughs—especially those of Darwin. In this social ambience that combined insecurity and naivete, Theosophy thrived. In Washington's telling, Blavatsky's writings served to

> ... embody the secrets she was being taught by the Masters, in forms that would make them accessible to a wider public while making it clear that those who subscribed to the doctrine were an elite.[16]

A harmless indulgence? We are no longer in a position to think so. Whether or not the general public in the West is more educated than a century ago, it has been rudely divested of its pretensions to innocence. Living at the beginning of the 21st century, schooled by grainy and horrific images of the Holocaust, we are in a position to know what Blavatsky could not have imagined: that ideas and ideologies have consequences that extend beyond the fashionable drawing rooms and salons with which she was familiar. And beneath the silliness of some of her presentation, there crouches what we have come to recognize as an ugly and *dangerous* disposition. To Blavatsky (and, as mentioned earlier, to many Europeans who considered themselves to be sophisticated and fair) Jews were taken to personify all that was antithetical to spiritual values—they were materialistic and sensual, concerned only with price, indifferent to value. To many people, the educated among them not excepted, Blavatsky would have been making sense when she claimed: "Strictly speaking, the Jews are an artificial Aryan race, born in India, and belonging to the Caucasian division."[17] Unfortunately, so also would her more strident words on the matter have made sense—words that most folks at the beginning of the 21st century find unpleasant reading:

> With the Semite, that *stooping* man meant the *fall* of Spirit into matter, and that *fall* and *degradation* were apotheosized by him with the result of dragging Deity down to the level of man. For the Aryan, the symbol represented the divorce of Spirit from matter, its merging into and return to its primal Source; for the Semite, the wedlock of spiritual man with material female nature, the physiological being taking pre-eminence over the psychological and the purely immaterial. The Aryan views of the symbolism were those of the whole Pagan world; the Semite interpretations emanated from, and were pre-eminently those of a small tribe, thus marking its national features and the idiosyncratic defects that characterize many of the Jews to this day—gross realism, selfishness, and sensuality.[18]

In light of such attitudes, even the optimistic pronouncements of Blavatsky take on a sinister overtone. Evolution by way of *reincarnation,* an account that according to Theosophy is the deeper story of nature than the one proposed by Darwin's views grounded in natural selection, leads inexorably to a higher version of humanity. Wonderful—but as in Darwin's combative scenario, there will be casualties. Consider Blavatsky's words:

> On the law of parallel history and races, the majority of the future mankind will be composed of glorious Adepts. Humanity is the child of cyclic Destiny, and not one of its Units can escape its unconscious mission, or get rid of the burden of its co-operative work with nature. Thus will mankind, race after race, perform its appointed cycle-pilgrimage. Climates will, and have already begun, to change, each tropical year after the other dropping one sub-race, but only to beget another higher race on the ascending cycle; while a series of other less favored groups—the failures of nature—will, like some individual men, vanish from the human family without even leaving a trace behind.[19]

"Less favored groups"—groups that will "vanish from the human family." Our knowledge of the agenda of National Socialism invests Blavatsky's words with ominous resonance. The law of karmic consequence is taken to pertain not only to individuals, but also to *groups*. To see how this was incorporated into Theosophical doctrine, we move forward in time a few years. Blavatsky died in 1891, and in 1895 her successor as leader of the Theosophical Society was Annie Besant (1847-1933). Besant made the following claim about the relation between individual karma and the destiny of groups of humans. In this passage, the term "sub-race" refers to what are today referred to variously as ethnic groups or races.

> Where long series of incarnations have been followed, it has been found that some individuals progress from sub-race to sub-race very regularly, whereas others are more erratic, taking repeated incarnations perhaps in one sub-race. Within the limits of the sub-race, the individual characteristics of the man will draw him towards one nation or another, and we may notice dominant national characteristics re-emerging on the stage of history *en bloc* ... thus crowds of Romans reincarnate as Englishmen, the enterprising, colonizing, conquering, imperial instincts reappearing as national attributes. A man in whom such national characteristics were strongly marked, and whose time for rebirth had come, would be drafted into the English nation by his karma and would then share the national destiny for good or evil, so far as that destiny affected the fate of an individual.[20]

Thus the individuals in groups, especially those groups marked by strong characteristics or tendencies, had a karmic tendency to reincarnate back into the group—or one very like it—in which they had lived previous lives. Thus, a self-congratulating Englishwoman might assure herself, the ancient Romans (who were greatly admired at the time) came to be reborn as Englishmen. Certainly there is a preciousness here, but also evident are dynamics endemic to a belief in reincarnation and karma. Turning back to Besant for a moment, however, we find her offering, in a passage only a page after the one just quoted, a kind of disclaimer:

> The working out in detail of collective karma would carry us far beyond the limits of such an elementary work as the present and far beyond the knowledge of the writer ...[21]

Ms. Besant may not be able to work out the details of collective karma, but history can. I will press matters, now, deliberately but without malice. The Theosophical disposition to embrace reincarnation, karma, and specifically *collective* karma found further expression in another, still later, exponent.

Alice Bailey (1880-1949) joined the Theosophical movement in 1915, and soon claimed to be in contact with none other than Koot Hoomi. By 1920, however, disagreements with the entrenched hierarchy of the Theosophical Society led her to break away. Some of those disagreements were political and centered on issues of control. Others were doctrinal. She and her husband Foster Bailey founded what they called the Arcane School in 1923. In her autobiographical study, *The Unfinished Autobiography,* Bailey claimed that her teaching was founded on three points:

> I found that this universe of ours is not a "fortuitous concurrence of atoms" but that it is the working out of a great design or pattern which will be all to the glory of God ... that there are Those Who are responsible for the working out of that Plan ... that the Head of this Hierarchy of spiritual Leaders was the Christ ... The third teaching I came across ... was the dual belief in the law of re-birth and the law of cause and effect, called Karma in Reincarnation by Theosophists who, so often, like to sound learned.[22]

A dismissive tone toward Theosophists is evident here; but more significant is a new emphasis—on Christ. This was a major point of divergence in the Arcane School approach from that of Theosophy. As the historian Bruce F. Campbell puts it: "The Arcane School believes humanity is entering a new age and that the messiah of the new age is Christ, who is about to make an appearance."[23] Of course, such beliefs are emphatically *old age* vintage, having been at the heart of the Christian view from its inception. Just that was pointed out by more orthodox Theosophists, who saw Bailey's teaching as a form of *Christianity,* and as such an abandonment of the universalist teaching of Blavatsky. The differences were irreconcilable. But while Bailey broke with the Theosophical Society, she did not abandon the general outlook of Theosophy, however much she both criticized and Christianized it. Like the Theosophical thinkers before her, the influence of the Hidden Masters was vital to Bailey's teaching. About the time when she broke with Theosophy, she was directed by Koot Hoomi to establish contact with another Master, one called The Tibetan, also known as Djwhal Khul. As Campbell says,

> She agreed to be his amanuensis [a scribe who took dictation], and between 1919 and her death in 1949 wrote two dozen books on occult philosophy, most of which claimed to be his teachings.[24]

4

Returning to our focus on karma and reincarnation, now, we find that The Tibetan (let's take Bailey's word here) had some profoundly distressing things to say. And this, too, is part of the legacy of Theosophy—an extrapolation of ideas we've encountered in Blavatsky and Besant. As we turn to these ideas, it is important to note that they were written—or transcribed—not in the 19th century or even the early 20th century. They were put to paper *after* World War II. The topic under discussion is *group karma* and the dynamics of reincarnation; the question at issue is that of *responsibility*. We are informed by The Tibetan:

> The outstanding evidence of the Law of Cause and Effect is the Jewish race. *All nations prove this Law,* but I choose to refer to the Hebrew peoples because their history is so well known and their future and their destiny are subjects of worldwide, universal concern ... Today the law is working and the Jews are paying the price, factually and symbolically, for all they have done in the past. They are demonstrating the far-reaching effects of the Law.[25]

Yes, Bailey allows, the Jews are victims. But she goes on to insist that they are not *innocent* victims. They have been historical accessories to their tragic situation in the mid-twentieth century. She continues:

> They [the Jews] have never faced candidly and honestly (as a race) the problem of why the many nations, from the time of the Egyptians, have neither liked nor wanted them. It has always been the same down the centuries. Yet there must be some reason, inherent in the people themselves, when the reaction is so general and universal.[26]

People throughout all time and in all places have disliked the Jews. Never mind for the moment the historical inaccuracy of the claim—just note that it is a feature of Bailey's (or The Tibetan's) psychological landscape. The plight of the Jews is not beyond repair, however; a change in Jewish national karma is possible. But, we are told, the Jews must do their part in changing it:

> ... it will come when selfishness in business relations and the pronounced manipulative tendencies of the Hebrew people are exchanged for more selfless and honest forms of activity ... The evil karma of the Jew today is intended to end his isolation, to bring him to the point of relinquishing

material goals, of renouncing a nationality that has a tendency to be somewhat parasitic within the boundaries of other nations, and to express inclusive love instead of separative unhappiness.[27]

The Jew as voluntary outsider, the Jew as materialist, the Jew as parasite; just such characterizations of "the Jew" are found in speeches made by Nazi Minister of Propaganda, Joseph Goebbels. More: the Jews as reaping the collective consequences of past behavior; the Jews as *benefitted* by the suffering they endured, the Jews as "working out their karma." We must remind ourselves that what is being explained here—and make no mistake, what is being *justified* here—is the Nazi attempt at the total extermination of the Jews, popularly known as the Holocaust.

In impatience and anger, we might be tempted to assert an equivalency between Nazi doctrines and those of Theosophy. But to do so would be a serious mistake, for it would be to disregard the important *differences* between Bailey's (and Blavatsky's) attitudes toward Jews and those of the Nazis. And this would blind us to the dangerous 21st century appeal of the doctrines of karma and reincarnation. As we saw in our discussion of India in Chapter 3, one of the most disturbing things about contempt for groups in the context of karma and reincarnation is that such contempt—even deadly contempt—is always provisional. Neither Blavatsky nor Bailey would see the fate of the Jews in the mid-20th century as an *ultimate* injustice. Indeed, understood in a proper perspective, the Holocaust is not an affront to justice, but an expression of justice—justice on a deeper level. This is just the kind of thinking that we found in India. The contempt for Jews evident in Blavatsky and Bailey does not confront us with "bigotry as usual." This is one of the most maddening aspects of it. Individual Jews, for example, are what Blavatsky terms *monads*. These are actually *divine* spirits, spirits on the course of an evolutionary ascent. And however degraded and unfortunate they are at any given point in their trajectory of reincarnation, their misfortune is *temporary,* and is an elaboration of their karmic destiny. As the Theosophical view rejects the Darwinian version of evolution as concerned only with the gross, material level, so also it rejects a morality based on the assumption that any given human life is the *only* life of an individual. Recall Blavatsky's words: "MONADS [=individual psyches] … have to pass through the "Circle of Necessity," rewarded or punished by such rebirth for the suffering endured or crimes committed in the former life."

It will surprise no one that such reasoning found dark applications. In an acclaimed study of the mystical origins of National Socialism, historian

Nicholas Goodrick-Clarke traces the emergence of racist occult movements that served as precursors Nazism to Theosophy:

> The modern German occult revival owes its inception to the popularity of theosophy in the Anglo-Saxon world during the 1880s. Here theosophy refers to the international sectarian movement deriving from the activities and writings of the Russian adventuress and occultist, Helena Petrovna Blavatsky.[28]

A key figure in the occult revival spoken of by Goodrick-Clarke was Guido von List (1848-1919), a self-proclaimed conduit of ancient wisdom of the Germanic peoples. Like Blavatsky, he claimed to have had clairvoyant access to transcendent wisdom; he claimed, again like Blavatsky, an occult understanding of human genealogy grounded in reincarnation, an understanding entirely at odds with Darwin's views on natural selection. By the time List died, his views had been institutionalized in the List Society and the *Germanen Orden*—secret societies that promoted a racial mysticism that came to be the ideological heart of Nazism. List's most influential work, *Das Geheimnis der Runen,* was translated by Stephen E. Flowers as *The Secret of the Runes,* and in his introduction to that work, Flowers says:

> It is in the area of Theosophy, however, that we see the greatest single impact on the final form of List's occult vision. Principal among its influences on him were the concepts of Indian theology and mystical racial evolution—both of which Theosophy popularized—as well as the presence of "hidden masters" and the technique of gaining mystical vision of the remote past.[29]

Continuing in the same vein, Frederick Crews, in his review of Washington's *Madame Blavatsky's Baboon,* invites our attention to the parallels between Theosophy and National Socialism—not so much in regard to its historical development, but in regard to its philosophical orientation. He says:

> ... we should not overlook the broad epistemic likeness between Theosophical dreamers and the ideologues who smoothed the way for the terroristic Nazi state. The common factor was their shared rejection of rational empiricism. By pretending that reliable knowledge can be obtained through such means as clairvoyant trances and astrological casting, the original Theosophists encouraged their German colleagues to "uncover" in prehistory just what they pleased; and the resultant myth of how Aryan hegemony was broken by quasi-simian races formed a

template for the infectious post-World War I story of betrayal by Jewish materialists and the vindictive Allies. The whole visionary apparatus—the vitalistic sun cult, the mystic brotherhood, the pygmy usurpers, the lost ancient continents, the millennial cycles, even the idea of a conspiracy by a cabalistic "Great International Party" of diabolical anti-traditionalists—was already there in *The Secret Doctrine*.[30]

Are we to conclude, then, that the outcome of the Theosophical adventure was National Socialism? To do so, to insist on the point yet again, would be to blind ourselves to the real social dangers posed by widespread belief in karma and reincarnation. The social attitudes of those who believe in reincarnation are typically not rooted in a psychology of hate but in a psychology of *compassion*. Reincarnation theory serves to quiet the sense of outrage that manifest injustice evokes—and it does so through the soothing assurance that the perceived injustice is no *more* than a perception, that operative at a "deeper" level is a sublime and beneficent justice. And so we are tempted to a *laissez faire* state of mind. But as the 18th century social philosopher Edmund Burke warned us: "The only thing necessary for the triumph of evil is for good men to do nothing." And the concern here centers not on evil people, but on the consequences of ideas and doctrines.

At issue is compassion, but a toxic form of compassion. At issue is a compassion that sees, often with genuine sympathy, the painful consequences of *choices* that have been made—choices, for example, about which group to be born into. To suggest that Theosophy, or Theosophists, are to blame for the Nazi horrors would be an irresponsible oversimplification. Yes, Blavatsky held some of the negative attitudes toward Jews and Judaism that were endemic to the culture in which she lived. And it is beyond dispute that some of the ideas promoted by the Theosophical movement found employment in ideologies that led to National Socialism. But of itself, this does not constitute a decisive indictment of Theosophy. For it is also beyond dispute that the ideas like ecology, holistic health, the value of meditation, and a concern with healthy diet were also incorporated into the National Socialist vision. This is in no way a "give 'em a break" disposition on my part. What I take to be a balanced assessment of the role of Theosophical doctrines in Nazi ideology is found in a source that is unlikely to be in any way "soft" on Nazis or their philosophical fellow-travelers—the Simon Wiesenthal Center. In a position paper on the Museum of Tolerance website titled "Hitler's Racial Ideology: Content and Occult Sources," Jackson Spielvogel and David Redles write:

It is important to observe that there are also some striking differences between Blavatsky's doctrine and Hitler's later racial ideas. Blavatsky herself did not identify the Aryan race with the Germanic peoples. And although her racial doctrine clearly entailed belief in superior and inferior races and hence could be easily misused, she placed no emphasis on the domination of one race over another. She certainly did not advocate the use of force since human racial evolution was an inevitable process that operated primarily on the basis of spiritual laws. Nevertheless, in her work Blavatsky had helped to foster antisemitism, which is perhaps one of the reasons her esoteric work was so rapidly accepted in German circles.[31]

While some social critics accuse those in the Theosophy movement as being, in essence, fellow travelers with Nazis, the Wiesenthal Center's report is a more careful and perceptive analysis. Blavatsky's rejection of violence and domination and the essentially *spiritual* character of her thought are acknowledged. The article firmly directs our attention, however, to the idea that esoteric doctrines can have dreadful consequences on the exoteric level—out in the street. Here at the beginning of the 21st century, we are acutely sensitized to such language as is found in Blavatsky and other Theosophists. And well we should be. For good reasons, the idea of a "genteel anti-Semitism" is repugnant to us. And these *reasons* are historical: we now *know* things that the early Theosophists did not know; we know that ideology can easily move from the study or the classroom or the meditation hall into the streets. And out in the street, an ideology's consequences can find realization in extremes never dreamt of by its more refined advocates.

I pause to restate of thesis of this study. Religious ideas have consequences, and whatever the intentions of their formulators and promoters may have been, the *consequences* of these ideas are, in the last analysis, the only basis of judging their value.

5

The next figure in our survey of the dramatic history of the Theosophical outlook is Aleister Crowley (1875-1947). Crowley was born to a wealthy British family and, like many prominent Theosophists, led a life peppered with controversy. Also, like prominent Theosophists from Blavatsky to Bailey, Crowley claimed to channel higher wisdom that emanated from an ascended master. In 1904, he attained contact with such a master, and under circumstances that are by now familiar:

> There is a Being called Aiwaz, an intelligence discarnate, who wrote the *Book of the Law,* using my ears and hand. His mind is certainly superior to my own in knowledge and in power, for He has dominated me and taught me ever since.[32]

Crowley is not an attractive figure; the details of his life appear to be a sustained and desperate attempt to call attention to himself. My interest in his thought is that it serves as a segue between the Theosophical outlook and Social Darwinism. We'll explore Social Darwinism in greater detail in the next chapter. For now, I want to draw attention to the imperious tone of Crowley; any semblance of Buddhist compassion has been traded in for tough-mindedness. He both channels and comments upon Aiwaz's work, *The Book of the Law.* And in that work and its commentary, the thought of Crowley and Aiwaz—let's take Crowley at his word that there were in fact *two* of them—strongly reflect the Social Darwinism that was so fashionable in 1904. First, here's Aiwaz:

> We have nothing with the outcast and the unfit: let them die in their misery ... stamp down the wretched & the weak: this is the law of the strong: this is our law and the joy of the world. *The Book of the Law,* Ch.II, verse 21.

And here is Crowley's commentary on this verse:

> It is the evolutionary and natural view. Of what use is it to perpetuate the misery of tuberculosis, and such diseases, as we now do? Nature's way is to weed out the weak. This is the most merciful way, too. At present all the strong are being damaged, and their progress hindered by, and their progress hindered by the dead weight of the weak limbs and the missing limbs, the diseased limbs and the atrophied limbs ... Let the weak and wry productions go back into the melting-pot, as is done with flawed steel castings. Death will purge, reincarnation make whole, these errors and abortions. Nature herself may be trusted to do this, if only we will leave her alone.[33]

This is a tune different than the one we've heard in other spiritual teachers of the late 19th and early 20th centuries—certainly different from mainstream Theosophists like Blavatsky. Crowley brings together the aspirations to be both *scientific* and *spiritual,* the aspiration that so motivated the adherents of Blavatsky and her doctrines. But in Crowley there is no pretense to universal compassion—indeed, he regularly crows his disdain for compassion as being weak and, his ultimate term of disparagement, "Christian."

The significance of Crowley's thought to this survey is that he represents a convergence between the spiritualism and reincarnation doctrines that characterized the Theosophical movement on the one hand, and the tough-minded snarl we find in some—not all, but some—of the Social Darwinists to be considered in the next chapter. Indeed, I'll be suggesting that the brazen candor of Crowley and of the majority of Social Darwinists is preferable to the arcane philosophizing of the Theosophists. Crowley's brass-knuckle assertions are more honest than the honeyed compassion with which reincarnation doctrine is typically presented by Theosophy. The bottom line in both is that the wretched are in their state because they deserve to be there.

6

Theosophy was unsuccessful in its bid to become a major religious outlook in the West—and thereby institutionalize the doctrines of karma and reincarnation within mainstream Western thought. But the cause of its failure was not disgrace over association with unsavory company in figures connected to National Socialism. The demise of Theosophy's credibility occurred before the Nazis came to power in 1933. From the outset, the Theosophical movement was defined through the forceful personalities who claimed unimpeachable Sources for their pronouncements. Doctrinal commitments became blurred with personal allegiances. It is hardly surprising, in such an operatic ambience, that pettiness, personal jealousies, and vindictiveness came to prevail. It did so not only in the personal interactions among Theosophists, but also in their publications. Referring again to *The Unfinished Autobiography* of Alice Bailey, we read:

> The sectional magazines and the international magazine, called "The Theosophist," were pre-occupied with personality quarrels. Articles were given up to the attack or the defense of some individual ... [34]

Cronyism and cliquishness had come to dominate the Theosophical Society, and along with it, Bailey noted, came embarrassing claims by some of the leading Theosophists—claims that tilted toward childishness:

> Books were being published at Adyar by Mr. Leadbeater that were psychic in their implications and impossible of verification, carrying a strong note of astralism. One of his major works, *Man: Whence, How and Whither,* was a book that proved to me the basic untrustworthiness of what he

wrote. It is a book that outlines the future and the work of the Hierarchy of the future, and the curious and arresting thing to me was that the majority of the people slated to hold high office in the Hierarchy and in the future coming civilisation were all Mr. Leadbeater's personal friends. I knew some of these people—worthy, kind, and mediocre, none of them intellectual giants and most of them completely unimportant.[35]

We must recall, of course, that Bailey broke with the Theosophy movement, and under circumstances that were anything but friendly. And so it would be reasonable to suspect that Bailey's account reflects little more than personal pique on her part. But her assessments are corroborated in Peter Washington's study:

... Leadbeater added potent dashes of snobbery and family pride, calculated to appeal to class-conscious late-Victorians. For not only was everyone in the [Theosophical] Society found to be the reincarnation of past celebrities; it also turned out that they were all related to one another in bizarre combinations ... There was a surprising regularity in the pattern of reincarnations. Leadbeater traced sixteen past lives for each individual. Each life averaged fifty-five and a half years in length and each was separated from the next by 1,264 years. It happened that in every case the first three and the last seven existences were in male form, the intervening six female. That it might transpire that Leadbeater had been Annie's [Besant] daughter on Mars or her mother-in-law in ancient Egypt.[36]

An atmosphere of hokum had harried the image of Theosophy from its inception. Through her savvy and the force of her personality, Blavatsky was able maintain an air of authenticity that, for many Theosophists, covered over any embarrassments. With her death, Theosophy fell into less successful management. Annie Besant's tenure at the helm of the movement was conflicted throughout by the unstable and idiosyncratic influence of Charles Leadbeater. Restraint, self-critique, and caution were abandoned. One might say that the liabilities inherent in an organization crystalized around the ideals of mystical contact with higher powers asserted themselves. The Theosophical Society was predicated on the idea of *hierarchy:* a hierarchic structure of reality, a hierarchy of beings, a hierarchy of wisdom. This passion for hierarchy generated, throughout the course of the movement, an all-too-human concern with *status.* A spiritual status, suspiciously similar to the class consciousness of many of its most devoted adherents, came to be a matter of earnest and even anxious concern. There were those who were "in"—set apart from (and above) those who were *not* in—or at least not quite as in as they might be. And even among those who were "in," there were some who were *further* in than others. Badges and ribbons were issued. Something of a mystical *chic* evolved. Peter Washington describes the developments this way:

> The result of Annie's [Besant] enthusiasm for starting societies, combined with Leadbeater's interest in sacraments, orders and vestments, was a huge increase in theosophical paraphernalia. Though her own early writings ... put great stress on inwardness and the folly of mistaking appearance for reality, Annie Besant was not a little vain about her own appearance and enjoyed dressing up in the regalia of the various theosophical orders she and Leadbeater founded together. As the years passed, both of them became more and more besotted with ceremonies and uniforms, offices and decorations.[37]

And so, heavy with solemnity and decorations and an inflated sense of self-importance, Theosophy slowly sank from significance in Western culture. Having expressed her observations about the decline of the integrity of the movement, Alice Bailey concludes: "Owing to all these various causes many people were leaving the Theosophical Society in disgust and bewilderment."[38]

7

By far the most important of those who left in disgust was Jiddu Krishnamurti, the chosen heir to the mantle of leadership in the Theosophical Society. He was taken by some to be an incarnation of a divine Buddhist savior figure named Maitreya, by others to be an incarnation of the same spirit that had been incarnated as Christ. He was groomed to be, as the head of the Theosophical movement, the messiah for the modern age. But in 1929, Krishnamurti stunned the Theosophical Society by dissolving one of its innermost circles—The Order of the Star. He announced that he'd had enough. In a talk titled "Truth is a Trackless Land," he called attention to the belief in spiritual development that was at the core of the Theosophical movement:

> Consider, reason with yourselves, and discover in what way that belief has made you different—not with the superficial difference of the wearing of a badge, which is trivial, absurd ... [39]

There can be little doubt that in the passage above Krishnamurti refers to the foolish theatrics that had come to pervade the movement. But there were issues more substantial than fashion that troubled him. He saw honorific titles and chic regalia as symptomatic of a deeper misdirection in the religious quest—as a spiritual pride that is rooted in an infatuation with the ego. Invariably connected to an infatuation with the ego is a terror of death. And Krishnamurti firmly places the reincarnation theory that was so much at the heart of Theosophy into the category of metaphysical comforts through which we face the terrors of death—similar in this regard to Christian beliefs in resurrection and afterlife. Speaking of death, he says:

> So what is it that human beings are so dreadfully frightened of? They are frightened of something ending, of ending psychologically, inwardly. And knowing it *is* going to end we want comfort, so we say there must be a continuity. The ancient Hindus said there is a continuity, which is called reincarnation. They said you will be reborn next life according to what you have done in this life. If you have behaved properly, decently, morally, in the next life you are going to be better, and through a series of incarnations, and depending on your behavior, you will ultimately come to the highest principle. That is very comforting, and millions believe in that ... And of course the Christians have their own belief in the resurrection; they believe that their own deity woke up from death physically.[40]

Krishnamurti's departure from the Theosophical Society, then, was rooted in doctrine as much as in taste. And his departure signaled the end the Theosophical vision as a contender for global allegiance.

Theosophy had offered itself as a universal religion, as the religion of the future. Had it been successful in its bid, it might have mainstreamed its core doctrines of karma and reincarnation into Western culture. This was not to be. Theosophy went into eclipse, and it did so through *silliness*—perhaps the fate of all movements that are, in the last analysis, personality cults. And with Theosophy, the doctrines of karma and reincarnation went, however temporarily, into eclipse.

Notes

1. Blavatsky, H. P. *Isis Unveiled.* The Theosophical University Press Online Edition, http://www.theosociety.org/pasadena/isis/iu1-01.htm. Volume I, p.9. All quotations from *Isis Unveiled* will be from this edition.
2. Campbell, B. F. *Ancient Wisdom Revisited: a History of the Theosophical Movement.* Berkeley: University of California Press, 1980, p.32.
3. Washington, P. *Madame Blavatsky's Baboon: a History of the Mystics, Mediums, and Misfits Who Brought Spiritualism to America.* New York: Schocken Books, 1995, p.9.

4. *The Secret Doctrine*, Pasadena, California: The Theosophical University Press, 1999. Volume II, p.446. All quotations from *The Secret Doctrine* will be from this edition.
5. *The Secret Doctrine*, Volume II, p.255.
6. Washington, 1995, p.44.
7. Head, J. And S. L. Cranston, eds., *Reincarnation: an East-West Anthology.* Wheaton, Ill.: Theosophical Publishing House, 1975, p.62.
8. *Isis Unveiled.* Volume I, p.154.
9. Blavatsky, H. P. "Spiritual Progress." *Theosophist*, May, 1885. http://www.blavatsky.net/blavatsky/arts/SpiritualProgress.htm.
10. *The Secret Doctrine.* Volume I, p.634.
11. *The Secret Doctrine*, Volume II, p.303-4.
12. Hume, A. O. *"Mahatma Letter" to A. O. Hume*, November 1, 1880. Online edition: http://www.theosociety.org/pasadena/mahatma/ml-khaoh.htm.
13. Sinnett, A. P. *The Mahatma Letters to A. P. Sinnett.* Theosophical University Press, Online Edition. Letter no.60. http://www.theosociety.org/pasadena/mahatma/ml-60.htm.
14. *The Secret Doctrine*, Volume II, p.200.
15. Washington, 1995, p.53.
16. Washington, 1995, p.49.
17. *The Secret Doctrine*, Volume II, p.471 fn.
18. *The Secret Doctrine*, Volume II, p.470.
19. *The Secret Doctrine*, Volume II, p.446.
20. Besant, A. *Karma.* Wheaton, Ill.: Theosophical Publishing House, 1975, p.77-8.
21. Besant, 1975, p.79.
22. Bailey, A. A. *The Unfinished Autobiography of Alice A. Bailey.* New York: Lucis Publishing Co., 1951, p.139-140.
23. Campbell, 1980, p.153.
24. Campbell, 1980, p.151.
25. Bailey, A. *Esoteric Healing.* (Volume IV in *A Treatise on the Seven Rays.*) New York: Lucis Publishing Company, 1998, p.263-4.
26. Bailey, 1998, p.265.
27. Bailey, 1998, p.267-8.
28. Goodrick-Clarke, N. *The Occult Roots of Nazism: Secret Aryan Cults and their Influence on Nazi Ideology.* New York: New York University Press, 1992, p.18.
29. Flowers, S. E. *The Secret of the Runes, by Guido von List.* Rochester, Vermont: Destiny Books, 1988, p.29.
30. Crews, F. "The Consolation of Theosophy, II" in *The New York Review of Books:* Volume 43, Number 15 ; October 3, 1996, online edition. http://www.nybooks.com/articles/1403

31. Spielvogel, J. and D. Redles "Hitler's Racial Ideology: Content and Occult Sources." Simon Wiesenthal Center; Museum of Tolerance Online, 1997. http://motlc.wiesenthal.com/resources/books/annual3/chap09.html.
32. Crowley, A. *The Law Is For All: the Authorized Popular Commentary on Liber AL vel Legis sub figura CCXX, The Book of the Law.* Las Vegas, NV: 1996, p.13.
33. Crowley, 1996, p.102.
34. Bailey, 1951, p.170.
35. Bailey, 1951, p.170.
36. Washington, *op. cit.,* p.121.
37. Washington, 1995, p.127.
38. Bailey, 1951, p.170.
39. Krishnamurti, J. "Truth is a Trackless Land," in *Total Freedom: The Essential Krishnamurti.* San Francisco: HarperSanFrancisco, 1996, p.4.
40. Krishnamurti, 1996, "A Relationship with the World," p.313.

8

TOUGH JUSTICE FOR TOUGH MINDS: SOCIAL DARWINISM IN ITS SEASON

> The race is bound, from generation to generation, in an unbroken chain of vice and penalty, virtue and reward. The sins of the fathers are visited upon the children, while, on the other hand, health, vigor, talent, genius, and skill are, so far as we can discover, the results of high physical vigor and wise early training ... There is no other such punishment for a life of vice and self-indulgence as to see children grow up cursed with the penalties of it, and no such reward for self-denial and virtue as to see children born and grow up vigorous in mind and body.
>
> —William Graham Sumner[1]

1

While reincarnation theory is a newcomer to the popular mind in America, the general disposition underlying the theory is no stranger to the American historical scene. The underlying disposition to which I refer found expression in the movement known as Social Darwinism. In fact, there are important ways in which Social Darwinist theory is both like and unlike reincarnation—and its relevance to our discussion touches on both. First, *like* reincarnation theory, Social Darwinism serves to both explain and ethically endorse social conditions in which poverty and injustice are accepted as built in to the order of things. Reincarnation and Social

Darwinism have in common the assumption that people in wretched social circumstances have somehow *earned* their status in society—that there is a "rightness" to their unfortunate circumstances.

Second, this time *unlike* reincarnation theory, Social Darwinism leaves many people feeling badly. Relegating the poor to the dregs of the social order, the gritty "that's how it is" attitude of Social Darwinism, was for many Americans simply too heartless. Especially the more strident explicators of the movement—people like William Graham Sumner, quoted in the epigraph to this chapter—gave the impression of advocating outright cruelty. And yet, Social Darwinism can be seen as an extension of uniquely American attitudes.

American culture has historically been a matrix of opportunity. The question "How far can you go in life?" was answered by another question: "How *good* are you?" And the *good* spoken of is not a moral good, but a good that comprised savvy, toughness, and insight, a good that embodied above all else *survivability*. Over time, this disposition found callous expression on a sign that hung in many work-places: *"If you're so smart, why ain't you rich?"* There is clearly a sneer in this question. It may be said that Social Darwinism is an extrapolation of the question, complete with the sneer. Stated simply, Social Darwinism is the attempt to formulate public policy around the evolutionary theories articulated by Darwin. The essence of Social Darwinism is the assumption that the poor and the wealthy are in their respective social stations because they *belong* there. And they belong there because the rough sorting process of natural selection—the survival of the fittest—placed them there. If you're smart, if you have what in a later day was called "the right stuff," you're rich. And if not—not.

The relation between the theories of reincarnation and Social Darwinism is subtle, but important. I do not be suggest that people who espouse reincarnation theory are covert Social Darwinists—such a characterization would be both inaccurate and unfair. Yes, Social Darwinism and reincarnation theory have both served to justify deplorable social circumstances. But where Social Darwinism endorses a social policy of undisguised severity, reincarnation theory speaks the language of compassion and spiritual aspiration. Both equally serve to ethically endorse the status quo in society—as we saw in the last chapter, this makes the compassion that we find in reincarnation theory a sinister compassion indeed. We'll see that Social Darwinism, its severity notwithstanding, proposes a compassion of its own, and more, an honesty and candor.

2

Of the many ideas that have had their season on the stage of Western culture, some are relegated to the Rogue's Gallery. Social Darwinism is one of them. In his historical study, *Social Darwinism: Science and Myth in Anglo-American Social Thought,* Robert C. Bannister says, "social Darwinism is singular in that virtually no one adopted it as a badge of honor. A social Darwinist, to oversimplify the case, was something nobody wanted to be."[2] As we'll see, this was not always so, but it is certainly true today. There are good reasons for this. Social Darwinism has negative associations in the mind of most people—associations that run the gamut from mean-spirited to racist. If the ideas of Theosophy, discussed in the last chapter, are considered by some to be too soft-headed, then those of Social Darwinism are considered to be too hard-hearted. Yes, the wealthy are conspicuously advantaged; the impoverished live in destitution—but these facts reflect a rightness, in the view of Social Darwinism, in the same way that in India the privileges of the *Brahmins* and the misery of the *Shudras* and the Outcastes were taken to reflect a primordial rightness.

In fact, it might be said that Social Darwinism is in certain respects more plausible that Hinduism's caste system. To see why, it will be useful to briefly compare the two theories. Recall that it was Sarvepalli Radhakrishnan who attempted to justify the caste system using the language of Social Darwinism. His views were examined in Chapter Three, and are worth revisiting here. Invoking the debate over the role of genetics versus the role of environment in societal structure, we saw that Radhakrishnan critiqued the Enlightenment view that—

> ... held that men were molded by their environments as so much soft clay. Modern science, however, holds that this view exaggerates the influence of the environment. Progress does not depend on a mere change of surroundings. Darwin's teaching that evolution proceeds by heredity was taken up by Galton ...[3]

Again, the problem in this line of thinking is that the caste system in India takes the unique qualities that constitute individual character—the varying degrees of intelligence, industriousness, and so on—and ascribes them to *groups* of people. And, more, one is *born* into this or that group; one does not *earn,* through the efforts brought to this life, membership in a caste. An individual is at this station or that one by virtue of the parents to whom he or she is born, and that station is taken to be fixed for the entire life of the individual. The identity of the group takes precedence over the identity of the individual—that is, a person was defined by *group* membership rather than by *individual* triumphs and failures. By contrast, Social Darwinism, although it had racist and nationalist expressions, was committed to a focus on the individual: the gifted *individual* would rise out of the group to secure her or his proper place in society on the strength of unique qualities; the less than gifted individual would correspondingly be relegated to a proper, that is, a lower, place in society.

In this sense, Social Darwinism is more akin to Plato's rigorous meritocracy as it was presented in Chapter 4. Like Plato, Social Darwinist theory assumed that a selection process would take place that sorted out the gifted individuals from the not-so-gifted. The agenda of Social Darwinism is unlike that of Plato, however, in that the selection process would not be administered by the wisest of the Ruler class, but by nature itself—by means of natural selection. This is where Social Darwinism brings *Darwinism* into play.

3

We now take a closer look at the details of Social Darwinism. As stated above, today the doctrine stands in the Rogue's Gallery of ideas. But a century ago, this was not so. Social Darwinism was seen as scientific and realistic—and, by many of its proponents, as *beneficent*. The core of the doctrine can be stated simply enough: the human species, human civilization, and individual human well-being will be best served if the dynamics of nature are allowed to operate unfettered within society. What dynamics of nature? *Darwinian* dynamics: natural selection, the ceaseless winnowing for more effective adaptation, and—very important—a differential reproduction rate in favor of the most successful. The struggle and strife of Darwinian natural selection is what brought the human species to its present state. And, insists the Social Darwinian view, that rough struggle must be maintained, and maintained *within* society, or else. Or else: the human species itself will degenerate, human civilization will coarsen, and the prospects for individual well-being will be significantly diminished. Without the refreshing and strengthening struggle of natural selection operative *within* the social realm, we humans face disaster. Hence, *Social Darwinism*.

And all this occurred in the face of the poetically sublime anxieties expressed, as we saw in Chapter 6, by Alfred Lord Tennyson—anxieties over the baleful prospects for the human agenda should the bloody dynamics of nature be allowed to prevail in culture. Tennyson wrote in the 19th century; the same concerns are alive and well today. Indeed, no sooner is the term Social Darwinism spoken than an objection, more reflex than reflection, is raised. Darwin's theories suggested that humans are members in good standing in the animal kingdom. This was not, as we've already seen, cheering news to many. In Darwin's perspective, humans are beasts, and now Social Darwinists proposed that our beastliness be accommodated in the structure of society. Predation would be the order of the day. The brute reality of the street thug would be refined into the capitalist Robber Baron wearing a respectable business suit.

4

Those who are committed to Darwin's ideas typically bridle at the suggestion that Darwin himself contributed to anything so disreputable as Social Darwinism—that cruel doctrine is seen as a perversion of the Master's theories. However, the evidence indicates otherwise. In *Origin of Species,* Darwin restricts himself to discussing the evolution of nonhuman life. Although in that discussion he speaks of a process operative in the animal kingdom. But the process he described would be taken as the kernel of his position on human life in society; he speaks of "one general law, leading to the advancement of all organic beings—namely, multiply, vary, but the strongest live and the weakest die."[4]

Certainly there were presentations of the essential ideas of Social Darwinism before Darwin wrote—especially in the mid-19th century work of Herbert Spencer. For any thought properly designated Social *Darwinism,* however, we must wait until 1871. In that year Darwin published *The Descent of Man,* in which he applied the insights of his earlier work to the human species. And *pace* those who would rescue Darwin from himself, the fifth chapter of that work, titled "On the Development of the Intellectual and Moral Faculties," may be taken as the inaugural text of Social Darwinism. There, Darwin states what he takes to be the optimal situation in human society:

> ... the more intelligent members within the same community will succeed better in the long run than the inferior, and leave a more numerous progeny, and this is a form of natural selection. The more efficient causes of progress seem to consist of a good education during youth whilst the brain is impressible, and of a high standard of excellence, inculcated by

the ablest and best men, embodied in the laws, customs and traditions of the nation, and enforced by public opinion.[5]

The human species was brought to its present state of success through struggle and competition. And that present state is entirely provisional—humans, like all other forms of life, are ever in flux, ever in process of redefinition through interaction with its environment. Natural selection is at bottom, Darwin regularly reminds us, *sexual* selection; natural selection is a process that turns on differential reproduction—that the fittest leave behind *more* offspring; the less fit leave behind *less* offspring. That, at least, is the ideal. What we actually find when we look at society, however, is somewhat different:

... the reckless, degraded, and often vicious members of society, tend to increase at a quicker rate than the provident and generally virtuous members. Or as Mr. Greg puts the case: "The careless, squalid, unaspiring Irishman multiplies like rabbits: the frugal, foreseeing, self-respecting, ambitious Scot, stern in his morality, spiritual in his faith, sagacious and disciplined in his intelligence, passes his best years in struggle and in celibacy, marries late, and leaves few behind him. Given a land originally peopled by a thousand Saxons and a thousand Celts—and in a dozen generations five-sixths of the population would be Celts, but five-sixths of the property, of the power, of the intellect, would belong to the one-sixth of Saxons that remained. In the eternal 'struggle for existence,' it would be the inferior and less favoured race that had prevailed- and prevailed by virtue not of its good qualities but of its faults.[6]

For those keeping track, the squalid Irish are identified with the Celts, the provident Scots with the Saxons. Never mind the historical inaccuracy here (Scots too are a predominantly Celtic people, not Saxon), the alarm expressed was one heard with increasing urgency during the last two decades of the 19th century and the first two decades of the 20th. "Look at who's reproducing aplenty; and look who *isn't*. And what do those population dynamics bode for the future?" The problem, according to Darwin, is rooted in human nature, indeed, in one of the things we most admire in human nature—sympathy:

The aid which we feel impelled to give to the helpless is mainly an incidental result of the instinct of sympathy, which was originally acquired as part of the social instincts, but subsequently rendered, in the manner previously indicated, more tender and more widely diffused. Nor could we check our sympathy, even at the urging of hard reason, without deterioration in the noblest part of our nature ...[7]

But the result of this sympathy threatens not only society, but also the human species. In fact, it seems clear that for Darwin the line between sympathy and squeamishness tends to get blurred. In a passage that is both famous and notorious, he says:

> With savages, the weak in body or mind are soon eliminated; and those that survive commonly exhibit a vigorous state of health. We civilised men, on the other hand, do our utmost to check the process of elimination; we build asylums for the imbecile, the maimed, and the sick; we institute poor-laws; and our medical men exert their utmost skill to save the life of every one to the last moment ... It is surprising how soon a want of care, or care wrongly directed, leads to the degeneration of a domestic race; but excepting in the case of man himself, hardly any one is so ignorant as to allow his worst animals to breed.[8]

This passage may be said to embody the agenda of Darwin's theories with respect to society—that is, Social Darwinism. In the natural ambience of "the survival of the fittest," the term Darwin took from Spencer, society and the species are strengthened by the stern discipline of natural selection. Life in civilization is dedicated to easing the challenges that have terrified humans since humans first existed. There have been great successes, but those successes have had ironic consequences. Specifically, the challenges overcome by civilization have been the very sources of human excellences of every kind, from physical to emotional to intellectual. Our adversities, terrible as they have been, have made us what we are. Indeed, it was precisely those adversities that, through the rough processes of natural selection, forced us to become strong, to become smart, to develop all our virtues. Mitigate those adversities, and the strength, intelligence, and virtue to which they gave rise will correspondingly diminish. In the concluding chapter of *The Descent of Man,* Darwin sums up his position this way:

> The advancement of the welfare of mankind is a most intricate problem: all ought to refrain from marriage who cannot avoid abject poverty for their children; for poverty is not only a great evil, but tends to its own increase by leading to recklessness in marriage. On the other hand ... if the prudent avoid marriage, whilst the reckless marry, the inferior members tend to supplant the better members of society. Man, like every other animal, has no doubt advanced to his present high condition through a struggle for existence ... and if he is to advance still higher, it is to be

feared that he must remain subject to a severe struggle. Otherwise he would sink into indolence, and the more gifted men would not be more successful in the battle of life than the less gifted ... There should be open competition for all men; and the most able should not be prevented by laws or customs from succeeding best and rearing the largest number of offspring.[9]

The point made here by Darwin is as simple as it is alarming: the success of civilization has made life easier; that success has lowered the bar for survival and, by extension, has allowed the baleful propagation of the less-than-fittest. The easement of the human situation results in the diminishment of the health of the human species. We are faced, in Darwin's view, with a crisis. And while he sketched a description of that crisis in *The Descent of Man,* Darwin avoided extensive discussion of it in his published work. A more forceful and public analysis of the perceived crisis was spearheaded by the man who was to assume, especially in America, the mantle of the major prophet of Social Darwinism—Darwin's friend Herbert Spencer.

5

In his day, Herbert Spencer (1820-1903) was regarded as a preeminent philosopher; he was thought by some to be the Aristotle of his age. Spencer developed his social theories before the publication of Darwin's *Origin of the Species* in 1859. But with the rapid spread of Darwin's ideas, Spencer's theories gained an enhanced credibility; they were bathed in the allure of *science*—the new science, both exciting and disturbing, of evolution. Spencer's stature as a thinker was particularly magnified among readers in America, where his ideas proved more potent than those of Darwin himself. As the historian Richard Hofstadter put it in his 1944 study, *Social Darwinism in American Thought:*

> Spencer's philosophy was admirably suited to the American scene ... It offered a comprehensive world-view, uniting under one generalization everything in nature from protozoa to politics. Satisfying the desire of "advanced thinkers" for a world-system to replace the shattered Mosaic cosmogony, it soon gave Spencer a public influence that transcended Darwin's.[10]

And where Darwin's discussion of the social applications of his theories was circumspect, Spencer's was not. Here's what he says on the operation of natural selection within society:

> He on whom his own stupidity, or vice, or idleness entails loss of life must, in the generalizations of philosophy, be classed with the victims of weak viscera or malformed limbs ... Beings thus imperfect are nature's failures, and are recalled by her laws when found to be such. Along with the rest they are put on trial. If they are sufficiently complete to live, they do live, and it is well that they should live. If they are not sufficiently complete to live, they die, and it is best that they should die.[11]

This is not a diplomatic phrasing and Spencer doesn't intend it to be. In his view it is realism, not diplomacy, that is needed. At risk, in his view, is the well-being of the human species. And as Darwin was to claim later, the enemy of a healthy realism is sentimental and misguided sympathy. Here's how Spencer puts it:

> Sympathy with one in suffering suppresses, for the time being, remembrance of his transgressions. The feeling which vents itself in "poor fellow!" on seeing one in agony, excludes the thought of "bad fellow," which might at another time arise ... Those whose hardships are set forth in pamphlets and proclaimed in sermons and speeches which echo throughout society, are assumed to be all worthy souls, grievously wronged; and none of them are thought of as bearing the penalties of their misdeeds.[12]

Misdirected sympathy brings us to judge the wretched conditions of the foolish and improvident as *unjust*. Poverty and its attendant horrors, according to Spencer, are not an issue of social injustice, but of natural consequence. As we have seen with Darwin, Spencer too believed that civilization works *against* the dynamics of nature—civilization serves to mitigate the harshness of the natural selection process; it seeks to mitigate the very pressures that produce strength and virtue. Here's Spencer again:

> If to be ignorant were as safe as to be wise, no one would become wise. And all measures which tend to put ignorance upon a par with wisdom inevitably check the growth of wisdom. Acts of Parliament to save silly people from the evils [that result from their folly] ... are therefore bad. Unpitying as it looks, it is best to let the foolish man suffer the appointed penalty of his foolishness.[13]

And what comes between ignorance and its consequences, according to Spencer, are social programs designed to relieve the poor and unfortunate. For all that they may be well-intentioned, such programs are destructive. Is there no remedy to this dynamic by which the human species is weakened? Indeed there is, but that remedy entails the discipline and grit to allow the dynamics of nature to operate *within* society. It requires the ability to see nature and its ways as the *friend* of society and humanity, not as a menace. And it requires more than the ability to see this, it requires the ability to *act* on what is seen. Or to state the case more accurately, what is needed is the capacity to *refrain from action,* especially from so-called philanthropic action.

For Spencer, there is a deep irony in the word "philanthropy." As a social enterprise, philanthropy purports to act out of a love of humanity—hence its name. But because this enterprise is brought to the aid and support of the conspicuously unfit, it is in fact at *war* with humanity. Social welfare programs, however well-intentioned they may be, function as genetic time bombs for successive generations. These programs promote the careless reproduction of the careless; as such they burden talented and productive people with the maintenance of the inept. And this, for Spencer, is not philanthropy but *cruelty:*

> Fostering the good-for-nothing at the expense of the good is an extreme cruelty. It is a deliberate storing up of miseries for future generations. There is no greater curse to posterity than that of bequeathing them an increasing population of imbeciles and idlers and criminals. To aid the bad in multiplying is, in effect, the same as maliciously providing for our descendants a larger host of enemies.[14]

6

Spencer's thought was extremely popular in America, where Social Darwinism found strong support—and not just among intellectuals. Vice president Theodore Roosevelt delivered a speech in 1899 titled "The Strenuous Life," in which he clearly espoused the values of Social Darwinism:

> I preach to you, then, my countrymen, that our country calls not for the life of ease but for the life of strenuous endeavor. The twentieth century looms before us big with the fate of many nations. If we stand idly by, if we seek merely swollen, slothful ease and ignoble peace, if we shrink from the hard contests where men must win at hazard of their lives and at the risk

of all they hold dear, then the bolder and stronger peoples will pass us by, and will win for themselves the domination of the world.[15]

And in the world of economic power, figures like John D. Rockefeller and Andrew Carnegie were also staunch supporters of the doctrine of the survival of the fittest. In his study of Social Darwinism in America, Richard Hofstadter says this of Carnegie:

> The most prominent of the disciples of Spencer was Andrew Carnegie, who sought out the philosopher, became his friend, and showered him with favors. In his autobiography, Carnegie told how troubled and perplexed he had been over the collapse of Christian theology, until he took the trouble to read Darwin and Spencer.[16]

Another prominent supporter of Social Darwinism was William Graham Sumner (1840-1910). Sumner was trained as a minister, but later became a professor of sociology and economics at Yale University. A strident advocate of a capitalistic expression of "the survival of the fittest," Sumner was a one of the most prominent spokesmen of the doctrine at the turn of the century. To repeat a point made earlier, some Social Darwinists were bigots. But not all of them were, and one of the points emphasized by Sumner suggests that he was not. Speaking of what he took to be the key to *fitness* in the struggle for survival, he said in 1893:

> The evolution of intellectual power is consequent upon education, which is the great unfolding force. Hence, it follows, that those who command the largest educational advantages control those of inferior opportunities. To equalize these opportunities is the great purpose of the American free school system, to secure all mind evolution, the unfolding of its powers, so that the humblest citizen may become a thinker and be prepared to maintain his independence in all conflicts that may arise between contending classes.[17]

Power in the Darwinian struggle is, according to Sumner, *intellectual* power. It is intellectual power that determines a person's social station. Sumner was speaking of American culture a century ago, but his observation is one that, as we'll see in the next chapter, has even more relevance for the present than in 1893. Life in America does not reflect social equality, true. And Sumner is notorious for insisting that the existing social structure, with its class inequities, is exactly as it should be. Speaking against those who would institute fairness and equality in society, and who are critical of the rough stratifications found in the social order, Sumner says:

> They bring forward complaints which are really to be made, if at all, against the author of the universe for the hardships which man has to endure in his struggle with nature. The complaints are addressed, however, to society; that is to other men under the same hardships. The only social element, however, is the competition of life, and when society is blamed for the ills which belong to the human lot, it is only burdening those who have successfully contended with those ills with the further task of conquering the same ills over again for somebody else ... The law of the survival of the fittest was not made by man and cannot be abrogated by man. We can only, by interfering with it, produce the survival of the un-fittest.[18]

Disparate social circumstances do not compromise the American ideal of democracy, according to Sumner, because the equality that is essential to democracy is not an equality of *results,* but an equality of *opportunity.* And that equality of opportunity is established through none other than the public education system—which exists, in Sumner's words, "so that the humblest citizen may become a thinker." May—or may not. The education system is in place; it exists to provide equal opportunity to all. Those who are able to avail themselves of the advantages conferred by that system do so; those who are unable do not. And those who are not able to gain intellectual power through education gravitate to the lower level of society—a level that is appropriate to them, that is their *natural* place.

We may conclude, then, that the ideals of Social Darwinism were widely embraced in the halls of power in America. But the influence of these ideals was not restricted to the high levels. They also found popular expression; they served as the basis of the extremely influential novels of Horatio Alger.

7

Horatio Alger (1832-1899) wrote boys' novels that were exceptionally popular and influential—his books were intended, and were taken to be, educational and character-building stories. They were highly valued for conveying moral instruction to young minds in their formative phases. Although seldom read today except by academics, Alger's novels were hugely successful during his life and in the decades that followed it. Today, even people who know nothing of Alger or his novels use the phrase "Horatio Alger story" as a byword for American "do it yourself" success.

Alger's most famous novel was *Ragged Dick,* the story of a young boy living on the unfriendly streets of New York City. The protagonist goes from being an urchin with the street name "Ragged Dick" to being a budding success, Richard Hunter, Esquire. How is this extraordinary social ascent possible? The chief factors are presented by Alger this way, in a conversation between Ragged Dick and a fellow street-urchin named Johnny Nolan. We hear Johnny first:

> "I went to school once; but it was too hard work, so I give it up."
>
> "You're lazy Johnny—that's what's the matter. How'd you ever expect to know anything, if you don't try?"
>
> "I can't learn."
>
> "You can if you want to."
>
> Johnny Nolan was evidently of a different opinion. He was a good-natured boy, large of his age, with nothing particularly bad about him, but utterly lacking in that energy, ambition, and natural sharpness for which Dick was distinguished. He was not adapted to succeed in the life which circumstances had forced upon him; for in the street-life of the metropolis a boy needs to be on the alert, and have all his wits about him, or he will find himself wholly distanced by his more enterprising competitors for popular favor. To succeed in his profession, humble as it is, a boot-black must depend upon the same qualities which gain success in higher walks of life.[19]

It is important to note how Darwin's theories manifest themselves in Alger's story. I'll be talking for a moment now not about "our hero," Ragged Dick, but about poor Johnny Nolan. Johnny didn't try—Dick points that out to him regularly. But Dick doesn't really understand Johnny's problem. Johnny's real problem is not that he *won't,* but that he *can't.* The boy just wasn't born with sufficient grit. At the very beginning of the novel we read this comparison of the two boys:

> Now, in the boot-blacking business as well as in higher avocations, the same rule prevails, that energy and industry are rewarded and indolence suffers. Dick was energetic and on the alert for business, but Johnny was

the reverse. The consequence was that Dick earned probably three times as much as the other.[20]

Alger invites us to see that the differences in the two boys are differences that each was born with. To be sure, Johnny's a nice enough kid. He just wasn't lucky in what we would today call his genetic endowments. Life isn't fair; the social order of wealth and poverty reflects life's unfairness—it reflects the *natural* disparity in human talent. The wealthy have earned their wealth; the impoverished are where they are because, in the natural order of things, that's where they belong. Such is the view in Alger's popular novels.

8

In *Social Darwinism in American Thought*, Richard Hofstadter speaks of Social Darwinism as a phase, as something like a temporary trend—indeed the second chapter of his book is titled "The Vogue of Spencer." Why was Social Darwinism a *vogue*—and no more—in American thought? Certainly, the reason was not because the doctrine seemed unrealistic; on it own terms it clearly was. Indeed, as we've already seen, a call to *realism* was the watchword of the Social Darwinists. But no matter if the claims and agenda of Social Darwinism made sense to the head, they offended the heart. There is a certain irony here: Social Darwinists prided themselves on the gritty realism of their doctrine. But it was precisely the specifics of that realism—specifics realized not in theory, but all-too-visibly, in the street—that precluded Social Darwinism from having a lasting popularity in America. The doctrine couldn't take permanent root in the American psyche because it was simply too psychologically harsh. Its more candid proponents characterized it frankly as *cruel*. But they quickly added, by way of justification, that the ways of nature are cruel. Spencer's aspirations and optimism required a cold and clinical detachment toward the disturbing realities evident on the streets of most urban centers, and in rural areas as well. But what most Americans perceived in the doctrines was unvarnished heartlessness. And this perception was rooted in their core values—their religious values. Speaking of the obstacles faced by Social Darwinist theory in Europe, the historian Mike Hawkins characterizes the very points that worked decisively against the doctrine in America. Hawkins points out that implications of Social Darwinism go straight "to the fundamentals of Christianity itself. The truly valuable part of Christian teaching—the Golden Rule to love one's neighbor … the equality of men before God, charitable conduct towards the poor and wretched ... "[21] He also says:

> Modern 'savages,' children, women, criminals, the insane, epileptics—sometimes entire classes ... could be assigned inferior positions and substituted for one another on the evolutionary ladder. This tactic did not originate with Social Darwinism ... But Social Darwinism increased its plausibility and provided the value judgments implicit in these categorizations with a scientific mantle.[22]

Darwinism, especially in its social applications, smacked too much of a replacement of the law of God with the law of the jungle. The prescriptions of Social Darwinism were psychologically disturbing; pragmatic realism aside, most people do not want to embrace attitudes and policies that can feel, in midnight hours of reflection and candor, like nothing more than rationalized callousness and indifference. This psychological discomfort was then amplified to revulsion through an awareness of the horrific events of the mid-20th century in Europe. The sternness and dispassionate immunity to sentimentality recommended by Social Darwinist thinkers came to be reminiscent of the barbarous cruelty of Nazism. And so the appeal of Social Darwinism waned. In 1944, Richard Hofstadter had assumed that the views of Social Darwinism were *history:*

> What ever the course of social philosophy in the future, however, a few conclusions are now accepted by most humanists: that such biological ideas as the 'survival of the fittest,' whatever their doubtful value in natural science, are utterly useless in attempting to understand society ...[23]

But it seems that the winds are changing again. In his 1992 introduction to Hofstadter's book, Eric Foner makes the following observation:

> ... the most striking difference between Hofstadter's cast of mind and that of our own time lies in his resolute conviction that social Darwinism was an unfortunate but thankfully closed chapter in the history of social thought. Hofstadter wrote from the certainty that social Darwinism was demonstrably wrong, that biological analogies are "utterly useless" in understanding human society, that this episode had all been some kind of "ghastly mistake" ... But he could hardly have foreseen the resurrection in the 1980's of biological explanations for human development and of the social Darwinist mentality, if not the name itself ...[24]

In the next chapter we'll look at developments in American culture that once again invite calls to realism. Once again, even the most desperate of social circumstances may come to be seen as expressive of a deeper rightness, a justice deeper than the social order itself. But in the 21st century world, the sting of conscience will be quieted through the assurance that this "deep justice" is not the harsh, brutal realities of "nature, red in tooth and claw." Not the rough logic of natural selection, but a divine order is operative—one that will ultimately serve the well-being of even the most wretched individuals. In the long run, over the course of lives that follow the present one by way of reincarnation, all will be well. That assumption, again, is the concern of this book.

Notes

1. Sumner, W. G. "Socialism" in *Social Darwinism: Selected Essays of William Graham Sumner.* Englewood Cliffs, N. J.: Prentice-Hall, 1963, p.72.
2. Bannister, R. C. *Social Darwinism: Science and Myth in Anglo-American Social Thought.* Philadelphia: Temple Univ. Press, 1979, p.xii.
3. Radhakrishnan, 1965, p.73.
4. Darwin, 2003, p.262.
5. Darwin, C. *The Descent of Man and Selection in Relation to Sex.* Chapter 5. New York: The Modern Library, 1936, p.509.
6. Darwin, 1936, p.505.
7. Darwin, 1936, p.501-2.
8. Darwin, 1936, p.501.
9. Darwin, 1936, p.919.
10. Hofstadter, R. *Social Darwinism in American Thought.* Boston: Beacon Press, 1992, p.31.
11. Spencer, H. *Social Statics.* New York: Robert Schalkenbach Foundation, 1970, p.339-340.
12. Spencer, H. *The Man Versus the State.* Indianapolis: Liberty Classics, 1982, p.31.
13. Spencer, 1970, p.338.
14. Spencer, H. *The Study of Sociology.* New York: D. Appleton & Co., 1896, p.314.
15. Roosevelt, T. "The Strenuous Life," 1899. http://www.usembassy.de/usa/etexts/speeches/rhetoric/trlife.htm
16. Hofstadter, 1992, p.45.
17. Sumner, W. G. "What's Good for the Goose." *Locomotive Firemen's Magazine,* January 1893, 69. http://historymatters.gmu.edu/d/4999/
18. Sumner, 1963, p.16-7.
19. Alger, H. *Ragged Dick and Struggling Upward.* New York: Penguin Books, 1985, p.125.

20. Alger, 1985, p.8.
21. Hawkins, M. *Social Darwinism in European and American Thought: 1860 - 1945.* New York: Cambridge University Press, 1997, p.143.
22. Hawkins, 1997, p.81.
23. Hofstadter, 1992, p.204.
24. Hofstadter, 1992, p.xx.

9

O' BRAVE NEW WORLD—
COMPLETE WITH CASTES?

> I define globalization this way: it is the inexorable integration of markets, nation-states and technologies to a degree never witnessed before—in a way that is enabling individuals, corporations, and nation-states to reach around the world farther, faster, deeper and cheaper than ever before. This process of globalization is also producing a powerful backlash from those brutalized or left behind by this new system. The driving idea behind globalization is free-market capitalism ... Globalization means the spread of free-market capitalism to virtually every country in the world. Therefore, globalization also has its own set of economic rules—rules that revolve around opening, deregulating and privatizing your economy, in order to make it more attractive to foreign investment.
>
> —Thomas Friedman, *The Lexus and the Olive Tree*[1]

1

The processes described above by Thomas Friedman are historically unprecedented; globalization and its emerging effects are, quite literally, something new under the sun. And one of the most disturbing aspects of globalization is the rapid pace at which it is being asserted throughout the world. Put otherwise, one of the most important changes in the cultural world of the 21st century centers on change itself. Obviously, change is nothing new. Human civilization—life lived in some form of municipal organization—has been in a state of change since it first emerged in Mesopotamia some 8,000 years ago. But again, never has that change occurred at such an accelerated pace.

Rapid social change is not something that most people find congenial. We have seen how the evolutionary theories of Charles Darwin—with their emphasis on change over permanence—generated a sense of insecurity and disorientation in the 19th century. Evolutionary theory forced a rethinking of fundamental values. In a similar way, here at the beginning of the 21st century, the speed and the depth of changes precipitated by globalization is forcing a rethinking of fundamental values. And the values being challenged are not those of the marketplace alone. Like the Darwinian crisis of the 19th century, the change wrought by globalization challenges traditional understandings of human dignity and identity. And though the 21st century has not yet found its Tennyson to poignantly express its fears in verse, the sense of insecurity that permeates American culture, as well as many other cultures around the world, is tangible.

Amidst all the rapid changes, there are two trends that are particularly worrisome. Taken together, they threaten the continuance of representative democracy on the one hand, and our sense of human dignity on the other. The first of these trends is an acute vertical stratification of society along lines of both wealth and (more alarming) cognitive ability. The second is a predictable consequence of social transitions in which traditional modes of identity are destabilized. As Friedman describes it, globalization has an inherent dynamic that reorganizes society along corporate lines. Nations are depotentiated; identity rooted in the nation becomes tenuous. When that happens, people often seek identity in terms more primitive than the nation—in tribalism or religious extremism. Identity comes to be sought through an ideology of *difference,* through what separates us rather than what we have in common.

In this chapter, we will consider how these two trends—acute social stratification and tribalism—might interact. Each is dangerous enough on its own terms, taken together they are even more dangerous. But if combined with reincarnation theory, the blend might tip American culture into catastrophic developments.

2

We begin with social stratification. Like social change, social stratification is nothing new. But in the context of American history since World War II, it *feels* new, it *feels* unprecedented. And again, it is happening *fast;*

its rapid pace is one its most unsettling aspects. An important way in which globalization is forcefully asserting itself centers on the issue of employment, the work that people do. In America, work is more than a job, it is essential to a person's sense of identity. In his recent study of the American character, *Who Are We? The Challenges to America's National Identity*, historian Samuel P. Huntington makes these observations on the historical relation between identity and work in America:

> Bourgeois societies promote work. America, the quintessential bourgeois society, glorifies work. When asked "What do you do?" almost no American dares answer "Nothing" ... Throughout American history social standing has depended on working and earning money by working. Employment is the source of self-assurance and independence ... The concept of "the self-made man" is a distinctive product of this American environment and culture ... Americans have not only worked more than other peoples, but they have found satisfaction in and identified with their work more than others have.[2]

The work we do gives us a sense of identity and meaning. It serves to define us to others—and to ourselves. And right here is where the impact of globalization makes itself felt in acutely personal terms.

3

In addition to connecting and unifying the world, globalization is at the same time profoundly dividing it. And the boundaries of these new divisions are not national borders, but *neighborhoods*. We see the process dramatically evident in America. Communities are being crystallized along lines of economic status, yes. But of itself this doesn't tell the whole story. For in the new world of globalization, wealth will increasingly be the consequence of the capacity for high cognitive performance, a capacity that will be *the* decisive advantage in the fast-paced, high-tech ambience of the Information Age. And this brings us back to the concept of work. Former Secretary of Labor Robert B. Reich, in *The Work of Nations: Preparing Ourselves for 21st Century Capitalism*, calls the high cognitive performers "symbolic analysts," and offers this disturbing prediction of their future relationship to the less gifted members of society:

> By 2020, the top fifth of American earners will account for more than 60 percent of all the income earned by Americans; the bottom fifth, for 2 percent. Symbolic analysts will withdraw into ever more isolated enclaves

> ... Distinguished from the rest of the population by their global linkages, good schools, comfortable lifestyles, excellent health care, and abundance of security guards, symbolic analysts will complete their secession from the union. The townships and urban enclaves where they reside ... will bear no resemblance to the rest of America; nor will there be any direct connections between the two. America's poorest citizens, meanwhile, will be isolated within their own enclaves of urban and rural desperation; an ever-larger proportion of their young men will fill the nation's prisons.[3]

Reich's baleful assessment, published in 1991, reads more like a *description* than a prediction in the middle of the first decade of the 21st century. Some say that we are witnessing the evaporation of the middle class, and worse, the proliferation of an intransigent, impoverished class already being cynically referred to as a *postmodern peasantry*. Whatever the phrasing, one thing is undeniable: American society is undergoing acute vertical stratification. Besides the changing nature of work, there is another key to understanding this stratification—education. Public education has historically taken to be the guarantor of representative democracy in America. But as with work, things are changing. Mickey Kaus, in *The End of Equality*, speaks of the changing significance of education in America:

> For decades after World War II, guidance counselors told high-schoolers that without a college education they'd be sunk, and for decades the guidance counselors were wrong. In the sixties and early seventies ... the economic advantage of a college degree actually diminished. In 1973, 30-year-old men with four years of college made, on average, just 15 percent more than 30-year-old men who only had high-school degrees. But then the advantage of the college-educated grew rapidly until, by 1986, the gap in earnings had widened to 49 percent. The world the guidance counselors warned us about has finally arrived.[4]

Now, at the beginning of the 21st century, education matters as it has never mattered before. Jobs that require moderate education yet pay reasonably well are disappearing. High-pay, low-skill employment had its heyday in the decades following World War II. The prevalence of assembly-line factory industries, coupled with successes of labor unions, made possible good wages—and hence good lifestyles—for people who may even have lacked a high school education. Indeed, the income of many factory workers with a high school diploma (or less) was often higher than that of the school teachers who had attained an undergraduate degree. But as Kaus points out, those days are over:

> For an American auto worker, a strong back was once a valuable attribute. Increasingly, it's not, as "routine production" jobs ... move overseas. Meanwhile, American brainworkers ... are still competitive. They include the usual suspects: lawyers, investment bankers ... research scientists, academics ... architects, writers and editors, musicians, and television and film producers ... What becomes of American production workers, if they lack the necessary skills to become "symbolic analysts"? They are forced to compete for the remaining non-intellectual jobs that can't be shipped overseas ... They work as store clerks, restaurant workers, nurses, cabdrivers, custodians, and security guards. Unfortunately, these service workers don't get paid very well ... [5]

This disparity of wealth is based not on inherited privilege but on *education*—and a bit more problematically, on a willingness and ability to embrace education. The gulf between the well-educated and the ill-educated is redefining America, according to many informed commentators. As Nicholas Lehmann puts it in *The Big Test: the Secret History of the American Meritocracy:*

> Here is what American society looks like today [1999]. A thick line runs through the country, with people who have been to college on one side of it and people who haven't on the other. This line gets brighter all the time. Whether a person is on one side of the line or the other is now more indicative of income, of attitudes, and of political behavior than any other line one might draw: region, race, age, religion, sex, class.[6]

Note that higher education (or the lack of it) is taken to be a more reliable indicator of socio-economic status than even *race*. This is an extremely important point. Certainly we must remain vigilant, as the issue of race has a deeply conflicted history in America. But although it remains an object of progressives' doubts and bigots' hopes, a racial basis of the cultural divide is not supported by the evidence. For one thing, as Kaus points out, the cultural stratification underway emphatically includes blacks in the higher strata:

> Middle-class blacks, especially, joined the exodus [from the cities during the 1990's] during these years. As affluent taxpayers left, urban tax bases shriveled, which meant there was less money available for central city schools to educate their increasingly intractable student populations, which in turn caused more taxpaying parents to leave.[7]

In addition, the cultural divide underway is leaving under-educated whites on the lower side of the "thick line" referred to by Lehmann as surely as it is leaves under-educated blacks and others. The under-educated are being left behind; their communities are abandoned by the educated, and consequently more affluent, people who were raised there. The affluent leave to find better housing and more upscale communities. And one of the most important reasons for their leaving centers on *education*. Parents recognize very quickly that children are deeply influenced by their peers—in this case, by the children with whom they attend school. They realize, as Kaus puts it, that

> ... my kid's education obviously depends, to some degree, on the attitudes and actions of the other children he goes to school with. He will learn from them as well as from his teachers ... That means parents also want schools that exclude the "wrong" kind of people. A lot of this is snobbery, some of it is racism, but the point is it's not just snobbery and racism. To at least some extent, kids will learn more math and speak clearer English if they're surrounded by kinds who care about learning math and who speak clear English.[8]

This concern has resulted in a determination to *separate,* says Kaus, and there is more at stake than separate schools. With the ideal of common schools, the ideal of social equality—not economic equality, now, but social equality—is being abandoned. Kaus again:

> Common schools, ideally, are places where children of all incomes actually meet under conditions of equal dignity. They curse the same teachers, play on the same football fields, chase after the same dates for the prom.[9]

The situation at the beginning of the 21st century, then, may be summarized as follows. The shift to high technology employment has placed a premium on higher education. The less educated are left in lower income jobs, and as a result their communities are coming to be increasingly impoverished. And although these communities are becoming isolated, their under-educated residents are visible everywhere: to cite only one example, they staff the shopping malls that are omnipresent in American society. There they work in what is called the "service sector," and they typically do so for little more than minimum wage. They are not expected to be happy in their circumstances.

A combination of low-wage employment and unemployment has produced communities that are coming to be defined in terms of *difference*. The term "underclass" is being used with increasing frequency. We must not confuse the concept of *underclass,* as Kaus and other social critics use the term, with the working poor. It used to be assumed that the poor are pretty much like the rest us, just short of money. With the emergence of the concept of the underclass, however, we are coming to suspect that at least some of the poor are not a bit like us—they are ensnared in personal and social habit patterns that are acutely self-destructive. The processes of globalization has brought about, the suspicion goes, a class of people who are *different*. Different, but different in a pejorative and disturbing sense. With the emergence of the underclass we are witnessing the simultaneous emergence of an new attitude toward the unfortunate in society—an attitude of distrust and fear.

And nowhere do such feelings hold sway so much as in regard to education—not education in the abstract, now, but the education of children that are beloved and cherished. In such circumstances, parents are compelled to think realistically. They are, Kaus tells us, forced to face a new set of facts:

> ... the reality is that the underclass does exist, and it is the underclass that transforms the suburbs' natural exclusionary impulse into a primordial demand. All it takes is a single drive-by shooting, or the sight of metal-detectors in school hallways, to make the virtues of class-mixing seem fairly theoretical. It will be one thing for social egalitarians to ask a $150,000-a-year lawyer to risk sending his child to school with the children of $15,000-a-year working-class families. It's another thing to ask him to send his kids to a school where they might be stabbed by crackheads. The Civic Liberal ideal of class-mixing in the classroom is quite hopeless as long as the underclass is one of the classes to be mixed.[10]

Nor is this concern restricted to the white or Asian educated classes—it emphatically includes those blacks who leave behind the poverty of urban neighborhoods: "The point of schools is to transmit culture, and nobody (in the black middle class, especially) wants his kids immersed in a culture of poverty."[11] If the impulse to separate is, for the educated classes, what Kaus calls "a primordial demand," then social stratification threatens to take on a rigid and impassible aspect. What then of the great hope offered by American society—equality not of *results,* but of *opportunity?*

Do not, warns Kaus, be seduced by hoary ideals. Do not trust in the hope that, while there may not be equality of results, we can still have equality of *opportunity* in the context of globalization and its free-market capitalism. The world of the 21st century has exhibited a nasty tendency that has attended capitalism from the start. Specifically, capitalism has an inherent bias against equality. As Kaus puts it, to embrace capitalism is to embrace *inequality:*

> ... you cannot decide to keep all the nice parts of capitalism and get rid of all the nasty ones. You cannot have capitalism without "selfishness," or even "greed," because they are what make the system work. You can't have capitalism and material equality, because capitalism is constantly generating extremes of *in*equality as some individuals strike it rich—and then use their success as the basis for still further riches—while others fail and fall on hard times. Even if you are willing to settle for "equality of opportunity," you can't really have it under capitalism unless ... you're also prepared to get rid of the family. One of the motives that drives the system, after all, is the idea of giving one's children a better life—but if that is allowed, then the children of capitalism's "winners" start out their lives with an inevitable advantage in resources.[12]

What is one of the first things wealthy folk do with their money? They enhance the opportunities of their children. Parents will inevitably seek to privilege their children—they don't want their children to be just "one of the class," they want them to be at the *head* of the class, or as close to that position as possible. Recall Plato's eugenic hopes as discussed in Chapter 4. Plato may have been one of the most brilliant minds in history, but we've seen that he was deeply and dangerously naive in his hope to manipulate the best and brightest in his Republic into being conned into a rigged breeding lottery, and further into being blithely indifferent as to the identity of their offspring. Such naivete is not supported in the culture of America today: the ideals of a common culture are being swept aside by parents' concern for the education of their children. Never mind economic equality, the aspiration to social equality is being swamped in concerns over differences that are indisputable. And that brings us to the second trend wrought by the rapid transitions of globalism referred to earlier—a reversion to more primitive modes of identity.

4

The dynamics of social stratification are abetted significantly by another trend—a tendency to construe identity through *difference* that has become fashionable. This is a *difference* actively embraced by population sub-groups, not an identity ascribed to them by others as a disparagement. This is perhaps a predictable effect of the dizzying pace of globalization. The social vertigo is succinctly described by Walter Truett Anderson:

> We must understand—and the kindly hoards of liberals, New Agers, and one-worlders who think globalism is the end to all our troubles need to understand—that it is one of the most psychologically and politically threatening events in all of human history ... The collapse of a belief system can be like the end of the world ... Even those who are most oppressed by a belief system often fear the loss of it. People can literally cease to know who they are.[13]

And people typically don't deal gracefully with such feelings: in the face of such widespread insecurity, primitive and simplistic models of identity become increasingly attractive. Benjamin Barber, in *Jihad vs. McWorld: How Globalism and Tribalism Are Reshaping the World*, uses the metaphor of McWorld to represent the forces of corporate globalism, and the metaphor of Jihad represent the predicable reactions to McWorld that take the forms of religious fundamentalism, political extremism, and tribalism. Here's how he puts it:

> In being reduced to a choice between the market's universal church and a retribalizing politics of particularist identities, peoples around the globe are threatened with an atavistic return to medieval politics where local tribes and ambitious emperors together ruled the world entire, women and men ... lived out isolated lives in warring fiefdoms defined by involuntary (ascriptive) forms of identity.[14]

The reaction that Barber characterizes as Jihad is at bottom a desperate quest for meaningful identity in a context in which familiar models of identity are in rapid process of evaporation—a quest that finds resolution in any of the fashionable varieties of identity politics. And, it is important to note, this essentially *pre*-modern mode of identity is generated by the *post*-modern realities of corporate globalization; McWorld and Jihad, in Barber's view, have a reciprocal development:

> Jihad pursues a bloody politics of identity, McWorld a bloodless economics of profit. Belonging by default to McWorld, everyone is a consumer; seeking a repository for identity, everyone belongs to some tribe.[15]

And he continues:

> The phenomena to which I apply the phrase [=Jihad] have innocent enough beginnings: identity politics and multicultural diversity can represent strategies of the free society trying to give expression to its diversity. What ends as Jihad may begin as a simple search for a local identity, some set of common personal attributes to hold out against the numbing and neutering uniformities of industrial modernization and the colonizing culture of McWorld.[16]

Jihad, then, is resistance to the homogenizing and threatening global reality of McWorld. Nor is this mentality restricted to underdeveloped countries. Barber drives home this point in regard to the Oklahoma City bombing in 1995:

> The authorities immediately suspected Jihad. They were right, although mistakenly they thought Jihad meant foreign: Islamic or Arab or Iranian. But Jihad had come home to American in all its native ferocity. Homegrown, it stalks the heartland.[17]

It is clear that Americans are in no way immune to the identity crisis brought on by the galloping pace of change. The sociologist Todd Gitlin, in *The Twilight of Common Dreams,* also speaks of the growing tendency to seek identity through an ideology of difference, a tendency that he sees as rooted in insecurity:

> ... the contemporary passion for difference is also the consequence of unsettled psychological states. The American pace of change constantly eats away at identity—and just as reliably kicks up materials for manufacture, the stitching together, of new possibilities. The search for hard-edged social identities is surely an overcompensation. Americans have gravitated toward racial, ethnic, religious, sexual, and subcultural distinctions partly to build ramparts against confusion ... An intolerance for one's own confusion generates a frantic search for hard-and-fast identity labels. Beneath the flux, America has developed the countertendency toward a fundamentalist identity culture.[18]

Understandable though it may be, this development accomplishes more than half the leg-work and heavy-lifting needed for the institutionalization of a caste system in America. For the essence of a caste system is the assumption that people are *different,* really different—and that they are at different places in society because they were *born* different. Just this is the concern expressed by Mickey Kaus:

... the wealthiest 20 or 30 percent of Americans are "seceding," as Robert Reich put it, into separate, often self-sufficient suburbs, where they rarely even meet members of non-wealthy classes, except in the latter's role as receptionists or repairmen. And is it the gnawing sense that, in their isolation, these richer Americans not only are passing their advantages on to their children, but are coming to think that those advantages are deserved, that they and their children are, at bottom, not just better off but better?[19]

If we refer back to the apologists for caste in India reviewed in Chapter 3, we saw that they too insisted on identity through *difference*. And of course difference among humans is indisputable. But, as I asserted in my discussion of caste in India, such differences pertain to *individuals*, not groups. What identity politics shares in common with Indian caste theory is the tendency to impute the differences so evident among individuals to *groups*.

During the past decade, a popular admonition has been to "Celebrate Diversity!" But it is clear that the diversity to be celebrated is not philosophical diversity, or individual diversity of any kind. The diversity at issue is a *collective* diversity, a diversity of groups—specifically, ethnic and racial groups. And our celebration of *that* type of diversity is likely to be a very grim party. My concern here is that the proudly asserted claim that "We're different!" may well come to be met with a condescending rejoinder—"Indeed you are ... "

This is where claims of difference and identity politics meet fatefully with the vertical stratification discussed earlier. Given the dramatic changes in employment and the enhanced role of higher education described earlier, it is inevitable that those individuals capable of advanced education will earn more money and will live differently and, worry many like Kaus, separately. In the 21st century, it is inevitable that disparate cognitive skills will yield disparate standards of living—standards of living that are radically disparate. These twin forces—economic stratification speaking the language of *inevitability,* and identity politics speaking the language of *ethnic pride* and *authenticity*—have brought about a cultural ambience in which it is commonplace to *think*, if not to speak in public, of "those people." For a while now, we'll be in some ugly territory.

5

The reader may sensibly be wondering what the foregoing concerns about recent developments in American culture have to do with the central issue of this book—the social consequences of the doctrine of reincarnation. The relevance may be seen in a book published in 1994, a book that created a scandal in American intellectual circles. Titled *The Bell Curve: Intelligence an Class Structure in American Life,* the book was co-authored by the psychologist Richard J. Herrnstein and the social scientist Charles Murray. The thesis of the book was seen by many as a public statement of a disturbing suspicion in American culture. I treat the book here because it is my contention that both the assumptions and the predictions found in it are given significant impetus by the current rise in popularity of reincarnation.

But I want to be careful. In the Introduction to this study, I insisted that to subscribe to reincarnation theory is not thereby to be wicked. I reassert that view now. At the same time, my purpose in this book is to sound an alarm: widespread belief in reincarnation carries with it consequences that would horrify the typical American adherent to the doctrine.

And so we proceed. The background to *The Bell Curve* is the developments that have already been covered in this chapter. We've seen that high technology and globalization have decisively transformed the nature of employment. High-salary jobs now require high cognitive capacities. Increasingly, intelligence will determine income, which in turn will determine social class. And according to the hypothesis advanced in *The Bell Curve,* this means that society will be naturally segregated in terms of cognitive capacity. This is nothing new. But unlike social critics like Nicholas Lehmann and Mickey Kaus, who see black Americans on *both* sides of what Lehmann calls the "thick line" of higher education that divides American society, Herrnstein and Murray take high cognitive capacity to be reflected in *race.* One of the many points argued in their book is that intelligence is unevenly distributed among the racial groups comprising America—a disappointing assertion, and one utterly unnecessary to their major thesis. It was this racist assertion that deafened most American intellectuals to any other points the book presented. As a culture, we are so harried by guilt, paranoia, and insecurity around race that we don't really know how to think about it. The book was roundly—and in the view of many informed experts, rightly—condemned for misuse of genetic theory, for distorted statistical assessment, and most of all for its racist bias. As I said, we'll be in some ugly territory for a while.

Herrnstein and Murray do not celebrate social polarization. Consistent with my concerns, they predict the emergence of a caste system in America, a development they deplore—and there's no reason to doubt their sincerity on this point. They rehearse the developments of "an increasingly isolated cognitive elite" and "a deteriorating quality of life for people at the bottom end of the cognitive ability distribution." And they conclude:

> Unchecked, these trends will lead the U.S. toward something resembling a caste society, with the underclass mired ever more firmly at the bottom and the cognitive elite ever more firmly anchored at the top, restructuring the rules of society so that it becomes harder and harder for them to lose. Among the other casualties of this process would be American civil society as we have known it.[20]

These altered circumstances will necessitate the institution of what they call a *custodial* state. The transition to a custodial state will be rationalized and defended, Herrnstein and Murray predict, through an emphasis on the government's moral responsibilities—responsibilities to provide for the human needs of the underclass, responsibilities to provide for security requirements of the cognitive elite. But above all, the agenda will be driven by an insistence that the limitations of the underclass must be frankly acknowledged—and must be accommodated with equal frankness. For example, they predict:

> It will be agreed that the underclass cannot be trusted to use cash wisely. Therefore policy will consist of greater benefits, but these benefits will be primarily in the form of services rather than cash.[21]

The enhanced benefits to be provided will include, speculate Herrnstein and Murray, things like the following. Child care, in which the care, education, and social training of children will be taken from the family and assumed by the government. Housing will be provided at low or no cost, but this will be *controlled* housing in which behavior can be monitored through various surveillance options, including the issuance of identity cards. There will be a standardization of vigorous, low-tolerance policing of both public and private behavior. The successful implementation of such benefits will require one other thing:

> *The underclass will become even more concentrated spatially than it is today.* The expanded network of day care centers, homeless shelters, public housing, and other services will always be located in the poorest

part of the inner city, which means that anyone who wants access to them will have to live there.[22]

This custodial state will assume a lack of responsibility on the part of the underclass housed and "cared for." All this will proceed under the banner of "for their own good." The policies implemented will no doubt be scripted as both caring and responsible. It will be useful to remind ourselves again that apologists for the caste system in India also spoke of it as being caring and responsible—as protecting the weak and less capable. Recall the claims cited above in Chapter 3:

> Radhakrishnan calls for *realism* in the face of indisputable differences in intellectual abilities, the very circumstances described by Herrnstein and Murray, and the very call to realism voiced by them. Further, Radhakrishnan claims that the caste system is a means of humanely accommodating these disparities: "Blood tells. We cannot make genius out of mediocrity or good ability out of inborn stupidity by all the aids of the environment. It does not, however, mean that nature is all and nurture is nothing. The kind of nurture depends on the group and its type. So long as we had the caste system, both nature and nurture co-operated ... "

> Vivekananda claimed that "In Europe, it is everywhere victory to the strong and death to the weak. In the land of Bharata (India), every social rule is for the protection of the weak. Such is our ideal of caste ... "

By contrast, Herrnstein and Murray offer no such comforting assurances about the emergence of social castes that they see as imminent in America. The situation will be, they predict, like "a high-tech and more lavish version of the Indian reservation."[23] They further point out that the negative effects of this caste structure will not remain neatly contained on underclass reservations. American culture, they say, will be reshaped to its roots:

> It is difficult to imagine the United States preserving its heritage of individualism, equal rights before the law, free people running their own lives, once it is accepted that a significant part of the population must be made permanent wards of the state.[24]

Again, Herrnstein and Murray see this as an acutely deplorable development, and they lament the prospect of a custodial state as the means by which a caste system may come to be institutionalized. Not everyone, however, is troubled at the prospect. Some welcome it. What could such people be thinking? Meet Ian Angell.

6

Ian Angell is a British information scientist. In *The New Barbarian Manifesto: How to Survive the Information Age,* he argues that the fate of workers is bound up with the modes of the production of wealth. There was a time when workers—and the particular skills entailed in being a worker—were needed. But that time is at and end. And the end will not be pleasant. Here's how Angell sees it:

> Because the masses were needed in that [older] production process, the bourgeoisie was forced to share the wealth around, and this eventually led to the present dependency culture. But in the Information Age, who are the new bourgeoisie, now that production takes place inside a human head rather than in a factory of machines? And what are their attitudes toward to the masses now they no longer need them?[25]

What will happen to those displaced masses in the upcoming shifts in the production of wealth? What will happen to those in the Information Age, amidst the dynamics of globalization, who are no longer needed? Angell answers his own questions by referring to Herrnstein and Murray's book:

> Societies are stratifying. New elites are appearing. Something inevitably self-selecting is happening. In his book *The Bell Curve* ... libertarian Charles Murray predicts that society will polarize, as the rich or intelligent will choose breeding partners only from within their own social group, and the masses likewise. The future is about inequality, and at the very bottom of the heap, Western societies are already witnessing the emergence of a rapidly expanding underclass ... In the transition to inequality we can expect massive civil unrest and disorder. Those with nothing have nothing to lose.[26]

Where Robert Reich speaks of "symbolic analysts," Angell speaks of "new barbarians." These are the high cognitive performers who will constitute a new elite, and he extols them as

> ... barbarians who care nothing for the polite society of the 20th century, for its arbitrary logic, its models and moralities, its philosophies, its politics, its genteel manners and bourgeois sentimentality—for its degeneracy. The barbarians are at the gate. Our Rome is burning! The barbarians know that societal evolution is not benign. Evolution is "nature red in tooth and claw." It spawns carnivores as well as herbivores. The

carnivorous barbarians care nothing for democracy or the rules of parliament, that representative of herbivores. Grass eaters beware, the jackals are circling; the hyenas are laughing.[27]

Hyenas indeed. There are clearly elements of showmanship and swagger in what Angell says. And as so often in political theatrics, his presentation seems to be geared more to shock than to inform or communicate. Angell seems more than a little anxious to have us see him as *bad*—bad-to-the-bone. Amidst all his strutting and crowing he issues a call not so much to realism as to *Schadenfreude*. Throughout his book, he is concerned less with celebrating the triumph of the strong than relishing the misery of the less-than-strong.

7

We turn again to social critic Walter Truett Anderson. In his 2001 analysis of globalization, *All Connected Now: Life in the First Global Civilization,* he takes Angell and his swagger seriously. He does not endorse Angell's views, but expresses concern that these views are finding a more sympathetic hearing that we might expect. He says:

> There are no apologies for the inequalities of rich and poor in *The New Barbarian Manifesto;* rather, there is a conviction that business should be running the world together with a Darwinian acceptance of the inevitability of winners and losers—big winners and big losers ... although this particular take on reality may not be frequently expressed in public discourse, it is the way many people actually see the world.[28]

I do not agree. There will always be *some* that find the gloating disposition espoused by Angell attractive. Some, but not many—at least not a demographically significant *many*. And there is a reason for this. As we saw in the last chapter, a majority of Americans have historically been repulsed by theories, like Social Darwinism in its more strident expressions, that scripted social indifference as "realism." Americans recoil from the notion that social conscience is for sissies. And so it seems to me unlikely that the celebration of cruelty endemic to Angell's position will find broad acceptance in America.

And yet the situation is not so simple. It would be naive to ignore the fact that American culture is confronted with grave challenges. As discussed above, globalization is transforming the nature of employment in favor of cognitive ability and education. The ensuing vertical stratification of American society is threatening the fabric of common citizenship. A national identity crisis is underway, and one response to this crisis is the emergence of identity politics—an ideology that celebrates *group* identity over individual identity. But there's more, and worse: group identity is taken to embody differential cognitive abilities, those very abilities that are proving increasingly decisive to success in the emerging corporate global culture that Benjamin Barber calls *McWorld*.

It is not my concern in what follows to issue a call to avert the transitions that are so rapidly transforming American society. Few among informed social commentators doubt that momentous change is at hand, change that for a variety of reasons is seen as imminent. Corporate globalism has a momentum that suggests inevitability. Supercharged by the internet and satellite broadcasts, corporate values are (often subliminally) permeating culture throughout the world, subtly subverting traditional values. Again, my concern is not to decry the transitions at hand, but to draw attention to the ways in which they will make reincarnation extremely attractive—and disastrous.

Reincarnation will not of itself precipitate this dystopian scenario; that, as just stated, is likely to be wrought through the effects of globalization. But widespread belief in reincarnation will promote the *acceptance* of this scenario. It will disarm the impulse to avert it. The doctrine will sabotage the one force that can bring about a more humanitarian 21st century society—the traditional American sense of *outrage* at human misery. Humanitarian progress has typically marched on the feet of indignation. "We won't *have* this!" Reincarnation theory tranquilizes that vital indignation. Reformers have typically sought to awaken our conscience. Where the theories of an Ian Angell serve to affront the social conscience, the theory of reincarnation serves to anaesthetize it. The doctrine of reincarnation frames the outrageous not just in terms of necessity, but in terms of *rightness*. It provides comfort and assurance that the intolerable is a manifestation of "deep justice." The people at the bottom end of the incipient vertical stratification of society will come to be seen as people who by dint natural law or divine order are relegated to the lower orders, to the lower *castes* of society. These people, we will be assured, have made choices; they have karmic *business* to work out—at least in this particular life. All is well.

And how could such psychological legerdemain occur on a mass scale? Americans would do well to remind themselves that if caste could arise in India, a culture steeped in reflection and ethical sensibilities, if caste could seem a good thing to minds like Vivekananda, Radhakrishnan, and Gandhi, then we in the postmodern West are by no means immune. Our consciousness is conditioned to unsuspected depths by the commercialism that so expertly enfolds us, and we cannot sensibly assume that we are magically resistant to the psychological comforts and assurances that reincarnation doctrine carries with it. The monstrous realities of caste in India are well documented, as is the persistence of those realities into the 21st century. And Americans can ill afford a smug condescension toward the lamentable history and present plight of India in regard to the institution of caste: with the incipient popularity of reincarnation theory we may be faced with nothing less.

8

Let me review my concerns. Although it is fairly widespread (27% of the population, according to 2003 polls), belief in reincarnation has not yet reached that critical point at which it might significantly impact American cultural dynamics. It is my contention that, should such a critical point in popular belief be reached, it would be bad, indeed disastrous for America. I make this claim because the psychological dynamics inherent in the doctrine of reincarnation tend to ease a transition toward a *de facto* caste system. To make my case, I have presented and assessed a series of historical developments relevant to a rise in popularity of the belief in reincarnation. I have analyzed the circumstances in which reincarnation theory successfully took root—as, for example, in India. I have also analyzed the historical circumstances in the West in which the theory arose but did not successfully take root. There was the Greek fluorescence of the doctrine, culminating in Plato's philosophy, which was swept aside by the Christian promise of personal immortality. And there was the more recent popularity of reincarnation in the Theosophical movement, a flowering that failed to take root, as we saw, largely because of the tom-foolery of the leading Theosophists.

Even without the inclusion of the theories of karma and reincarnation into the American mind-set, we've seen in this chapter that the tendencies toward a *de facto* caste structure of American society are increasingly undeniable. But these tendencies are, historically, grounded in a kind of Yankee tough-mindedness—in some variant of Social Darwinism. What belief in karma and reincarnation contributes to these emergent tendencies, as has been stated above, is a softening of focus. That is, the cold call to realism on the part of Social Darwinism come to be presented in a kinder, gentler light. The ways of the world are, on closer consideration, not really cruel, but *just*—people have earned and even somehow *chosen* their respective stations in life. And more than merely just, the ways of the world reflect a deeply *spiritual* reality.

Here is born a tolerance of dehumanizing conditions that masks itself as compassion. But if it is to be termed compassion, then it is a bitter compassion indeed—compassion for those who are working their way to beatitude through "working out their karma." In this connection it will be useful to recall the observations, previously cited in Chapter 2, of Christopher W. Gowans. Speaking of the wrenching specter of a child stricken by cancer, Gowans argues that "we probably would not think this cruel if the child was the rebirth of Joseph Stalin."[29] And as with that child, so we might come to see entire classes of people in desperate straits as working off the karmic effects of hateful behavior in previous lives. And—this is the important part—we could come to see these people in the miserable conditions that they'd earned for themselves not through the eyes of contempt, but through the eyes of *compassion*.

This point is so important because it constitutes one of the greatest challenges posed by the doctrines of karma and reincarnation: the harm that such doctrines portend is not motivated by evil or malice, but by compassion and spirituality. And how can one object to compassion? To spirituality? It is possible, of course; this book is a sustained attempt to make just such an objection. But the odds are stacked against the effort, ironically, because of the very *goodness* of the intentions at issue. To say it again, those who believe in reincarnation are typically among the best of us.

We've seen that Social Darwinism serves to *legitimate* acute social disparities. But except for the few, the tough-minded, Social Darwinism doesn't allow us to feel good about those social disparities. Or about *ourselves* as we live among those disparities. In this regard, the doctrine of reincarnation does much better. It does not demand toughness, instead it invites us to sensitivity—it allows us to *feel good* as we live among people in dire circumstances. It is a telling point (and here is an echo of Herder's concern cited in Chapter 5) that the conjunction of karma and reincarnation allow us to be more comfortable witnessing human misery than in eating, say, a chicken salad or a hamburger.

The high-mindedness that underlies reincarnation theory is what serves to make it so impervious—and not only to those well-intentioned folk who tolerate savage circumstances with equanimity. The doctrine of reincarnation will also serve to psychologically empower those who would actively *perpetrate* those circumstances. An iron-fisted conqueror, or a hard-hearted captain of industry, can be brought over time to be reflective and more sensitive. Sooner or later, powerful people want to see their power as grounded not merely in might, but also in *right*. Battle hymns that celebrate victory and conquest change, over time, into anthems of praise for peace and fairness. Robber barons come, over time, to act philanthropically—they build libraries, they fund charitable foundations. Manifest injustice is a thorn in the psyche of those who are in any degree responsible for it. But if desperate social circumstances are scripted as an expression of "deep justice" rather than injustice, then the impetus for reflection and self-assessment—that thorn in the psyche—is removed.

Notes

1. Friedman, T. L. *The Lexus and the Olive Tree.* New York: Anchor Books, 2000, p.9.
2. Huntington, S. P. *Who Are We?: the Challenges to America's National Identity.* New York: Simon & Schuster, 2004, p.71-2.
3. Reich, R. B. *The Work of Nations: Preparing Ourselves for 21st Century Capitalism.* New York: Alfred A. Knopf, 1991, p.302-3.
4. Kaus, M. *The End of Equality.* New York: Basic Books, 1992, p.30.
5. Kaus, 1992, p.38.
6. Lemann, N. *The Big Test: the Secret History of the American Meritocracy.* New York: Farrar, Straus and Giroux, 1999, p.6.
7. Kaus, 1992, p.53.
8. Kaus, 1992, p.108-9.
9. Kaus, 1992, p.52.
10. Kaus, 1992, p.109.
11. Kaus, 1992, p.108.
12. Kaus, 1992, p.9.
13. Anderson, W. T. *Reality Isn't What It Used to Be.* New York: Harper and Row, 1990, p.27.
14. Barber, B. *Jihad vs. McWorld: How Globalism and Tribalism Are Reshaping the World.* New York: Ballantine Books, 1995, p.7.
15. Barber, 1995, p.8.
16. Barber, 1995, p.9.
17. Barber, 1995, p.214-5.
18. Gitlin, T. *The Twilight of Common Dreams.* New York: Metropolitan Books, 1995, p.160.
19. Kaus, 1992, p.17.
20. Herrnstein, R. J. and C. Murray *The Bell Curve: Intelligence and Class Structure in American Life.* New York: The Free Press, 1994, p.509.
21. Herrnstein and Murray, 1994, p.523.
22. Herrnstein and Murray, 1994, p.524. Emphasis in the original.
23. Herrnstein and Murray, 1994, p.526.

24. Herrnstein and Murray, 1994, p.526.
25. Angell, I. *The New Barbarian Manifesto: How to Survive the Information Age.* London: Kogan Page Limited, 2000, p.115.
26. Angell, 2000, p.116.
27. Angell, 2000, p.26.
28. Anderson, W. T. *All Connected Now: Life in the First Global Civilization.* Boulder, Colorado: The Westview Press, 2001, p.208.
29. Gowans, C. W. *Philosophy of the Buddha.* New York: Routledge, 2003, p.111.

10

POSTSCRIPT: THE EMERGENCE OF BUDDHISM IN AMERICA

My survey explored Western [Buddhist] attitudes toward ... beliefs common to Asian Buddhism: karma [and] rebirth ... The strongest agreement was with the idea of karma. Ninety-three percent of the respondents agreed or strongly agreed with the statement, "What happens to us in this life is determined by the kind of karma we create." Even though it is not a traditional part of the Western view of death, 81 percent also agreed that "after death, we are reborn into another life."

—J. W. Coleman[1]

My own questioning of Zen Buddhist teachers on this point leaves no doubt about it. I have not found one that believes in reincarnation as a physical fact, still less one who lays claim to any literally miraculous powers over the physical world. All such matters are understood symbolically.

—Alan Watts[2]

1

There is clearly disagreement in regard to the place of reincarnation in Buddhism in the West. We have no reason to doubt the accuracy of Coleman's findings; the majority of Buddhists in America remain committed to reincarnation. But this is not a unanimous commitment; with increasing insistence an alternative view is finding expression among some of the most influential voices in Western Buddhism. One of the most articulate and effective advocates for the emergence of Buddhist in the West, Alan Watts, vigorously rejected reincarnation—and a significant number of other prominent Western Buddhists are following his lead on this crucial point. It makes sense, here at the outset of the 21st century, to speak of *American* Buddhism. What is the relevance of this development? Let's begin with some numbers.

Buddhism is presently the most popular of Asians religions in America. In addition, according to the respected "American Religious Identification Survey" of the City University of New York, the number of people who identified themselves as Buddhists underwent a dramatic increase between the years of 1990 and 2001—from 401,000 to 1,082,000.[3] That's an impressive 159% increase. Granted that this is impressive, is it not also a disturbing development? Because since its inception, Buddhist doctrine has incorporated reincarnation theory. Again: in light of my concerns about the consequences of reincarnation, can the fluorescence in America of a religion so powerfully associated with reincarnation be anything but bad news? The answer to this question is not obvious.

Religious influence is never a one-way street. The incorporation of Buddhism into American culture will bring about changes in that culture, yes—but it will also bring about changes in Buddhism. Buddhism in America will come to be, in time, American Buddhism. The transitions at hand are not without precedent; we can profitably consider the history of how Buddhism arrived in China from its original home in India. This arrival took place in the first century CE, and is described by the historian Fung Yu-lan this way:

> ... the terms, "Chinese Buddhism" and "Buddhism in China," are not necessarily synonymous. There were certain schools of Buddhism which confined themselves to the religious and philosophical tradition of India, and made no contact with those of China ... Schools like this may be called "Buddhism in China." Their influence was confined to restricted groups of people and limited periods ... On the other hand, "Chinese Buddhism" is the form of Buddhism that has made contact with Chinese thought and thus has developed in conjunction with Chinese philosophical tradition.[4]

What Fung characterizes as "Buddhism in China" might be characterized as cultural and religious *outposts* of India settled within China's territory. And while these outposts were a kind of Buddhism, they were not truly "Chinese Buddhism." The distinction is an important one and is relevant to the arrival of Buddhism in America. Throughout the earlier phases of its arrival, Buddhism in America was typically "Asia in America." Buddhist centers were *outposts;* in the context of mainstream Western culture they have been *exotic*—often replete with costume and fascinating but alien ritual. But according to Fung, immigrant religious outlooks are appropriated as a culture's *own* through integration with that culture's own philosophical and religious traditions.

What facilitated that process of assimilation in ancient China were some strong commonalities between the native Chinese religious traditions and Buddhist views. As the historian of Buddhism, Heinrich Dumoulin, puts it:

> During this period of assimilation there was steady progress in the adaptation of Buddhist doctrine to Chinese forms of thought, or in the integration of the Chinese way of thinking into the Buddhist religion ... the deepest roots for this remarkable affinity between the basic ideas of Buddhism and Taoism suggest a naturalistic view of the world and of human life that inspires the Mahayana sutras as well as Chuang-tzu, Lao-tzu and other Chinese thinkers.[5]

The process under consideration is one of cultural change with all its attendant complexities, and it cannot by its very nature be sudden. In ancient China it took centuries for Buddhism to manifest itself as a *Chinese* religion. So in America, the manifestation of Buddhism as an *American* religion will take time. But not nearly so much time as the transitions took in ancient China. As discussed in the previous chapter, cultural change during the past fifty years is proceeding at an unprecedented pace. What took centuries in the China of two thousand years ago is taking mere decades in late 20th and early 21st century America.

The question under consideration in this chapter is, What will a Western Buddhism, or more specifically an American Buddhism, look like as it continues to rapidly develop in the 21st century? Is Buddhism without reincarnation a possibility? Would such a variant of Buddhism—even if theoretically conceivable—meet the psychological needs of Americans who are turning to Buddhism?

2

There are those traditionalists who insist that one cannot be a Buddhist without embracing reincarnation theory—that reincarnation is as inextricably bound to Buddhism as it is to Hinduism. And according to accounts like that of J. W. Coleman, cited in the epigraph to this chapter, the conjunction of Buddhism and reincarnation is holding fast among American Buddhists. In what follows I will consider some voices of dissent. As a prelude to doing that, it will be useful to go back to the roots of the tradition in question—back to the teaching of the Buddha.

To begin, Buddhism does not present itself as divine revelation. The founder of Buddhism, Siddhartha Gautama (563-483 BCE), was a human being—a man of extraordinary insight and determination, certainly, but a human being nonetheless. Buddhist doctrine does not come down from the heavens, it is born of human analysis and acumen. The Buddhist teaching is not an "eternal Truth," but a human truth, rooted in the human condition, addressed to human realities. The Buddhist scholar Walpola Rahula, in his influential *What the Buddha Taught,* puts it this way:

> Among the founders of religions the Buddha ... was the only teacher who did not claim to be other than a human being, pure and simple. Other teachers were either God, or his incarnations in different forms, or inspired by him [God]. The Buddha was not only a human being; he claimed no inspiration from any god or external power either. He attributed all his realization, attainments and achievements to human endeavour and human intelligence. A man and only a man can become a Buddha.[6]

And what of the teaching of this man who came to called "the Awakened One"—the Buddha? None of the seminal texts question the reality of reincarnation. But these texts do make evident a dispositional readiness to reject the dogmatic acceptance of *any* point of doctrine. To an extent that is extraordinary among founders of a religion, the Buddha invests the individual with an authority that supercedes that of either tradition or hierarchy. It is the individual's assessment of her or his own experience that is the final authority. Consider what are reported to be the last words spoken by the Buddha:

> "I am now grown old, O Ananda, and full of years; my journey is drawing to its close, I have reached the sum of my days, I am turning eighty years of age ... Therefore, O Ananda, be ye lamps unto yourselves. Rely on yourselves, and do not rely on external help. Hold fast to the truth as a lamp. Seek salvation alone in the truth. Look not for assistance to any one besides yourselves ... Those who, either now or after I am dead, shall be lamps unto themselves, relying upon themselves only and not relying upon any external help, but holding fast to the truth as their lamp, and seeking

their salvation in the truth alone, and shall not look for assistance to any one besides themselves, it is they, Ananda, among my bhikkhus, who shall reach the very topmost height! But they must be anxious to learn."[7]

Rely on yourself rather than anything external. Let *nothing*—not sages nor scripture nor tradition—take the place of your own assessment of your situation. One of the Buddha's most famous injunctions is stated here: "Be ye lamps unto yourselves." Think things through for *yourself*. I emphasize that these words are revered by Buddhist tradition as the Buddha's own. *Innovation* is native to Buddhist tradition at its deepest root. *Dissent* is native to Buddhist tradition at its deepest root. And the final words of the Buddha are not unique in this emphasis.

The Buddhist scholar/practitioner Stephen Batchelor provides a refreshingly candid account of his own rethinking of his relation to Buddhist tradition. He reports coming across an ancient text not translated into Tibetan, and hence not a part of the Tibetan Buddhist tradition to which he was an adherent. The text was the *Discourse to the Kalamas,* or the *Kalama Sutra.* Here is the passage he cites:

> "Yes, Kalamas, it is proper that you have doubt, that you have perplexity, for doubt has arisen in a matter which is doubtful. Now, look you Kalamas, do not be led by reports, or tradition, or hearsay. Be not led by the authority of religious texts, nor by mere logic or inference ... nor by the idea 'this is our teacher.' But, O Kalamas, when you know for yourselves that certain things are unwholesome, and wrong, and bad, then give them up ... And when you know for yourselves that certain things are wholesome and good, then accept them and follow them."[8]

Certainly there are many faces of the Buddhist tradition, and they differ as much as do the multiple faces of other traditions. But the *Kalama Sutra* presents a face of the tradition, and a very ancient one, that is particularly interesting from the standpoint of our concerns in this book. Here is an approach to Buddhism in which *doubt* is more highly prized than *belief.* Wisdom is grounded not in the authority of sages or scripture or tradition, but in the individual's own experience.

It is understandable that the *Kalama Sutra* is being cited with increasing frequency by Buddhists interested in establishing a Western version of Buddhism. If tradition is not to become a proverbial "dead hand," then it must be refreshed through critical analysis and candor. The Buddha's advice to the Kalamas represents a direct mandate to do just that. It was his meditation on this passage, among other things, that brought Stephen

Batchelor to reassess his relation to the Tibetan Buddhist tradition. His account seems entirely in keeping with the spirit of the ancient sage whose analysis of experience gave rise to what is called Buddhism:

> ... Tibetan Buddhism [is] a sealed, hermetic system of thought and practice that makes excellent sense if studied in its own terms but gets problematic if looked at from outside its own parameters ... Once inside the system, there is no room for doubt. The teacher is enlightened, the path complete and perfect. Everything you need to know has been accounted for ... [Through my analysis] I gained the security to entertain doubts. Although my Tibetan preceptors did not encourage this interest, they did tolerate it ... For myself, I felt stronger in my Buddhist faith, but this very strength started to undermine my need to feel devoted to any one of its many traditions.[9]

One thread within the history of Buddhism tells the story of a determined resolution to subvert the tendency to make a fetish or an idol out of the Buddhist tradition, the Buddhist scriptures, or even the Buddha himself. One expression of this resolution is especially vivid—yet also disquieting because of its resonance with the capricious madness that so lionizes the news media in 21st century America. It was a statement by a 9th century Chinese Buddhist monk named Lin Chi: "If you should meet the Buddha on the road, *kill* him!" Kill him: that is, when your mind produces an attractive image of the sacred and wise Buddha, don't let that image become an impediment to the *enlightenment* that is the goal of what the Buddha taught. The object of the Buddhist teaching is not to idolize the Buddha, but to attain enlightenment; should the image of the Buddha arise, treat it like any other distraction—put it aside, *kill* it. And if one should meet not the Buddha, but the sacred tradition of *reincarnation* on the road?

3

Kill it. And this brings us back to the present, to America. While still in the minority, many Western Buddhists are ready to treat the venerable doctrine of reincarnation as one more iconic trapping of the Buddhist teaching. They are ready, in Lin Chi's terms, to *kill* it. They are, to say it again, a minority. But they are the focus of my attention here, because they represent a hope (and, I'll suggest, a plausible hope) that the growing popularity of Buddhism in America is *good* news rather than bad.

The proposal to embrace Buddhism while rejecting reincarnation theory is not a new one: we've seen in Chapter 5 that as early as 1819 Arthur

Schopenhauer was announcing Buddhism as the religion of the future in the West. At the same time, however, he insisted that reincarnation doctrine was a superfluous and patronizing appendage to the teaching. Recall his words:

> The proper and, so to speak, esoteric doctrine of Buddhism, as we have come to know it through the most recent researches, also agrees with this view, since it teaches not metempsychosis, but a peculiar palingenesis resting on a moral basis, and it expounds and explains this with great depth of thought ... Yet for the great mass of Buddhists this doctrine is too subtle; and so plain metempsychosis is preached to them as a comprehensible substitute.[10]

Almost a century and a half later, one of the most potent voices in the development of Western Buddhism, the widely read author and Zen priest Alan Watts, said something quite similar. In *Psychotherapy East and West*, first published in 1961, he said this about reincarnation:

> The vast majority of Asian Hindus and Buddhists continue to believe that reincarnation is a fact, and most Westerners adopting Vedanta or Buddhism adopt belief in reincarnation at the same time. Western Buddhists even find this belief consoling, in flat contradiction to the avowed objective of attaining release from rebirth ... I wish, therefore, to commend what many students of these doctrines may seem a startling thesis: that Buddhists and Vedantists who understand their own doctrines profoundly, who are in fact liberated, do not believe in reincarnation in any literal sense.[11]

Never mind the somewhat presumptuous claim on the part of both Schopenhauer and Watts about what profound Asian Buddhists and Vedantists *really* understood. If we are to credit the dispositions spelled out in the *Kalama Sutra* and the Buddha's final words, it really doesn't matter what profound Buddhists of other times and places thought. What is important for Schopenhauer is that he, Schopenhauer, found the idea of reincarnation to be philosophically incoherent and unworthy. Likewise Alan Watts. And what is important for our purposes is their *disposition* toward the teaching of Buddhism, a teaching that they both embraced. Their disposition is the one recommended by the Buddha in his last words, "Be ye lamps unto yourselves." Such an approach, seasoned in no small part by audacity, will prove to be indispensable to the formulation of a uniquely American Buddhism. And we find a splendid specimen of this audacity in the writing of the American Zen priest Steve Hagen. He stoutly rejects reincarnation as being entirely inconsistent with Buddhism. Reminiscent of Schopenhauer's critique of reincarnation, Hagen finds the doctrine philosophically incoherent with the core of the Buddhist outlook. In a book tellingly titled *Buddhism Is Not What You Think: Finding Freedom beyond Beliefs,* he supports his claim—that reincarnation has no legitimate place in Buddhism—by making reference to Nagarjuna, the illustrious *Madhyamika* Buddhist. He says:

> Nagarjuna, the great second-century Indian Buddhist philosopher, pointed out that there's nothing persisting from moment to moment. In fact, there's nothing that endures, even the least bit, to *be* impermanent ... This observation, which is based solely on immediate, direct experience, is simply incompatible with any notion of reincarnation, since reincarnation assumes the persistence of some kind of self or embodied entity. *There is no way to hold a view of reincarnation without holding a view of permanence.* Thus any view of reincarnation is antithetical to what the Buddha taught.[12]

For all that such a direct rejection of the legitimacy of reincarnation doctrine within Buddhism will be troubling to some Buddhists, it will, I suspect, be music to others. Historically, as we've seen, reincarnation has not been a mere ornament on the Buddhist teaching. It cannot be denied that, historically, reincarnation has been a core aspect of the teaching, with direct and momentous implications for the practicing Buddhist. And yet for many Buddhists, I suspect, Hagen's rejection of reincarnation, a rejection stated right out loud, will be spiritually refreshing.

This should not be surprising. We find a similar situation in regard to traditional Christianity and doctrine and heaven and hell as afterlife destinations of individual souls. As with Buddhism and reincarnation, it cannot be denied that, historically, the doctrine of heaven and hell has been a core aspect of Christian teaching, with direct and momentous implications for the practicing Christian. Yet for all its centrality and momentousness, for all that it can be argued that the doctrine of heaven and hell is the *raison d'etre* of Christianity—for all that, many modern Christians prefer to keep the doctrine at a distance, psychologically. In light of developments made not only in science, but also in psychology and ethics, the doctrine of heaven and hell feels to educated modern folk more than a little implausible, even a bit *foolish,* perhaps even unworthy. To *insist* on the doctrine, as today's plethora of Fundamentalists seem bent on doing, is distasteful to many Christians. A demand that the doctrine of heaven and hell is mandatory for the authentic Christian elicits, for many sincere modern

Christians, just the opposite—it elicits the odor of *inauthenticity*. And so it is not surprising that, for such Christians, a rejection of the doctrine of heaven and hell, stated right out loud, is spiritually refreshing.

An insistence on outdated points of doctrine can come, over time, to poison one's relationship to a religious teaching. It is a recipe for cynicism and nihilism. I propose that it is just the insistence that "to be a Christian is to believe X, Y, and Q" that has contributed in large part to the spiritual death, so widely decried, that characterizes postmodern American culture. Rampant consumerism plays a role, yes, but the allure of the shopping mall is so potent because for too many people, being "religious" entails assent to what they see as a passel of nonsense. And so values and insights that can be realized only through in reflection, self-assessment, silence, and perhaps solitude are sought with increasing desperation at shopping malls or through online diversions. Fulfillment in life comes to be sought through a psychological state that cannot possibly yield it—a state that the poet T. S. Eliot described as "distracted from distraction by distraction."

Buddhism is in no way exempt from the psychological dynamics that have so compromised Christianity for many who would like to be Christians in the 21st century. To insist upon traditional doctrine, especially when that doctrine is implausible in light of critical analysis and science, is to kill the spirit. As problematic—and this returns us to the central concern of this book—doctrines like heaven and hell in traditional Christianity, or reincarnation in traditional Buddhism, are not only able to pollute a person's spiritual aspiration, they can also bring about an ethical indifference. This is just the point made by Stephen Batchelor:

> To cling to the idea of rebirth can deaden questioning. Failure to summon forth the courage to risk a nondogmatic and nonevasive stance on such crucial existential matters can also blur our ethical vision. If our actions in the world are to stem from an encounter with what is central in [this] life, they must be unclouded by either dogma or prevarication ... shifting concern away from a future life and back to the present ... demands an ethics of empathy rather than a metaphysics of fear and hope.[13]

The "metaphysics of fear and hope" spoken of by Batchelor can equally characterize both the traditional Christian belief in heaven and hell, and also the traditional Buddhist doctrine of reincarnation. Both doctrines shift our concerns away from the present and toward a future existence. The despised and the desperate—they'll be better off in a future life. They're just working out their karma. And again, this concern is not new. In Chapter 5, we saw that this liability was recognized in 1784 by Johann Gottfried von Herder, who worried that while reincarnation theory created "a false compassion towards every living creature, it diminished real sympathy for the miseries of our fellows."

4

Buddhism is being pushed to reform, in America and throughout the world, by its own inner dynamics. Change is natural to Buddhism as flow is to water; from the Buddha to his 21st century American adherents, the Buddhist teaching is taken to be perpetually *incomplete*. The idea of a "final word" in alien to the spirit of Buddhism. In this, Buddhism is like the practice of science. Typically, Buddhist thinkers do not immunize any aspect of Buddhism from the chilly interrogations of the scientific method. Again, it is the inner dynamics of Buddhism—its resistance to dogmatism, its commitment to experiment and verification, its compatibility with science—that results in a process of ongoing rethinking of what Buddhism is about. It is just this process that allows doctrines like reincarnation, however bound up with the historical Buddhist tradition, to be set aside. This is what the philosopher of science and Buddhist monk B. Alan Wallace refers to when he says:

> Judging by the trends ... of Buddhist practice in the West, it would appear that a kind of Buddhist protestant reformation is in the making ... Some Westerners who practice Buddhism and who may even regard themselves as Buddhist discard the Buddhist assertions of the continuity of consciousness following death and the efficacy of karma from one life to the next, on the grounds that *they are too incompatible with modern science.*[14]

It is important to note here that in the minds of many contemporary Buddhists, the demand for a compatibility between Buddhism and science is not a demand that Buddhism should compromise itself, bow to the inevitable, and march to a postmodern tune. On the contrary, in asserting its compatibility with science, Buddhism is seen as remaining true to its own nature. One of the most compelling aspects of the Buddhist teaching over the ages has been that it is *scientific*. Thus the scholar and historian of Buddhism, Nolan Pliny Jacobson, remarks that:

> As different as Buddhism and modern science may seem, they are in some important respects alike. Both have considerable power to shift the conduct of life *away from* established beliefs, however reliable and legitimate, *over to* the self-corrective mode of behavior.[15]

And the time for that self-corrective mode is at hand, according to Jacobson. The fact that this shift away from tradition beliefs does not constitute a rift between Western and non-Western Buddhists is one of the most remarkable things about it—there is nothing uniquely American about an insistence that Buddhism and science are compatible. No less an authority within the Buddhist tradition than the Dalai Lama agrees. Recall his interview with Carl Sagan, cited in Chapter 1, in which he allowed that if reincarnation were to be disproved by science, then Buddhism would have to change. In another interview, this time with an American Buddhist, the systems theorist and ecologist Joanna Macy, the Dalai Lama states his position regarding the possible relation of reincarnation theory to Western Buddhism. Macy explains to him how Buddhism has informed her environmental work, and how she illustrates to her students a sense of "deep interconnections" by recalling to them their *former lives*. This reference to former lives elicits a question from the Dalai Lama:

"How can Western people know this if they do not believe in rebirth?" His Holiness asked.

"For rebirth we substitute evolution," I said. And to illustrate I took his hand and led him on a two-minute evolutionary remembering. "Each atom in each cell in this hand goes back to the beginning of time ... to the first explosion of light and energy, to the formation of the galaxies and solar systems, to the fires and rains that bathed our planet, and the life-forms that issued from its primordial seas ... We have met and been together many times."
"Yes, of course," he said quietly. "Very good."[16]

The theme of grounding Buddhist vision and practice in an evolutionary context—an emphatically scientific understanding of the world—is gaining popularity. And it is in the view of many Buddhists a most promising development: it not only weds Buddhist theory to the analysis and falsifiability that is the lifeblood of scientific integrity, it also serves as an effective replacement for the doctrine of reincarnation that is seen by many Buddhists as outdated and problematic. This trend to incorporate evolutionary theory into Western Buddhism is entirely serious. But because Buddhism from it inception has valued doubt over belief and candor over reverence, it is able to allow for *playfulness*. A light touch, yet one that is grounded in common sense, has typically characterized the American pragmatic approach. And we find that approach nicely exemplified by the environmental activist and Buddhist poet Gary Snyder. In his "Smokey the

Bear Sutra," he whimsically brings Buddhism and evolutionary cosmology into single vision. Here is an excerpt:

> "In some future time, there will be a continent called
> America. It will have great centers of power called
> such as Pyramid Lake, Walden Pond, Mt. Rainier, Big Sur,
> Everglades, and so forth; and powerful nerves and channels
> such as Columbia River, Mississippi River, and Grand Canyon.
> The human race in that era will get into troubles all over
> its head, and practically wreck everything in spite of
> its own strong intelligent Buddha-nature.
>
> "The twisting strata of the great mountains and the pulsings
> of great volcanoes are my love burning deep in the earth.
> My obstinate compassion is schist and basalt and
> granite, to be mountains, to bring down the rain. In that
>
> future American Era I shall enter a new form: to cure
> the world of loveless knowledge that seeks with blind hunger;
> the mindless rage eating food that will not fill it."
>
> And he showed himself in his true form of
>
> SMOKEY THE BEAR.
>
> A handsome smokey-colored brown bear standing on his
> hind legs, showing that he is aroused and watchful.[17]

Whimsical, but entirely serious. The Sutra emphasizes *connectedness;* our lives are the result of all that has been, our lives are intimately bound up with everything that presently exists. Past lives? As many as you'd like—but like Joanna Macy, Snyder invites us to understand those past lives in terms of our evolutionary trajectory. By playfully merging into a single focus the locutions of ancient Buddhist scripture and the even more ancient vistas of paleontology, the "Smokey the Bear Sutra" calls our awareness to the sacred that is immediately before us. Our task is not to fret over past and future lives, but to see the world around us, present and familiar, in a broader and more realistic context.

5

Our discussion has taken an optimistic turn—at least in contrast to the tone of concern that has animated this study. We've looked at some influential Buddhist thinkers who firmly reject reincarnation. But hasn't something been left unaddressed? To restate the question posed in the opening section of this chapter: is an American Buddhism, free of reincarnation doctrine, able to meet the psychological needs of Americans who, in looking for alternatives to traditional Western religion, turn to Buddhism? No doubt a postmodern Buddhism configured along evolutionary lines would find acceptance among scholars, Zen philosophers, and other intellectuals. But would it be sufficiently compelling to the popular mind? Specifically, would it appeal to the same minds and hearts that were set aflame by Shirley MacLaine's *Out on a Limb?*

We cannot know that Buddhism will exert a powerful impact on the American religious consciousness. And even if it does, we cannot know that in America Buddhism will come to jettison the ancient doctrine of reincarnation. But if it should exert influence, and if it should divest itself of reincarnation, then American Buddhism (precisely because it carries the traditional religious authority of being Buddhism) might be effective in deflating the dangerous infatuation with reincarnation that is spreading through American culture.

Reincarnation *ala* Shirley MacLaine—or the Apocalyptic visions presented in the hugely successful *Left Behind* series of novels referred to earlier—enjoy a popularity that the thinking represented by the authors cited in this chapter will never outvote. This would seem to prompt an unfurling of the "Abandon all hope" banner from Dante's gate into hell. Yet I propose that it would be inappropriate to do so. The eminently pragmatic character of the American mind has historically asserted itself. Common sense and science has regularly trumped superstition and other forms of unscientific enthusiasm. Clearly there is more than a small element of hopeful thinking in this reasoning. But without such hope, we've already passed through Dante's gate. An important step in making that hope realistic rather than foolish turns on *awareness*. If we are aware of the social consequences toward which the doctrine of reincarnation inclines a culture, then hope is alive and realistic. This book has been an attempt to spark that awareness.

Notes

1. Coleman, J. W. *The New Buddhism: The Western Transformation of an Ancient Tradition.* New York: Oxford Univ. Press, 2001, p.122.
2. Watts, A. *Psychotherapy East and West.* New York: Vintage Books, 1975, p.59.
3. The Graduate Center, CUNY: "American Religious Identification Survey" http://www.gc.cuny.edu/studies/key_findings.htm
4. Fung Yu-lan, *A Short History of Chinese Philosophy.* New York: The Free Press, 1968, pp.242-3.
5. Dumoulin, H. *Zen Buddhism: a History, vol.1, India and China.* New York: Macmillan Publishing Co., 1988, p.67-8.
6. Rahula, W. *What the Buddha Taught.* New York: Grove Press, 1974, p.1.
7. The Buddha's Farewell Address." In Carus, P. *The Gospel of Buddhism,* Ch.93. Online edition. http://www.mountainman.com.au/buddha/carus_93.htm
8. Batchelor, S. *The Faith To Doubt: Glimpses of Buddhist Uncertainty.* Berkeley: Parallax Press, 1990, p.9. The formal title of this sutra is *Anguttara Nikaya III.65,* and the full text may be found at http://www.buddhist information.com/the_kalama_sutra.htm
9. Batchelor, 1990, p.9.
10. Schopenhauer, *The World as Will and Representation,* Vol. II, ch.41, p.502-3.
11. Watts, A. 1975, p.52.
12. Hagen, S. *Buddhism Is Not What You Think: Finding Freedom beyond Beliefs.* San Francisco: HarperSanFrancisco, 2003, p.46. Emphasis in the original.
13. Batchelor, S. *Buddhism Without Beliefs*, New York: Riverhead Books, 1997, p.38.
14. Wallace, B. A. "The Spectrum of Buddhist Practice" in C. S. Prebish and M. Baumann, eds., *Westward Dharma: Buddhism Beyond Asia.* Berkeley: Univ. of California Press, 2002, p.46. Emphasis in the original.
15. Jacobson, N. P. *Buddhism and the Contemporary World: Change and Self-Correction.* Carbondale: Southern Illinois University Press, 1983, p.133.
16. Macy, J. "The Council of All Beings" in J. Macy *World as Lover, World as Self.* Berkeley: Parallax Press, 1991, p.202.
17. Snyder, G. "Smokey the Bear Sutra," in Strong, J. S. *The Experience of Buddhism: Sources and Interpretations.* Belmont, Ca.: Wadsworth Publishing Co., 1995, p.350.

BIBLIOGRAPHY

Abelsen, P. "Schopenhauer and Buddhism." *Philosophy East and West*, 43: Ap. 1993. Internet version.

Alger, H. *Ragged Dick and Struggling Upward.* New York: Penguin Books, 1985.

American Religious Identification Survey. The Graduate Center, CUNY. http://www.gc.cuny.edu/studies/key_findings.htm

Anderson, W. T. *All Connected Now: Life in the First Global Civilization.* Boulder, Colorado: The Westview Press, 2001.

Anderson, W.T. *Reality Isn't What It Used to Be.* New York: Harper and Row, 1990.

Angell, I. *The New Barbarian Manifesto: How to Survive the Information Age.* London: Kogan Page Limited, 2000.

Augustine, St. *The City of God.* Translated by M. Dods. New York: The Modern Library, 1950.

Bach, R. *Jonathan Livingston Seagull.* New York, MacMillan Co., 1970.

Bache, C. M. *Dark Night, Early Dawn: Steps to an Ecology of Mind.* Albany: SUNY Press, 2000.

Bailey, A. *Esoteric Healing.* (Volume IV in *A Treatise on the Seven Rays.)* New York: Lucis Publishing Company, 1998.

Bailey, A. A. *The Unfinished Autobiography of Alice A. Bailey.* New York: Lucis Publishing Co., 1951.

Bannister, R. C. *Social Darwinism: Science and Myth in Anglo-American Social Thought.* Philadelphia: Temple Univ. Press, 1979.

Barber, B. *Jihad vs. McWorld: How Globalism and Tribalism Are Reshaping the World.* New York: Ballantine Books, 1995.

Basham, A. L. *The Wonder That Was India.* Calcutta: Rupa and Co., 1967.

Batchelor, S. *Buddhism without Beliefs.* New York: Riverhead Books, 1997.

Batchelor, S. *The Awakening of the West: The Encounter of Buddhism and Western Culture.* Berkeley: Parallax Press, 1994.

Batchelor, S. *The Faith To Doubt: Glimpses of Buddhist Uncertainty.* Berkeley: Parallax Press, 1990.

Bereman, G. D. "The Concept of Caste" in the *International Encyclopedia of Social Sciences, v.II.* New York: Crowell, Collier, and Macmillan, 1968.

Besant, A. *Karma.* Wheaton, Ill.: Theosophical Publishing House, 1975.
Besant, A. *A Study in Karma,* 1917. "Perfect Justice." http://www. theosophical. ca/StudyKarma.htm.
Bhattacharji, S. *Fatalism in India.* Calcutta: Sarmistha Roy, 1995.
Blavatsky, H. P. *Isis Unveiled.* The Theosophical University Press Online Edition, http://www.theosociety.org/pasadena/isis/iu1-01.htm.
Blavatsky, H. P. "Spiritual Progress." *Theosophist,* May, 1885. http://www. blavatsky.net/blavatsky/arts/SpiritualProgress.htm.
Blavatsky, H. P. *The Secret Doctrine,* Pasadena, California: The Theosophical University Press, 1999. Two volumes.
Bloom, H. *The Lucifer Principle: a Scientific Expedition into the Forces of History.* New York: Atlantic Monthly Press, 1995.
Campbell, B. F. *Ancient Wisdom Revisited: a History of the Theosophical Movement.* Berkeley: University of California Press, 1980.
Carus, P. *The Gospel of Buddhism,* Ch.93. "The Buddha's Farewell Address." Online edition. http://www.sacred-texts.com/bud/btg/btg94.htmhttp://www. mountainman.com.au/buddha/carus_93.htm.
Catholic World News Online. http://www.cwnews.com/ news/ viewrec.cfm? RefNum=8270, 8-13-98.
Coleman, J. W. *The New Buddhism: The Western Transformation of an Ancient Tradition.* New York: Oxford Univ. Press, 2001.
Conze, E. *The Memoirs of a Modern Gnostic, Parts I & II.* Sherborne, England: Samizdat Publishing Co., 1979.
Cornford, F. M. *From Religion to Philosophy: a Study in the Origins of Western Speculation.* New York: Harper Torchbooks, 1957.
Crews, F. "The Consolation of Theosophy, II" in *The New York Review of Books:* Volume 43, Number 15 ; October 3, 1996, online edition. http://www.nybooks. com/articles/1403.
Crowley, A. *The Law Is For All: the Authorized Popular Commentary on Liber AL vel Legis sub figura CCXX, The Book of the Law.* Las Vegas, NV: 1996.
Dalrymple, W. *Out of India.* PBS Documentary, 2000.
Danielou, A. *Gods of Love and Ecstasy: the Traditions of Shiva and Dionysus.* Rochester, Vermont: Inner Traditions Press, 1992.
Darwin, C. *The Origin of Species by Means of Natural Selection of the Preservation of Favored Races in the Struggle for Life.* New York: Signet Classic, 2003.
Darwin, C. *The Descent of Man and Selection in Relation to Sex.* New York: The Modern Library, 1936.
Dawkins, R. *Unweaving the Rainbow: Science, Delusion, and the Appetite for Wonder.* New York: Mariner Books, 2000.
Desmond, A. and J. Moore, *Darwin.* New York: W. W. Norton and Co., 1994.
Deussen, P. *Sixty Upanishads of the Veda.* Delhi: Motilal Banarsidass, 1980.
Diogenes Laertius *Live of Eminent Philosophers, v.2,* translated by R. D. Hicks. Cambridge, Mass.: Harvard Univ. Press, 1979.

Doniger-O'Flaherty, W. , translator. *The Rig Veda* 10.90, *Purusha Sutra.*
Dumoulin, H. *Zen Buddhism: a History, vol.1, India and China.* New York: Macmillan Publishing Co., 1988.
Edwards, P. *Reincarnation: a Critical Examination.* Amherst, NY: Prometheus Books, 1996.
Flowers, S. E. *The Secret of the Runes, by Guido von List.* Rochester, Vermont: Destiny Books, 1988.
Freud, S. *The Future of an Illusion.* New York: W.W. Norton & Co., 1961.
Friedman, T. L. *The Lexus and the Olive Tree.* New York: Anchor Books, 2000.
Fung Yu-lan, *A Short History of Chinese Philosophy.* New York: The Free Press, 1968.
Galanter, M. *Competing Equalities : Law and the Backward Classes in India.* Berkeley: University of California Press, 1984.
Gallup, G., Jr. and D. M. Lindsay *Surveying the Religious Landscape: Trends in U.S. Beliefs.* Harrisburg, PA: Morehouse Publishing, 1999.
Gandhi, M. K. *Collected Works of Mahatma Gandhi.* Delhi: Ministry of Information, Govt. Of India, 1958.
Gardiner, P. *Schopenhauer.* Baltimore: Penguin Books, 1971.
Gitlin, T. *The Twilight of Common Dreams.* New York: Metropolitan Books, 1995.
Goodrick-Clarke, N. *The Occult Roots of Nazism: Secret Aryan Cults and their Influence on Nazi Ideology.* New York: New York University Press, 1992.
Gould, S. J. *Ever Since Darwin: Reflections in Natural History.* New York: W. W. Norton & Co., 1977.
Gowans, C. W. *Philosophy of the Buddha.* New York: Routledge, 2003.
Gress, D. *From Plato to NATO: the Idea of the West and Its Opponents.* New York: The Free Press, 1998.
Griffiths, P. *Modern India.* New York: Frederick A. Praeger, 1957.
Grof, S. *The Cosmic Game: Explorations of the Frontiers of Human Consciousness.* Albany: SUNY Press, 1998.
Guthrie, W. K. C. *A History of Greek Philosophy, v.1-2.* New York: Cambridge Univ. Press, 1978.
Guthrie, W. K. C. *Orpheus and Greek Religion.* Princeton: Princeton Univ. Press, 1993.
Hagen, S. *Buddhism Is Not What You Think: Finding Freedom beyond Beliefs.* San Francisco: HarperSanFrancisco, 2003.
Harrison, J. *Prolegomena to the Study of Greek Religion.* New York: Meridian Books, 1966.
Hawkins, M. *Social Darwinism in European and American Thought: 1860 - 1945.* New York: Cambridge University Press, 1997.
Head, J. And S. L. Cranston, eds., *Reincarnation: an East-West Anthology.* Wheaton, Ill.: Theosophical Publishing House, 1975.
Herder, J. G. *Outlines of a Philosophy of the History of Man (1784).* Translated by T. Churchill. New York: Bergman Publishers, 1800.
Herodotus, *The Histories.* Translated by George Rawlinson.

http://www.herodotuswebsite.co.uk/Text/Book2.htm

Herrnstein, R. J. and C. Murray *The Bell Curve: Intelligence and Class Structure in American Life.* New York: The Free Press, 1994.

Hirshson, S. P. *General Patton: A Soldier's Life.* New York: HarperCollins, 2002.

Hofstadter, R. *Social Darwinism in American Thought.* Boston: Beacon Press, 1992.

Hume, A. O. The so-called "Mahatma Letter" to A. O. Hume, November 1, 1880. Online edition: http://www.theosociety.org/pasadena/mahatma/ml-khaoh.htm.

Huntington, S. P. *Who Are We?: the Challenges to America's National Identity.* New York: Simon & Schuster, 2004.

Jacobson, N. P. *Buddhism and the Contemporary World: Change and Self-Correction.* Carbondale: Southern Illinois University Press, 1983.

James, W. *Pragmatism.* Buffalo, New York: Prometheus Books, 1991.

Kaus, M. *The End of Equality.* New York: Basic Books, 1996.

Klostermaier, K. K. *A Survey of Hinduism.* Albany: State Univ. of New York Press, 1989.

Koestler, A. *The Sleep Walkers: A History of Man's Changing Vision of the Universe.* New York: Macmillan, 1959.

Krishnamurti, J. "Truth is a Trackless Land," in *Total Freedom: The Essential Krishnamurti.* San Francisco: HarperSanFrancisco, 1996.

Kristof, N. D. "Jesus and Jihad." New York Times, July 17, 2004, online edition.

Kushner, H. *When Bad Things Happen to Good People.* New York: Random House, 1990.

Laws of Manu, translated by G. Bühler. *Sacred Books of the East,* v.25. http://www.sacred-texts.com/hin/manu.htm.

LaHaye, T. and J. B. Jenkins *Glorious Appearing.* Wheaton, Ill.: Tyndale House Publishers, 2004.

Lemann, N. *The Big Test: the Secret History of the American Meritocracy.* New York: Farrar, Straus and Giroux, 1999.

Lilla, M. *The Reckless Mind: Intellectuals in Politics.* New York: New York Review Book, 2001.

Machiavelli, N. *The Prince.* Adams, R. M., editor and translator. New York: W. W. Norton and Co., 1977.

MacLaine, S. *Out on a Limb.* New York: Bantam Books, 1983.

Macy, J. "The Council of All Beings" in J. Macy *World as Lover, World as Self.* Berkeley: Parallax Press, 1991.

McDermott, J. P. "Karma and Rebirth in Early Buddhism," in O'Flaherty, W. D. *Karma and Rebirth in Classical Indian Traditions.* Berkeley: University of California Press, 1980.

Mill, J. S. *Autobiography.* New York: Bobbs-Merrill Co., Inc., 1957.

Murphey, R. *A History of Asia.* New York: HarperCollins Publishers, 1992.

Nietzsche, F. *The Gay Science,* translated by W. Kaufmann. New York: Vintage Books.

O'Flaherty, W. D. "Karma and Rebirth in the Vedas and Puranas," in O'Flaherty, W. D. *Karma and Rebirth in Classical Indian Traditions.* Berkeley: University of California Press, 1980.
O'Neill, T. "Untouchable." *National Geographic,* June 2003.
Peters, F. E. *Greek Philosophical Terms: a Historical Lexicon.* New York: New York University Press, 1967.
Plato: The Collected Dialogues. Hamilton, E. and H. Cairns, eds. Princeton: Princeton Univ. Press, 1961.
Postman, N. *Amusing Ourselves to Death.* New York: Penguin Books, 1986.
Power, C. *Plight of the "Untouchables" Newsweek,* 25 June, 2000.
Puligandla, R. *Fundamentals of Indian Philosophy.* New York: Abington Press, 1975.
Radhakrishnan, S., translator. *The Bhagavadgita.* New York: Harper & Row, 1973.
Radhakrishnan, S. *The Hindu View of Life.* New York: The Macmillan Co., 1965.
Radhakrishnan, S. *History of Philosophy: Eastern and Western, 2 volumes.* London: Allen & Unwin, 1952.
Radhakrishnan, S., translator. *The Principal Upanishads.* New York: Humanities Press, 1969.
Rahula, W. *What the Buddha Taught.* New York: Grove Press, 1974.
Rajagopalachari, C., translator and editor. *Ramayana.* Bombay: Bharatiya Vidya Bhavan, 1968.
Reade, W. *The Martyrdom of Man.* 1872. Online edition. http://www.exclassics.com/martyrdom/martcnts.htm
Reich, R. B. *The Work of Nations: Preparing Ourselves for 21st Century Capitalism.* New York: Alfred A. Knopf, 1991.
Reichenbach, B.R. *The Law of Karma: a Philosophical Study.* Honolulu: Univ. of Hawaii Press, 1990.
Reston, J. *The Last Apocalypse: Europe at the Year 1000 A.D.* New York: Anchor Books, 1998.
Robinson, J. M., ed. and transl., *An Introduction to Early Greek Philosophy: The Chief Fragments and Ancient Testimony.* Boston: Houghton Mifflin Co., 1968.
Rogo, D. S. *The Search for Yesterday: a Critical Examination of the Evidence for Reincarnation.* Englewood Cliffs, NJ: Prentice-Hall, 1985.
Ramayana, The Translated by K.M.K. Murthy. http://www.valmikiramayan.net/ayodhya/sarga9/ayodhya_9_frame.htm.
Roosevelt, T. "The Strenuous Life," 1899. http://www.usembassy.de/usa/etexts/speeches/rhetoric/trlife.htm
Roy, A. *The God of Small Things.* New York: HarperPerennial, 1997.
Safransky, R. *Schopenhauer and the Wild Years of Philosophy.* Cambridge: Harvard Univ. Press, 1991.
Sagan, C. *The Demon-haunted World: Science as a Candle in the Dark.* New York: Ballantine Books, 1996.
Schopenhauer, A. *Parerga and Paralipomena,* 2 volumes. Translated by E. F. J. Payne. New York: Oxford University Press, 1974.

Schopenhauer, A. *The World as Will and Representation*, 2 volumes. Translated by E. F. J. Payne. New York: Dover Publications, 1969.

Singh, S. "A Cosmetic Approach To Malignancy: Gandhi and Casteism" http://www.sikhe.com/gsdno/articles/opinion/11212001_sundeepsingh_gandhiandcasteism.htm

Sinnett, A. P. *The Mahatma Letters to A. P. Sinnett.* Theosophical University Press, Online Edition. Letter no.60. http://www.theosociety.org/pasadena/mahatma/ml-60.htm.

Shivanada, Swami. The Divine Life Society. http://www.hinduism.co.za/dharma.htm.

Sivananda, Swami. *Practice of Karma Yoga.* Divine Life Trust Society, 1995. Online edition. http://www.SivanandaDlshq.org/.

Snyder, G. "Smokey the Bear Sutra," in Strong, J. S. *The Experience of Buddhism: Sources and Interpretations.* Belmont, Ca.: Wadsworth Publishing Co., 1995.

Spencer, H. *The Man Versus the State.* Indianapolis: Liberty Classics, 1982.

Spencer, H. *Social Statics.* New York: Robert Schalkenbach Foundation, 1970.

Spencer, H. *The Study of Sociology.* New York: D. Appleton & Co., 1896.

Spielvogel, J. and D. Redles "Hitler's Racial Ideology: Content and Occult Sources." Simon Wiesenthal Center; Museum of Tolerance Online, 1997. http://motlc.wiesenthal.com/resources/books/annual3/chap09.html.

Sumner, W. G. "Socialism" in *Social Darwinism: Selected Essays of William Graham Sumner.* Englewood Cliffs, N. J.: Prentice-Hall, 1963.

Sumner, W. G. "What's Good for the Goose." *Locomotive Firemen's Magazine*, January 1893. http://historymatters.gmu.edu/d/4999/.

Taylor, A. E. *Plato: the Man and His Work.* New York: Meridian Books, 1964.

Tennyson, A. "In Memoriam: A. H. H." Published 1850. Online edition: http://charon.sfsu.edu/tennyson/inmemoriam.html.

Toynbee, A. J. *Civilization on Trial.* New York: Oxford Univ. Press, 1948.

Underhill, E. *The Essentials of Mysticism and Other Essays.* New York: E. P. Dutton & Co., 1920.

Vivekananda, S. "The Caste Problem in India" from *Swami Vivekananda on India and Her Problems.* Online at http://www.sivanandadlshq.org/messages/caste.htm.

Wallace, B. A. "The Spectrum of Buddhist Practice" in C. S. Prebish and M. Baumann, eds., *Westward Dharma: Buddhism Beyond Asia.* Berkeley: Univ. of California Press, 2002.

Walsh, R. N. And F. Vaughan, "A Comparison of Psychotherapies" in *Beyond Ego: Transpersonal Dimensions in Psychology,* ed. Walsh, R. N. and F. Vaughan. Los Angeles: Jeremy Tarcher, Inc, 1980.

Washington, P. *Madame Blavatsky's Baboon: a History of the Mystics, Mediums, and Misfits Who Brought Spiritualism to America.* New York: Schocken Books, 1995.

Watts, A. *Psychotherapy East and West.* New York: Vintage Books, 1975.

Whitehead, A. N. *Process and Reality.* New York: The Free Press, 1978.

Wright, R. *The Moral Animal: the New Science of Evolutionary Psychology.* New York: Vintage Books, 1994.

INDEX

A

Abelsen, P., 122
Achilles, 92, 100
Advaita Vedanta (Hinduism), 73
Alger, Horatio, 178-180
All Connected Now: Life in the First Global Civilization (Anderson), 200
Ambedkar, B.R., 76-77, 79, 80
anamnesis, 97
Anderson, Walter Truett, 8, 193, 200
Angell, Ian, 198-200, 201
Anquetil-Duperron, Abraham, 116, 122
Apocalypse, 4, 19, 20
Arcane School, 154
Aristotle, 128, 174
Aryan, 55, 56, 63, 74, 150, 152, 159
Augustine (Saint), 42, 108

B

Bacchus *see* Dionysus
Bach, Richard, 17, 25
Bache, Christopher M., 39, 40
Bailey, Alice, 154, 155, 156, 159, 161, 162, 163
Bannister, Robert C., 169
Barber, Benjamin, 193-194, 201
Basham, A.L., 70
Batchelor, Stephen, 30, 117-118, 211, 215
Bell Curve: Intelligence and Class Structure in American Life (Herrnstein & Murray), 196, 199
Beowulf, Epic of, 6
Bereman, G. D., 3
Besant, Annie, 153, 155, 162, 163
Bhagavad-Gita, 69, 79-80
Bhattacharji, Sukumara, 27, 54-55
Big Test: the Secret History of the American Meritocracy (Lehmann), 189
Blavatsky, Helena Petrovna (Madame), 141-164
  attitude toward Jews, 150-151, 158-159
  on karma and reincarnation, 143-144, 152
  relationship with Olcott, 145
  see also Theosophy
Bloom, Howard, 44
Book of Dzyan (Blavatsky), 144-145
Book of the Law (Crowley), 160
Brahman, 60-61, 68, 70, 120, 121, 123, 124

Brahmavaivarka Purana, 61
Brahmin (priests/scholars), 57, 59, 64-65, 66, 67, 169
breath of life *see* psyche
Britten, Emma, 142,143
Buddha, The
    as a man, 210
    last words, 210-211
    rejecting Hinduism, 77
Buddhism
    American, 127, 208-219
    Chinese Buddhism, 208-209
    statistics on growth, 208
    without a belief in reincarnation, 208, 209-210, 212, 216
    lack of idolatry, 212
    and science, 216-217
    Tibetan Buddhism, 212
Buddhism Is Not What You Think: Finding Freedom beyond Beliefs (Hagen), 214

C

Campbell, Bruce F., 142, 154
cannibalism, 88, 91, 94, 98
Carnegie, Andrew, 177
Caste Problem in India (Gandhi), 73-74, 75-76
caste system, 3, 4, 51, 59-60, 64, 65-66, 67, 68-69, 70, 72, 75, 81
    attacked by B. R. Ambedkar, 76-77, 79, 80
    caste classifications, 56
    compared to Social Darwinism, 169
    defined by Bereman, 3
    examined by Plato, 104
    defended by Vivekananda, 73-75
    defended by Gandhi, 72
    defended by Radhakrishnan, 72-73
    viewed by Herder, 117
Chandala, 59, 65, 66, 67-72, 150-151
    as executioners, 68
    Christian, 70
    see also Dalit, Outcaste, Untouchable
Chandogya Upanishad, 59, 60, 65-66,
Christ *see* Jesus Christ
Christianity, 6, 7, 9, 14, 18, 23, 107, 108, 109, 112, 118, 150, 154, 180, 214-215
City of God (St. Augustine), 42
Clement of Alexandria, 9
Clockwork Orange (Kubrick), 97
Coleman, J.W., 207, 210
collective karma, 39-40, 153, 154
Conze, Edward, 21, 22, 24, 25, 89, 93, 117, 120
Cornford, F.M., 53-54, 92
Cosmic Game: Exploration of the Frontiers of Human Consciousness (Grof), 28
Crews, Frederick, 157
Critique of Pure Reason (Kant), 11
Crowley, Aleister, 159-161

D

Dalai Lama, 32, 217
Dalit, 53, 65, 67, 71, 72, 74, 76, 77, 79, 104
    see also Chandala, Outcaste, Untouchable
Dalrymple, William, 70
Danielou, Alain, 75, 95
Darwin, Charles, 47, 116, 126, 127-138, 144,146, 171, 186
    Devil's Chaplain, 132
    misgivings, 132, 133
    on natural selection, 129-130
    on natural selection as regards humanity 172-174

Das Geheimnis der Runen (Flowers), 157
Dawkins, Richard, 31
Descent of Man (Darwin), 128, 171-172, 173-174
Desmond, Adrian, 132
determinism, 58-59
Deussen, Paul, 116
Dionysus, 93, 94, 95
    God of Orphic religion, 93
    possible origins of cults, 94, 95
    origins with Shiva, 95
Discourse to the Kalamas (Kalama Sutra), 211, 213
Djwhal Khul *see* The Tibetan
Dravidians, 55, 63
Dumoulin, Heinrich, 209

E

Ecclesiastes, 48
Edwards, Paul, 46-47
Egyptian belief in reincarnation, 86-87
Eliot, T. S., 215
Empedocles, 87, 88, 89, 91, 92, 98
End of Equality (Kaus), 1, 188-192
Enlightenment (philosophical movement), 7, 117, 137, 169
enlightenment (Buddhist), 212
Epic of Beowulf, 6
Er (Myth of), 99-101, 102, 107
eugenics, 105, 107, 192
evolution, 116, 126, 127-138, 141, 144, 152, 186
    by means of reincarnation, 152, 217
    contrasted with Christian concepts, 135-136

F

Fatalism in India (Bhattacharji), 27

Flowers, Stephen E., 157
Foner, Eric, 181
Forbes, James, 69-70
Ford, Henry, 22, 25
Freud, Sigmund, 29-30, 43, 44, 62,
Friedman, Thomas, 185, 186
From Plato to NATO: The Idea of the West and It's Opponents (Gress), 5
fundamentalism, 80, 81, 134, 148, 193, 194, 214
Fung Yu-Lan, 208, 209
Future of an Illusion (Freud), 43

G

Galantner, Marc, 74
Gandhi, Mohandas, 73, 75, 76-77, 80, 201
    defense of caste system, 72
Gautama, Siddhartha, 210 *see also* The Buddha
General Patton: A Soldier's Story (Nye), 22
Genesis, 128, 129, 136
genetics, 38-39
Germanen Orden (secret society), 157
Gilbert & Sullivan, 26-27
Gitlin, Todd, 194
globalization, 2, 185, 186, 192, 196, 199, 200, 201
Glorious Appearing (Jenkins & LaHaye), 19, 20
God and the New Physics (Davies), 31
Gods of Love, Gods of Ecstasy: The Traditions of Shiva and Dionysus (Danielou), 95
Goodrick-Clarke, Nicholas, 157
Gould, Stephen Jay, 133, 136, 137
Gowans, Christopher W., 49-50, 203
Greek Philosophical Terms: A

Historical Lexicon (Peters), 90
Gress, David, 5
Grof, Stanislav, 28-29, 30, 32, 149
Guthrie, W.K.C., 86, 91-92, 93

H

H.M.S. Pinafore (opera), 26-27
Hagen Steve, 213-214
Hahn, Helena Petrovna *see* Blavatsky
Harappa, 55, 56
Harrison, Jane, 86-87
Hawkins, Mike, 180-181
Herder, Johann Gottfried von, 116-117, 119, 203, 216
Herodotus, 86-87
Herrnstein, Richard J., 196, 197, 198, 199
Hindu View of Life (Radhakrishnan), 72-73
History of Asia (Murphey), 75
Hofstadter, Richard, 174, 177, 180, 181
Homer, 63, 90, 92
human sacrifice, 56, 94
Hume, A.O., 149
Humphreys, Christmas, 21, 25
Huntington, Samuel P., 187
Hymn of Man (Purusha Sutra), 56, 57, 59, 65, 74

I

Iliad, 63
In Memoriam (Tennyson), 134-135
International Encyclopedia of Social Sciences, 3
Irenaeus, 108
Isis Unveiled (Blavatsky), 143, 146-147

J

Jacobson, Nolan Pliny, 216-217
James, William, 12-13, 14
Jefferson, Thomas, 7
Jenkins, Jerry B., 19
Jews, as victims of karma, 80, 150-151, 152, 155-156
Jihid vs. McWorld: How Globalism and Tribalism are Reshaping the World (Barber), 193-4
jiva (soul), 54-61
Jonathan Livingston Seagull (Bach), 17, 26
justice, 35, 36, 40, 41, 42, 43, 48, 50, 58, 201, 204
Justin Martyr, 108

K

Kaikeyi (Queen), 63-64
Kalama Sutra (Discourse to the Kalamas), 211, 213
Kant, Immanuel, 11
karma, 35-52
    as anti-Semitic justification, 80, 150-151, 152, 155-156
    as a color (race) issue, 57, 63, 67, 71
    collective, 39-40, 153, 154
    as statistical law, 46-48, 49, 79
    as mechanical law, 48-50, 51, 79
    role in nature (Blavatsky), 143-144
Kaus, Mickey, 1, 2, 188, 189, 190, 191, 192, 194-195, 196
Klostermaier, Klaus K., 54, 55-56, 57
Koestler, Arthur, 94
Koot Hoomi, 143, 144, 149-150, 154
Krause, Karl Friedrich, 119

Krishnamurti, Jiddu, 163-164
Kristof, Nicholas D., 19-20
Kshatriya (warrior caste), 56, 59
Kushner, Harold S., 48

L

LaHaye, Tim, 19
Law of Karma (Reichenbach), 57
Laws of Manu, 62, 64, 65, 66-67, 69
Leadbeater, Charles, 161-162, 163
Lehmann, Nicholas, 189, 190, 196
Lexus and the Olive Tree (Friedman), 185
Lilla, Mark, 111
List, Guido von, 157
Locke, John, 7
Lucifer Principle (Bloom), 44
Luther, Martin, 42, 122

M

MacBeth, 15, 45
Machiavelli, Nicolo, 111
MacLaine, Shirley, 25, 26, 27, 219
Macy, Joanna, 217, 218
Madame Blavatsky's Baboon (Washington), 145, 151, 157
Manusmriti, see Laws of Manu
Martyrdom of Man (Reade), 127
McDermott, James P., 61-62
meat eating, 87-88, 91
Meno (Plato), 97, 101, 102
meritocracy, 103, 107, 110
Mill, John Stuart, 7, 42
Mohenjo Daro, 55
Moore, James, 132
The Moral Animal (Wright), 42-43
Morya, 143, 144
Murray, Charles, 196, 197, 198, 199
Murthy, K.M.K., 63

Myth of Er (Plato), 99-100, 101, 102, 107
Myth of the Cave (Plato), 96, 98

N

National Socialism, 79, 161
  origins in Theosophy, 153, 156, 158
natural selection, 129, 152, 172, 175
New Barbarism Manifesto: How to Survive the Information Age (Angell), 199, 200
Newtonian Laws, 47, 49, 131
Nietzsche, Friedrich, 138
noble lie (Plato), 103
Nye, Roger H. (Colonel), 22

O

O'Flaherty, Wendy Doniger, 38, 61
Olcott, Henry Steel (Colonel), 141, 142, 145
On the Language and Wisdom of the Indians (Schlegel), 117
O'Neill, Tom, 71
Order of the Star (Theosophy), 163
Origin of Species by Means of Natural Selection (Darwin), 128, 129, 131, 132, 134, 171
Orpheus, 91, 93
Orpheus and Greek Religion (Guthrie), 91
Orphism (religion), 91, 92, 93, 94, 98
Oupnek'hat (Anquetil-Duperron), 116, 117
Out of India (PBS documentary), 53, 70
Out on a Limb (MacLaine), 25-26, 219
Outcaste, 57, 59, 65, 67, 169

see also Dalit, Chandala, Untouchables
Outlines of a Philosophy of the History of Man (Herder), 116-117

P

palingenesis, 54, 86, 119, 120, 121
Parerga and Paralipomena (Schopenhauer), 118, 119, 120
Patton, George (General), 22
Paul of Tarsus (St. Paul), 108
Peirce, Charles S., 12
personal immortality, 23, 108, 109, 202
Phaedo (Plato), 90, 98, 99
Philosophy of the Buddha (Gowans), 49-50
Plato, 9, 26, 85, 86, 87, 90, 91, 95-112, 192
   and Social Darwinism, 170
   basis for a well-ordered society, 102-103
   Myth of Cave, 96
   Myth of Er, 99-100, 101, 102, 107
   on equality for women, 105
   on reincarnation, 93, 97, 99, 100, 109-111
   on selective breeding, 105-106, 107, 192
plutocracy, 105
Postman, Neil, 10-11
Pragmatism (philosophical movement), 12, 13, 14
Prolegomena to the Study of Greek Religion (Harrison), 86-87
Psychotherapy East and West (Watts), 213
Puligandla, Ramakrisha, 50-51
Purusha Sutra (The Hymn of Man), 56, 57, 59, 65, 74
Pythagoras, 26, 87, 89, 90, 98
   and beans, 89, 91
   death of, 91
   on reincarnation, 89

R

Radhakrishnan, Sarvepalli, 41, 58-59, 72-73, 75, 76, 78, 80, 123, 169, 198, 201
Ragged Dick (Alger), 179-180
Rahula, Walpola, 210
Rajagopalachari, Chakravarti, 63
Rama-Lila, 63, 64
Ramayana, 63, 64
Reade, Winwood, 127, 128
Reckless Minds: Intellectuals in Politics (Lilla), 111
Reich, Robert B., 187-188, 195, 199
Reichenbach, Bruce R., 57-58
reincarnation, 5, 7-8, 9, 117, 127
   as basis for evolution, 127
   Egyptian belief, 86-87
   master idea, 3, 4, 18, 20, 27, 35
   origins of belief in Greece, 86, 91, 93, 94, 109-111
   Platonic views, 93, 98-99, 100
   Pythagorean view of, 89-90
   statistics on western belief, 1, 8, 207
   Theosophical concept of, 144-145, 152, 153
   western rejection of Platonian view, 107-109
Reincarnation: A Critical Examination (Edwards), 12, 47
Republic (Plato), 96, 104, 110
   basis of a well-ordered society, 102-103, 104
   equality of women, 105
   Myth of Er, 99-100, 101, 102, 107
   Myth of the Cave, 96, 98
   selective breeding, 105-106

Reston, James, 6
resurrection of the body, 108, 109
Rig Veda, 55, 56, 57, 59, 65, 74
River of Forgetfulness, 101, 102, 103
Rogo, D. Scott, 24-25
Roosevelt, Theodore, 176-177
Roy, Arundhati, 53, 70

S

Sagan, Carl, 24, 32, 217
salvation (Christian doctrine), 42, 44
Satan, 4, 19
Schlegel, Friedrich, 117, 122
Schopenhauer, Arthur, 115-126, 133-134, 138, 146, 148
   on Buddhism, 119-120, 122
   as influenced by von Herder, 116
   rejection of reincarnation, 119-120, 212-213
   rejection of Western religious thought, 118
Secret Doctrine (Blavatsky), 143, 147-148, 157-158
Secret of the Runes (Flowers), 157
Shakespeare, 36, 45
Shiva, 95
Shivanada (Swami), 39-40, 71, 72
Siddhartha Gautama, 210, *see also* Buddha
Simon Wiesenthal Center, 158, 159
Sinnett, A.P., 149
Sixty Upanishads of the Veda (Deussen), 116
Smokey the Bear Sutra (Snyder), 217-218
Snyder, Gary, 217-218
Social Darwinism, 73, 160, 161, 167-182, 200, 202, 203
Social Darwinism in American Thought (Hofstadter), 174, 180

Social Darwinism: Science and Myth in Anglo-American Social Thought (Bannister), 169
Socrates, 9, 90, 97-98, 111-112
Spencer, Herbert, 129, 171, 173, 174-176
spiritualism, 142, 143
St. Augustine, 42, 108
St. Paul (Paul of Tarsus), 108
St. Thomas Christians, 70
Stalin, Joseph, 50, 203
Study in Karma (Besant), 35
Sumner, William Graham, 167, 168, 177-178
survival of the fittest, 129, 130, 131, 173, 177
Symposium (Plato), 111, 112

T

Taylor, A.E., 104, 105
Tennyson, Alfred Lord, 134-135, 136, 138, 144, 148, 170, 171, 186
The Tibetan (Djwhal Khul), 154, 155
Theosophical Society (formation of), 141-142, 145
Theosophy, 125, 126, 127, 138, 141-164
   and National Socialism, 153
   and Nazism, 156
   as backlash to evolutionary theory, 144
   as contrasted to evolutionary theory, 144, 146-148
   attitude toward Jews, 150-151, 152, 155-156
   demise of, 161-164
   origins in Indian religious thought, 150-151
   views on karma and reincarnation, 144-148, 150-151, 152, 153

Toynbee, Arnold, 9
Twilight of Common Dreams
   (Gitlin), 194

U

underclass, 191, 197-198
Underhill Evelyn, 13-14
Unfinished Autobiography (Bailey),
   154, 161
Untouchables, 65, 70, 71
Untouchables See also Outcastes,
   Chandalas, Dalits
Upanishads, 59, 60, 116, 119, 121,
   123, 124

V

varna, 57, 63, 67, 71
Vasubandhu, 61-62
Vaughan, Frances, 31-32
Vedas, 31, 55
Vikings, 5-6
Vivekananda, Swami, 73-74, 75-
   76, 77, 78, 80, 198, 201

W

Wallace, Alfred Russel, 132
Wallace, B. Alan, 216
Walsh, Roger N., 31-32
Washington, Peter, 143, 145, 151,
   157, 162, 163
Watts, Alan, 207, 208, 213
What the Buddha Taught (Rahula),
   210
When Bad Things Happen to Good
   People (Kushner), 48
Whitehead, Alfred, North, 85, 110
Who Are We? Challenges to
   America's National Identity
   (Huntington), 187
Wonder That was India (Basham),
   70
Work of Nations: Preparing
   Ourselves for 21st Century
   Capitalism (Reich), 187-188
World as Will and Representation
   (Schopenhauer), 118, 119, 121,
   133-134
Wright, Robert, 42-43